YOUR BEST YEAR YET!

*365 days of little changes that
add up to big results!*

Karen Ann Kennedy

ISBN: 1500808156
ISBN 13: 9781500808150
Library of Congress Control Number: 2014914363
CreateSpace Independent Publishing Platform
North Charleston, South Carolina

INTRODUCTION

Why do people get so excited about a new year? For me, it's the thrill of 365 new days, a blank slate to learn, create, grow, and make change. But the problem for most people is that they go into the new year with an "all or nothing," approach. They feel like they have to make all their changes on January 1st. They go from sixty to zero; from New Year's Eve, eating and drinking and staying up all night to celebrate, to New Year's Day, where they try to detox their bodies, clean their entire house from top to bottom, run ten miles, and become exceptionally organized all in one day. It's as if we forget that we have 364 more glorious days in the New Year. **We don't have to do it all in one day!**

This book was inspired by a seminar I conducted called "New Year, New You." The seminar was all about breaking down your year, month by month, to tackle the most common things that people list in their Yew Year's resolutions.

A 2014 study by the University of Scranton, Journal of Clinical Psychology, ranked the Yop 10 New Year's Resolutions. They are, in order:

1. Lose weight
2. Get organized
3. Spend less, save more
4. Enjoy life to the fullest
5. Stay fit and healthy
6. Learn something exciting
7. Quit smoking
8. Help others in their dreams
9. Fall in love
10. Spend more time with family

Their study also showed that 45% of Americans **usually** make resolutions and 17% **infrequently** make resolutions, but only 8% are **successful** in achieving their resolutions. The study went on to say that people who explicitly make resolutions are 10 times more likely to attain their goals than people who don't explicitly make their resolutions. This means making goals that are concrete, specific, and measurable.

1. Lose thirty-five pounds **vs.** lose weight
2. Find a "home" for every item and put items back in their "home" every time **vs.** get organized
3. Save 20% of my take home salary **vs.** spend less, save more
4. Spend at least six days per month on my hobbies **vs.** enjoy life to the fullest
5. Work out consistently four days per week **vs.** stay fit and healthy
6. Take skydiving lessons **vs.** learn something exciting
7. Research smoking cessation options with a target quit date of April 1st **vs.** quit smoking
8. Research mentoring programs and aim to mentor 2 or 3 students this year **vs.** help others with their goals and dream

9. Make a plan to "put myself out there," via dating sites, net-working events etc., with a goal to meet new people, and perhaps a potential partner **vs.** fall in love
10. Institute Sunday night dinners at home; take the family on two vacations this year **vs.** spend more time with family

It's good to have all of these goals, and good to put them into place, but it doesn't mean you have to do it all in the first week in January.

Through my work as a Certified Health Coach, I help people un-derstand that small changes really do add up to big results. It's not the big sweeping changes that make a difference in our lives; it's the little things we do.

The way we live our lives is a result of all the things we do each day, and every day is an opportunity to do something that will get us one step closer to living the life we really want to live. This is your chance to get your life, your health, your finances, and your rela-tionships in order and make this your **best year yet!**

Don't start next year with the same resolutions you had this year. Make a commitment to yourself to start now working towards your goals and dreams.

> *"The problem is we think we have time!"*
> *~Karen Ann Kennedy*

I've broken down this book by month, tackling the most common New Year's resolutions that people make.

January	Prepare For a New You
February	Master Your Finances
March	Organize Your Home and Your Life
April	Detox Your Life
May	Get Started on a Healthy Eating Plan
June	Focus on Fitness
July	Nurture Your Relationships
August	Meditate and Relax
September	Keep Learning
October	Get Cooking
November	Practice Gratitude
December	Reflect and Reset for the Coming Year

You can certainly buy a cookbook, a financial planner, a book on organizing, and any number of diet books that are out there on the market, but here, you will find it all!

So, Happy New Year! And Happy New You!

It's time to get started on *Your Best Year Yet*!

How to Use this Book

Each day will give you one new concept that you can put into practice. You may choose to work on the item that's given, or not; it's completely up to you. You can also switch days around, so if your January 7th is full, you can do that exercise on January 29th. The object is to get you thinking and doing, but it's your year and your life, so you need to be comfortable with the pace.

Each month is broken down by a different theme, as explained. If saving money isn't an issue for you, you may choose not to spend as much time working on those concepts. But, I urge you to at least go through and read each day. Remember, there is always room for improvement, and who knows…you might pick up some interesting information that will inspire you or cause you to think about your situation in a new way.

At the end of each month, there is a checklist to go through and track your progress for the month. You may choose to check off the items in your book, or, photocopy the page, check off the boxes, and put the page in your journal. This second option is good for those of you that plan to use this book again next year!

This is NOT a sit-on-the-beach-and-relax kind of book! This book is meant to inspire you into action! You'll be using this book in conjunction with other tools, such as a planner and a journal, and you'll be asked to do some exercises during the year.

DON'T SHORTCHANGE YOURSELF!

Take the time to work through the exercises and use the tools, tips, and techniques in this book to get you on the path to reaching your goals and dreams.

This is YOUR time, this is YOUR year! Get out there and make things happen!

ACKNOWLEDGMENTS

Writing a book has been a life-long dream of mine, and I certainly have many people to thank for helping to make my dream a reality.

To Paul, Kathy, Jade, John, and Josh: Thank you for making me feel like part of the family.

To Colleen: Thank you for encouraging me and holding me accountable every step of the way. Our early morning coffee dates are such an inspiration to me.

To Sherman: The best confidant, sounding board, and friend that anyone could ever ask for. The world is a better place because you're in it.

To Gina: For being my day-dreaming partner, and for encouraging me to keep moving forward with my dreams. Bali is not that far away!

To Mark: For all the friendship, fellowship, and business advice. As you always say, "It's on!"

ACKNOWLEDGMENTS

To my Nephew Marc: You are definitely the coolest Dude on the planet! I'm truly honored to be your Aunt.

To my Sister Lynn: My very first friend on this Earth and the best sister that anyone could ever hope to have. Thank you for loving me and encouraging me not just through the book-writing process, but throughout my whole life. P.S. You are the best damn proofreader a writer could ever ask for! I couldn't have done this without you.

To my Mom: Thanks for everything, and I do mean, everything; from countless breakfasts, lunches, and dinners, to all your help with the book. Thanks for always encouraging me. I couldn't have done it without you, and I'm really, truly grateful.

JANUARY – PREPARE FOR A NEW YOU

January is a great time to get into the mindset of starting anew. Instead of jumping in feet first to the New Year and trying to do everything all at once, I prefer to use January as a time to set myself up for a year of success!

Depending on your geographic location, the weather may be cold and dreary, and planning activities outside the home may be problematic due to the weather conditions. Why not use a cold, dreary weekend to do some planning? Americans spend more time planning their annual vacation than they do planning their lives! Now is the time to gather your materials; buy a new day planner, journal, etc. and get to work laying the positive foundation that will guide the rest of your year.

January 1st – Happy New Year!

If you've gone out last night to celebrate, you may be feeling a little sluggish today. That's okay. Today is going to be a day to relax and spend some time with your own thoughts. If your New Year's celebration is spilling over into today, savor it! Perhaps you are surrounded by friends and family. Maybe you are going out to see a New Year's Day parade, or meeting with friends for a fabulous lunch or dinner. Whatever your plans, enjoy them and don't stress about the things you want to accomplish this year. But, if you can carve out a few minutes of quiet time today, do it! Grab a pen and some paper. DO NOT use a pretty journal or notebook (if you do, you'll want to make it look all pretty and perfect). Spend a few quiet minutes just jotting down some things that you'd like to accomplish this year. Don't worry about timelines, deadlines, or even what's realistic. Just do some free-form writing and write down everything you think of, no matter how ridiculous or unrealistic it may seem. Hold onto this piece of paper…we'll come back to it later.

January 2nd – Get yourself a planner.

If you haven't already bought yourself a planner for the New Year, now is a good time to run out and get one. Yes, I know that you can keep all this information on your smart phone, but there's nothing quite like writing things down. My friends call me a "dinosaur" for carrying around my paper calendar, but I'll tell you what…this" dinosaur" is never late and always knows exactly where she is supposed to be, and what she is supposed to be doing. Buy a planner that's functional, but also one that fits your style. You'll be using it a lot this year. When you use it properly, it will become an amazing

3

tool! Visit an office supply store or bookstore and spend some time browsing around to find the planner that's just right for you.

January 3rd – Get yourself a journal.

Get yourself a journal that, like your planner, is stylish and that you'll enjoy writing in. While you're out, get some fun pens too! Pens that feel good when you hold them, have colors that you like, and ones that you'll use only for writing in your journal. If you are not much of a "journaler," don't worry, I'm not either, and I'm not suggesting that you write everyday (unless that's your thing). But I am going to suggest that you write sometimes, and I'll help you figure what to write and how to utilize your journal shortly.

January 4th – Start scheduling.

Today, pull out your shiny new planner and take a good look at your schedule. Start filling in important dates like birthdays and anniversaries, and start to think about some of the things you want to do this year. Pull out that free-form writing list from New Year's Day and highlight a few things that you really want to accomplish this year. Want to go to the beach this summer? Look at the summer months in the planner and "pencil" that in. And when I say pencil, I mean, really write it in pencil. You aren't making a concrete plan yet, but if you don't at least start to mentally book your vacation now, if you're anything like me, it will never materialize come June, July, and August! Were there other goals on that list that you can tackle? Read more? Schedule a Saturday or Sunday to go book shopping! Run your first 5K? Get on the internet and look up some races in your local area. Remember, we're still in the planning stages so no need to stress yourself out!

January 5th – Clear out the holiday clutter.

Today, put away the holiday decorations, and return everything to its "home." Broken decorations? Throw them away now. Don't

put them in a box to deal with in December. If you aren't willing
to fix it now, you won't be any more inspired to do it later in the
year. Now is the time to be honest about the things that you have.
If there are items that you don't love, or can't find a place for, think
about donating them. This will make your life a lot simpler twelve
months from now. Once you've gotten the decorations put away,
put your home back in order and give it a good clean. Does your
space look empty now? Some people feel a little depressed when
the holiday decorations go bye-bye. If this is you, treat yourself
to a vase of pretty flowers and put them in a prominent spot to
brighten your space.

January 6th – Clear your kitchen of holiday leftovers.
Clean out your kitchen and get rid of any leftover holiday foods.
This is a good time to dump the leftovers that are past their prime
and clean out the fridge. Fill your sink (or a cooler if you have
one) with ice and take everything out of your fridge. Wipe down
the shelves and pop a box of baking soda in there to keep things
smelling fresh. Before you put items back in the fridge, check the
expiration dates. Has your ketchup been in there for two summers
now? Time to chuck it! And remember, the warmest place in your
fridge is the door, so be strategic about where you place your food
items as you put them away.

January 7th – Check in with your feelings.
We are one week into the New Year! How are you feeling about
the rest of the year ahead? Do you feel anxious, excited, hopeful,
scared? Spend a few minutes today with your journal and write
down how you are feeling. Do this in a space and at a time where
you won't be interrupted. Make this a special time. Brew some tea,
pour a glass of wine, or find a sunny spot in the quiet of the morning and write over a cup of really good coffee. Don't just write
down how you feel, but take the time to examine why you feel that

way. Are you overwhelmed with the number of things on your to-do list? Are you dealing with a health issue or a family issue? Are you excited about the blank slate that is the New Year? Remember, don't stress about what's to come. You can only live one day at a time; that's all we get!

January 8th – Start an inspiration jar!

This is such a fun project and will be a really nice gift to yourself at the end of the year. Invest in a pretty glass jar and a small colorful notepad (not post it notes). During the year, whenever something wonderful happens for you, write it on a note with the date, fold it up, and put it in your jar. What do you include? It's all up to you! A promotion at work? The perfect latte on a snowy morning? Someone paid you a lovely compliment? You signed your first book deal? Doesn't matter what it is; if it makes you feel great; include it in your jar. At the end of the year (most people do it on New Year's Eve), you will take a few quiet moments and go through your slips of paper. Looking back on all of your achievements, big and small, will encourage and inspire you as you go into the next year.

January 9th – Journaling, for people who don't journal.

Get that journal out again! If you are not someone that feels like writing in a journal every day, or, if your journal ends up becoming just a rehash of each mundane task from your day, use your journal as a gratitude journal. I am not much of a journal writer. I find that I am a "rehasher." But, I now use my journal as a gratitude journal and at the end of each day, I write down just three things.

1. <u>Something I am grateful for.</u> Believe me, even on your WORST days, there is ALWAYS something to be grateful for. When you are feeling sorry for yourself, it's the perfect time to stop and think about all that you have to be

thankful for. Even if all you can come up with is that you're thankful that you ate today, that's something!

2. <u>Something fun that I did today.</u> This is more of a way to remind myself to stop and have a laugh. I know that I'm going to have to think of something fun to write down in my journal and if it's getting to be the end of the day and I haven't laughed at least once then something is wrong... REALLY wrong! So I make it a point to seek out at least one sliver of fun each day. Maybe coffee with a friend, or just sharing a joke with someone. It's important that you infuse a little fun into every day.

3. <u>Something that I have done today to get me closer to my goals.</u> Each and every day I try to do at least one thing that will make an improvement in my life. Even if it's just reading a page or two from a book, every day is a day to strive for self-improvement. I'm either learning something, helping someone, building my business, taking care of my body, or taking care of my spiritual self. I know you are busy, we all are. But, we can all carve out at least ten minutes every day for the pursuit of advancement. Make this a conscious effort every day!

January 10th – Let's get an action plan together for those goals!
Now is the time to pull out that free from writing list again and start to sort out what you really want to accomplish this year. It's time to put together an action plan. Remember:

> *"A goal without a plan is just a wish."*
> *~Antoine de Saint-Exupery*

Pull out your list, your planner, and your journal, and then, follow the three steps below to get started.

1. **WRITE** down your goals.
2. **PRIORITIZE** your goals and decide which one you will tackle first, second, third, etc.
3. Write an **ACTION PLAN** and a **TIMELINE** for each goal.
4. Get out there and **START**!

Once you have done this, commit to spending the time and effort it takes to see things through. Look at your planner and start scheduling activities that support your goals. Want to go back to school? Schedule a time to research your options. Schedule time to go visit college campuses or meet with an admissions counselor. Be realistic about when you would start your classes. Once you've written all your goals out, **SIGN AND DATE** them. A deal is a deal, and once you've signed off on your goals you have made a deal; **don't cheat yourself**!

January 11th – Get into the organizing mindset.

Getting into the organizing mindset does NOT mean a $300 run to the Container Store to buy a bunch of fancy storage boxes and baskets; In fact, I don't want you to buy anything at all. I want you to start getting rid of things. During your usual weekly cleaning, pick just one junk drawer, one sock drawer, or one bathroom cabinet, and clean it out, discarding things you no longer want or need. Now is a good time to do this while you are riding the wave of wanting to start the year fresh.

January 12th – Spend some time in your space.

Whether you have a six-bedroom mansion, a one-bedroom apartment, or you live in a small RV, this space is your home and is a good time to become reacquainted with it. Grab your journal and walk around your home spending some time in each individual room. Sit in the room and look around. Do you always sit on the sofa? Sit on the chair this time. Look at the room from a different viewpoint. What items jump out at you? What are some of your favorite things in the space? What do you have that you don't love or that no longer serves a purpose?

Think about the color scheme in each room. Is it what you really want? Write down how you feel in each room, and, what you would like to be feeling. If your dining room also doubles as your home office (like mine does), how can you make that space work for you? Thinking about a home improvement project this year? Get a blank sketchbook from an art supply store and start looking at home and design magazines. Cut out the pictures that inspire you. Maybe this is the year that you'll redecorate and make your home the sacred, beautiful space you've always wanted it to be!

January 13th – Clean out the pantry.

We've already tackled cleaning out the fridge. Now it's time to tackle the pantry. Go through and take out all your items. Wipe down the shelves and maybe put down some functional and stylish shelf liner. Go through each food item and check the expiration date; discard anything old or unusable. Think about how you store things. If you eat oatmeal every day, put the oatmeal within easy reach. If you keep treats around, but don't want to eat them all the time, store them on a higher shelf and make it a little more challenging to get to them. Once you have your pantry cleared out, make a list of items that you need to buy. We're going to stock a winter pantry next!

January 14th – Stock a winter pantry.

I don't know how the weather is where you live, but for me, January is cold and dreary! Most of my favorite fruits and vegetables are out of season, and with the snow and ice, going out for my weekly shopping trip starts to resemble an event at the winter Olympics! If the thought of bundling up and braving the nasty, snowy weather for a trip to the grocery store isn't very appealing to you, then having a well-stocked pantry will be a huge help in keeping you cozy AND well-fed.

Protein in the pantry
- Beans, dried and canned, like chickpeas and kidney beans
- Canned tuna (or other fish like salmon)
- Peanut butter
- Nuts

Fruits and veggies
Many winter fruits and veggies have a longer shelf life than their spring and summer counterparts. Root vegetables and different varieties of squash are easy to keep on hand for those cold, stormy days. Go for:
- Roots and tubers such as potatoes, onions, and turnips
- Winter greens such as Swiss chard, kale, and mustard greens
- Winter squash, such as butternut, acorn, and spaghetti squash

Other hearty staples
- Canned soups and broths
- Crackers
- Olives and olive oil
- Pasta, rice, and other grains like quinoa and couscous
- Whole grain cereals

You'll also want to stock up on canned, dried, and frozen essentials:
- Canned and frozen selections of fruits and vegetables
- Canned tomatoes and sauce
- Dried fruit

- Juices such as orange, apple, tomato, and grape

And how about some treats for those cold winter nights?
- Hot chocolate
- Microwave popcorn
- Powdered gelatin mixes
- Pudding

And how do you use some of these winter staples?
Quinoa is packed with protein and has a nutty, but mild flavor, which makes it very versatile. It cooks up quickly and can be used in both sweet and savory dishes. Use it to make hot cereal for breakfast, or as a base for soup, veggie burgers, or weeknight stir fry dishes.

Canned tomatoes are great to have on hand for chilis, soups, and stews, as well as pasta and pizza sauces, and casseroles.

Wild rice is a cold-weather pantry staple that is gluten-free, has two times the protein of brown rice, and 30 times the antioxidants of white rice...plus...it's delicious!

Canned pumpkin is also extremely versatile and can be used in both savory and sweet dishes. Try mixing it with your morning oatmeal with some nutmeg, cinnamon, or pumpkin pie spice!

Flax oil is delicious drizzled over steamed vegetables with a little tamari, lemon juice, a pinch of cayenne, and some crushed garlic. It's also delicious drizzled over soup.

Oatmeal is a terrific choice for a hearty breakfast on a cold morning, but it's also great to have on hand to make cookies, breads, and other baked goods.

11

Broth such as beef, chicken, or vegetable, is one of the best pantry staples around. It's great in soups, of course, but it's also useful when making sauces, risotto, mashed potatoes, casseroles, or even sautéed veggies. Freeze it in ice cube trays so you'll have small portions available when you need it.

Chickpeas or any type of beans are handy to have around. Chickpeas taste amazing with spaghetti or other pastas, in tacos, mashed into burgers, or blended into hummus.

Lentils just lend themselves to cold-weather eating. They are low-cost and can be used as a tasty alternative to chickpeas. Make a thick, filling lentil soup, tasty, hearty lentil bread, add lentils to meatballs, or sprinkle them on top of a salad.

January 15th – Turn off the TV!
Turn off the TV and free up some time! We are all busy. People always say they don't have time to do things, but you have as much time in your day as Albert Einstein, the President, and Oprah! The issue isn't the amount of time you have, but what you are doing with it. If you have time to watch TV, surf the internet, and play Candy Crush, you have time to do the things that will help you reach your goals. Read a book. Take a walk. Spend some time with your family. Do something every day that stimulates your brain and that does NOT mean watching hours of mindless TV!

January 16th – Prepare to take care of your body.
While you are in prep mode, it's time to start thinking about how you will take care of your body this year. Taking care of yourself is not a luxury, it is a NECESSITY! You have to take care of yourself before you can fully take care of others. This is why they tell you on the airplane to put on your own oxygen mask before you help another person with theirs! You cannot be a good spouse, parent,

sibling, employee, boss, neighbor, or friend, when you are taking care of everyone else at the expense of your own health and well-being. So, you know what time it is…get that planner out! See if you can block off some time to treat yourself. Schedule a haircut, a manicure, a massage, a colonic, or whatever else will make you feel healthy and pampered. Whatever it is you do to treat yourself, get it on the books now before you get too busy. Can't afford to go out for these services? That's okay, I've got you covered in the next few days.

January 17th – You can pamper yourself at home.

You do not need to spend a lot of money to feel pampered. With just a few essential products, you can stock a home spa and turn your bathroom into a sanctuary. I'll show you how in a day or two, but today, your first challenge is to clean your bathroom to create your sacred space! You cannot feel relaxed and refreshed in a bathroom with hair all over the floor, dirty towels lying around, kid's bath toys strewn all over, and the cat's dirty litter box. Take some time today to give your bathroom a good scrub, get rid of the clutter, and make it relaxing and inviting. Soon, you'll invest in some luxurious items like candles and bath salts, but first, clear out your bathroom space and get it ready. Buy some new, fluffy towels. Replace your worn out shower curtain. Think of color palettes that help you relax. Pull out that sketchbook of home pictures and add some pictures of relaxing bath spaces. What color schemes speak to you? Now is the time to get your bathroom space in order.

January 18th – Now, we shop!

It's time to stock your bathroom with spa-like products to help you relax and unwind. Here are a few things to pick up to get you started:

- An assortment of shower gels, soaps, and body lotions with scents that you enjoy. When possible, opt for more natural and organic products without a lot of chemicals.

- Essential oils such as tea tree, lavender, orange, and peppermint can be used in a variety of ways. Just be sure to read product labels carefully, as essential oils can be harmful if used improperly.
- High-quality face, body, and hair care products that you enjoy. Look for things with extra moisturizing properties, if you live in a cold climate. Forced air heat and cold winter weather can wreak havoc on your skin and hair.
- If you're feeling really indulgent, and you have the budget for it, invest in a few other luxury items like hand mitts and foot booties for deep overnight skin hydration, a pillow for the bathtub, an eye mask, scented candles, or maybe an aromatherapy diffuser.
- Skin brushes, a loofah mitt, and a good-quality hair brush.
- Skin scrubs, bath salts, and other exfoliating products will help slough off dry winter skin and give you a healthy, natural glow.

Carve out some time to pamper yourself and take care of your body. You will feel relaxed and healthy and an at-home spa day will take the bite out of cold winter days.

January 19th – Examine your work.
Today is the day to think about your work. Notice I didn't say "job." Not everyone works outside the home, but everyone works. If you stay at home to take care of your family, you are working! If you go to an office every day, you are working! If you drive a truck, drive your elderly parents to run errands, or drive the carpool to soccer practice, you are working! Do you enjoy what you do? Get that journal out again. Spend some time writing about your work. Do you enjoy it? If not, why do you do it? For some people the answer will be, "because I need to earn a living," and I totally get that! I worked a long time in a job that no longer served me because I

needed to pay my rent and feed my cat! But since this is going to be such a transformative year for you, it's time to think about your work and how you really feel about what you do. There are no right or wrong answers, just start writing down how you feel. Write down what you like about your work, what you dislike, and why you do what you do. Put the list away when you're done. We're going to let it sit for a few days before we explore what you wrote.

January 20th – Think about the people in your life.

Research has shown that we become a lot like the five people we spend the most time with. Who are your five people? If the people in your life are negative, whiny, selfish and self-centered people; that is not going to serve you well. As I was preparing to launch my business (and write this book), I found an accountability partner, a fellow entrepreneur with a can-do attitude and a giving spirit. We spent countless hours together working on our businesses, encouraging each other through failure and setbacks, and cheering each other on at every positive step forward. Imagine how great it would be to have someone like that in your life; to be surrounded by people that are in your corner, that have your back, and that want you to be successful.

Think about the people you associate with. Are there NEDs in your world? NEDs are Negative Energy Drains. You know them; the people who are always depressed, always sulking, people that can never find the silver lining? I call these people "Energy Vampires" because they literally suck the life and energy out of you. Stop being friends with these people. Stop allowing yourself to get sucked into their drama. This goes for everybody in your life, including your Facebook friends. Cut the cord on the negativity and drama and surround yourself with positive people with whom you can form healthy and happy relationships built on mutual caring and respect.

15

January 21ˢᵗ – Are we having fun yet?

Have you been writing in your journal every night? Are you writing down what you are grateful for? Are you writing down the fun you are having? While we are talking about fun; have you had any lately? When is the last time you took in a movie or met your friends for lunch, or had friends over for a movie marathon? If you haven't done anything fun since New Year's Eve, now is the time to get something on the books! Pull out your planner and schedule something fun to do. When you do this, it gives you something to look forward to. It's much easier to bear a tough week at work when you know that Friday night is girls' night, or that Saturday night is date night! Take your fun as serious as you take your work, it's just as important for your well-being.

January 22ⁿᵈ – Clean out your closet.

So far, we've cleaned out the kitchen, the bathroom, and maybe tackled a couple of junk drawers. Now is the time to get in your closet and donate clothing and accessories that you no longer want or need. A good rule of thumb is if you haven't worn an item in six months, it might be time to let it go. Pick a day when you don't have to go to work, put on some good music, and get ready to get to work! TRY THINGS ON! If you're on the fence about an item, put it on and see how you feel about it. Have fun! Put on a fashion show for yourself. Try that black blazer with your green dress. Break up a suit and wear your suit jacket with a pair of fabulous jeans and cool shoes. Men, try that purple tie with the blue shirt! If you aren't sure what to keep and what to discard, invite a friend over to help you. Pick someone you trust to be honest with you and someone that will tell you when it's time to let an item go. Once you've cleared out the items you no longer want, take them to the Goodwill or Salvation Army, or call Purple Heart to come pick them up, and then, reward yourself for giving to charity. Treat yourself to a new pair of shoes, or a cool, funky belt, or a fabulous new tie. But just one item! You don't want to fill up your newly-cleaned closet, and you don't want to blow your budget!

January 23rd – State your intentions.

Are you clear yet on your goals for the New Year? Have you decided what you truly want the next year to be like? It's time to state your intentions. There is something miraculous that happens when you tell people what you are going to do; you actually do it! Once it's spoken, and you've put it out there in the universe, it becomes real. This has happened to me many times in my life. I've told someone something I was going to do, or something that I really wanted, and it came to fruition! Stating your intentions helps create a support system for you.

I remember when I decided to run my first marathon; I told everyone! And then, people would ask me, "So, how's your training going? How far did you run today?" It created a level of accountability in my life, so on those days that I didn't feel much like running thirteen or fourteen miles, I thought about what I would say when somebody asked me about my training. Sometimes that was all the motivation I needed to follow through. Accountability is a powerful thing. Once you are clear on your goals and aspirations for this year, start letting people know. You'll be surprised how much you'll get from this one simple act.

January 24th – Give back as a way to feel good.

Now is the time to start thinking about how you can enhance your life by giving to others. When you volunteer, when you give of yourself to help others, it is the epitome of a win-win situation. The person receiving the services benefits from what you have to offer and you benefit from the good feeling that comes from helping others. I hear lots of reasons why people can't help. There's never enough money or time; believe me, I understand.

At the time of my writing this book, I am working 60 hours a week at my full-time job, getting my business off the ground, writing my blog and my newsletter, training for another half marathon, and taking care of my home and my cat. I have very little time and even less money to give. But I have found ways to do for others. I spend about 4 hours a month clipping coupons for our troops overseas. I collect and donate pet items for a local animal shelter, and I help high school and college students write their resumes and cover letters and prepare for their job interviews. Even the small act of feeding a stray cat has shown me that I can give back and make a difference.

Don't know where to start? Go to www.volunteermatch.com to find volunteer opportunities in your area. It's like a Match.com for people interested in volunteering, and organizations looking for additional help. When you give to others, believe me, you will inevitably get back so much more than you give.

January 25th – Let's revisit our exercise about work.

Pull out your notes from January 19th. How do you feel about what you do? Is there something you would rather be doing? And, if that's the case; why not go out and do it? I never felt like I fit in anywhere in my life. For a long time I felt like a pinball just getting bounced around from place to place. I always worked hard and worked to give my all to my employer, but I never felt like I was in the right place. As I began to build my business, I felt, for the first time in my life, that I had found my purpose.

> *"The two most important days in your life are the day you are born and the day you find out why"*
> *~Mark Twain*

The day I figured out why I was here on this Earth was a powerful day for me. And once I started working toward my true passion I finally felt like I belonged. So what do you want your life's work to be? Perhaps you will find your calling through some of that volunteer work we talked about yesterday. Maybe you have a hobby that can be turned into a lucrative business. Now is the time to think about your work and find your true path. It's never too late to be what you always wanted to be.

January 26th – Establish your schedule.

Pull out your planner again and start establishing a schedule for yourself. Your schedule should be broken down into the following areas:

1. Time for work
2. Time for family/friends
3. Time for yourself/your hobbies/self improvement
4. Time for household chores
5. Time for exercise
6. Time for fun

It's important to make sure that you are not letting one area of your life lapse because of too much focus on another area. Of course there are going to be times when your family will have to fend for themselves while you are on a week-long business trip, or exercise gets pushed to the side to take care of a sick friend. The danger comes when we consistently neglect an entire area of our lives. The trick here is to find the balance. If you're at the top of your game at work, but your family is falling apart; there is imbalance. If you are enjoying your family and friends, lavish dinners, and expensive happy hours, but can't pay your bills; there is imbalance. If you are physically fit and can bench press 350 pounds, but are severely depressed and alone; there is imbalance.

So, pull out that planner and start figuring out a schedule that works for you. There are 168 hours in a week. Below is roughly what most of my weeks look like:

1. 45 hours each week for work
2. 56 hours each week for sleep
3. 20 hours each week for exercise
4. 5 hours each week for household chores
5. 22 hours each week for myself
6. 20 hours for friends, family, and fun

Does every week look like this? Of course not! I don't always sleep seven hours a night. Some weeks I work harder, some weeks, I take a day or two off. I don't always get all my workouts in, and sometimes, I don't see my friends and family as much as I'd like. But at least I have a framework and am making a conscious effort to get everything in. If I find myself working way too many hours and not working out, I adjust. If I have been spending lots of time with friends but haven't been reading or learning, I adjust. Start looking at your schedule and see where you can capture pockets of time to do the things that you both need and want to do. FIND THE BALANCE!

January 27th – Start thinking about your money.
Since we'll be diving into your finances next month, now is the time to start thinking about your money.

> *"I got my mind on my money and my money on my mind."*
> *~Snoop Dogg*

Do you know how much money you make? Stupid question? Trust me, it's not. I worked in human resources for many years and each year at my job, employees would have to fill out benefits paperwork including their salary information. I can't tell you how many people would come to my office and ask me, "How much do I make?" Now folks, I don't know a lot of things, but I can tell you one thing I know, and that's how much money I make! So how much do you make? How much do you owe? How much money do you have right now in your wallet, your bank account, and your retirement fund? If you don't know, FIND OUT! If you feel beat up right now, just wait until February 1st. There is no excuse not to know how much money you have. It's important. You work hard for it! Here's a quick exercise to get you into the right financial mindset. Write down your annual salary, now figure out what you make each month, each week, each day, and each hour.

Let's assume you make $40,000 a year.
That means you make $3,333 a month.
That means you make $833 per week.
Assuming you work a 5-day week, that's $166 per day.
Assuming you work an 8-hour day, that's roughly $20 an hour.

Why is this important? Because when you go out and buy that $300 pair of boots, you've essentially traded about two days of your life for them! Think about that! But don't think about it too long, we'll be tackling your finances in just a few days.

January 28th – It's time to start thinking about food.
How much do you cook at home and how much of your food intake is from eating out? Most people start the New Year on an instant diet. January is actually one of the worst times, in my opinion, to start a diet. Where I live, it's cold and dreary and snowy, so I can't get out and exercise, and there is a shortage of really good fresh fruits and vegetables, unless you don't mind eating apples and oranges all day long.

But January is a good time to start becoming mindful of what you eat. We'll be talking about food a lot this year, since losing weight is the most popular New Year's resolution on the planet. Get that journal out again. For the next four days, write down everything you eat. Don't worry about the calorie count, that's not the purpose of this exercise. I want you to write down everything you eat and then write down how it made you feel. Did you feel bloated? Sluggish? Did you have gas? Did you feel guilty? It's important to start paying attention to what you're eating and what it's doing to your body.

After the four days, look back and try to spot any patterns in your eating habits. Do you consistently feel bad after you eat chips? Do you feel sluggish when you overeat at lunchtime? Try adjusting what you eat and pay attention to the cues being given to you by your body.

January 29th – Save on your grocery bill.

Want to save some money on your grocery bill? I'm betting you do! That's why shows like *Extreme Couponing* on TLC are so popular! Who <u>wouldn't</u> want to save hundreds of dollars every week on their grocery bill? I've got a great tip that has helped me save over the years.

Most people grocery shop based on their meal plan for the week. I do the opposite; I meal plan based on the grocery store. I usually do all my cooking for the week on Sunday (we'll talk about that later in the book).

Before I decide what I'm going to cook, I get online and check out what my grocery store has on sale.

Say I want to make shrimp and orzo, well, that's fine, except shrimp isn't on sale and neither is the orzo for that matter. But on Saturday morning, before I hit the grocery store, I sit at my computer with a cup of coffee and pull up the sale circular. I see that tilapia is on sale, so is risotto, and asparagus! That sounds like a pretty fabulous dinner to me! And by buying based on the sales, I save a substantial amount of money. Combine those savings with my coupons and BAM…that's even more money in my pocket! Try it! See how much you can save with just this one simple adjustment.

January 30th – Budget your grocery money.
When I started to really pay attention to my food budget, I realized that I was spending for me and my cat what some people spend to feed a family of four! It was ridiculous and I was, quite frankly, embarrassed for myself. I decided right then and there that I would cut my grocery bill, and I did. I now have a weekly budget of $60. That $60 feeds me and the cat. It also pays for my household cleaning supplies, AND all my health and beauty products. And, please note that I only buy all-natural cleaning and beauty products, so I'm stretching that sixty bucks a long way. By the way, I eat healthy! We're not talking pop tarts and soda here! I eat lots of oatmeal, seasonal fruits and veggies, and whole grain pasta. IT CAN BE DONE!

The first step is to do what I suggested yesterday, and plan your meals based on the sales. The second step is clipping those coupons. When clipping coupons remember, it's not a deal if you buy stuff that you don't really want. Coupons work best when you use them for products that you truly need and plan to use. Utilize your freezer by stocking up on sale items and freezing them until you are ready for them. And buy only what you need and can use in a week's time.

January 31st – End of the month check-in
We've made it through the first month of the year! How do you feel so far? Pull out your journal and go back to January 7th. Go ahead

and read what you wrote about how you were feeling. Do you still feel that way? Do you feel more in control? Have you done any of the things that I suggested for you? Go ahead and check off below which items you tackled this month. Or photocopy this page and check off the boxes if you plan to use this book again next year. Take a few moments to write down how you feel now about the New Year. If you still feel anxious or overwhelmed, think about some strategies you can use to help you feel more in control. And please remember, the object is to take it one day at a time. That's the goal!

My January to-do list:

- ° I brainstormed what I want this year to be like
- ° I bought my planner
- ° I bought a journal
- ° I did some preliminary scheduling
- ° I cleaned out the fridge
- ° I checked in with my own feelings
- ° I started my inspiration jar
- ° I started writing down the things I'm grateful for
- ° I wrote down my goals
- ° I set up my action plan in order to meet my goals
- ° I organized at least one junk drawer
- ° I spent time in the spaces within my home
- ° I cleaned out the pantry
- ° I stocked the pantry
- ° I cut down on my TV watching
- ° I cleaned the bathroom
- ° I stocked my home spa
- ° I examined my work
- ° I thought about the people in my life
- ° I scheduled some fun activities for myself
- ° I cleaned out my closet
- ° I stated my intentions
- ° I explored some volunteer opportunities
- ° I did the salary exercise
- ° I wrote down what I ate for four days

FEBRUARY – MASTER YOUR FINANCES

Most people want to feel financially secure. Most people want to have enough money to pay their bills, feed their families, and have enough money left over to be able to do some fun things in life. Most people want to save for the future. What about you? Do you want to master your finances? And what does "mastering" your finances really mean to you? For some people, this means being able to meet all their financial obligations comfortably, for some it means having enough money to take their family on a fabulous vacation every year, for others it means becoming a multi-million-aire, or billionaire. Whatever your goals are, you can get there, if you start with some of the simple financial steps that we'll be going through together this month.

February 1st – Write it down.

Grab yourself a small notebook, something small and light that you can carry with you wherever you go. For the next month, you are going to write down everything you spend; and I do mean <u>everything!</u> When you pay your rent, write it down. When you buy your groceries, write it down. When you buy a pack of gum for 65 cents, write it down. This is going to be the most eye-opening experience for you! It's amazing to see where your money actually goes.

Many of the people I work with tell me that they "don't spend very much," but upon examining where their money has gone, I see that they've spent $5 each day at Starbucks, or $35 a week on lunch. I once worked with a client who spent $8 a day at the vending machine; that's $40 a week! You cannot master your finances when you don't know where your money is going. So, for the entire month of February when you spend, you write it down.

February 2nd – Know what you owe.

The first step to managing your debt is to know what you owe. So many people I know avoid opening their bills because they don't want to see how much they owe. There's a word for this; denial…and people in denial do not master their finances. The best starting point is to get an accurate list of all your bills and monthly expenses. You cannot effectively manage your money if you don't know how much you bring in and how much is going out. Let's start, just for today, with writing down a list of your major expenses; credit cards, housing, car loan, student loans, etc. Don't worry about the budgeting just yet, we're going to get to that.

February 3rd – Know your credit card debt.

Make a list of all your credit cards and what the interest rate is on each card. Then, create a chart, like the one below, and write down your cards by interest, with the highest rate card listed first. The goal is to pay off the credit card with the highest interest rate first. As you pay off each card, take that payment money and pay off the next card and the next card and the next card.

Feature	Card 1	Card 2	Card 3	Card 4
Issuer:				
Interest rate:				
Amount owed:				
Minimum payment:				
Credit limit:				

We're going to spend a lot of this month talking about debt, particularly credit card debt, so fill out your chart and put it away for now. Don't worry, we'll be coming back to it soon.

February 4th – Set up a budget.

Now that you know how much money you make and how much money you spend, it's time to set up a budget for yourself. Be realistic about how much you can afford to spend each month. Your budget should consist of fixed expenses (rent, mortgage, car payment, etc.) and variable expenses (groceries, gas, electric, etc.). If you find that you don't have enough to cover everything, your variable expenses will need to be adjusted.

Not sure how to allocate your money? Here's a guideline that you can follow:

50% of your earnings to towards your needs
30% goes towards wants
20% goes towards your savings

And let's establish a "need." You need to eat. You need to keep a roof over your head. You need reliable transportation to get to work. You need clothes to wear. You need insurance to cover your medical expenses.

You do not need a $6 latte every day on your way to work. You do not need a $500 leather purse. You do not need to spend $75 every Friday night to go to happy hour with your co-workers. That's not to say that you shouldn't have these things IF YOU CAN AFFORD THEM! But, it's important to make sure that you can be honest with yourself about a need versus a want.

The easiest way to budget your money is to categorize it. We've already done the first step (identifying your fixed versus variable expenses), now it's time to put each expense in the right category. Here are some expense categories to get you started. Obviously, you want to pick the categories that fit your actual expenses.

Housing
- Mortgage or rent

Utilities
- Phone
- Electricity
- Gas

- Water and sewer
- Cable
- Trash removal
- Maintenance or repairs

Transportation
- Car loan
- Bus/taxi fare
- Insurance
- Gas
- Maintenance

Insurance
- Home
- Health
- Life
- Other

Food
- Groceries
- Dining out

Pets
- Food
- Medical costs
- Grooming
- Toys
- Other

Personal Care
- Medical
- Clothing
- Dry cleaning

- Gym membership
- Other

Entertainment
- Movies
- Concerts
- Music
- Sporting events
- Live theater
- Other

Loans
- Personal
- Student
- Credit cards

Gifts and Donations
- Gifts
- Charity 1
- Charity 2
- Charity 3

At the end of the month, once you've written down everything you've spent, start working out your budget and then stick to it.

February 5th – Start paying cash.
In a recent study, the spending habits of a few hundred people were tracked. The findings showed that those who paid with cash spent less money overall. Why? Because forking over actual dollars is painful for most people. I know it is for me. Swiping your credit card, or even your debit card, doesn't equate for most people to spending "real money," because plastic doesn't look or feel like real money.

When participants of the study had to pay cash, they spent on average of 35% less at the grocery store, and an average of 50% less overall. Just be sure that if you're going to use cash that you get a receipt so you can still track what you've spent.

February 6th – Break the credit card cycle.

It's okay to have a credit card, or two, for emergencies, and it's even good to spend a little on the cards here and there to keep your credit score in good shape. But if you're going to use credit, charge only what you know you can pay off. Carrying extra money on your cards with some interest rates as high as 26% means that you're paying a lot more than you need.

February 7th – Know the warning signs of credit trouble.

If you are paying only the minimum amount due on your credit cards that is the first sign that you may be in over your head with credit card debt. Another tell-tale sign of trouble is when your total credit balance rarely goes down. If you feel stress when you use your cards, or know that you are charging more than you make in payments in each month, it's time to get serious and put the cards away. One trick is to put your spending "on ice." You've probably heard this before, and it may sound crazy to you, but it really works! If you can't be trusted not to use your cards for impulse buys, leave them at home, better yet, freeze your cards. You heard me right! Put your card in a freezer safe baggie, submerge your card in a freezer-safe container filled with water and put the whole thing in the freezer. When you want to use your card, it will take some work to get to it. Use that time to really think about whether or not you need to make that purchase, and if you do, think about whether it has to go on your card.

February 8th – Stop financing your living expenses.

Are you using your cards to pay for everyday items like gas and groceries? This is another sign of credit card trouble. There is, however, one exception…if you have a card that pays you points, and you can pay off the balance on your card EVERY MONTH, then go for it!

I have a friend who used his Discover card for everything, and I mean everything. If he ran to the local convenience store for a soda and a hot dog, he used his Discover card. He used it for gas, groceries, movie tickets, clothing, and online purchases. He racked up enough cash back points to almost completely finance his dream trip to Italy!

Now, keep in mind, you've got to be really disciplined to do this. You still have to spend only what you can afford, and you must pay off the balance each month, otherwise, you may start to slide into debt.

February 9th – Make more than the minimum payment.
Credit card companies love it when you pay the minimum payment and no more each month. That's how they make their money! When you carry a balance and pay only the minimum payment, you are only scratching the surface of your actual debt. What you are paying with the minimum payment is the interest, NOT the principal. Pay as much as you can over the minimum payment to bring that debt down faster.

February 10th – Keep the lines of communication open.
If you are in debt and cannot pay your creditors, this is not the time to go radio silent. Call your creditors, explain your situation, and work out a payment plan with them. If you have been a customer with a company for a long time, be sure to tell them so. There are still companies that will reward customer loyalty. Those that appreciate customer loyalty will sometimes go to great lengths to keep their customer base happy, and that means, working with you when you hit hard times.

If you've lost your job, experienced a health crisis, or have experienced some other crisis that causes you to not be able to keep up with your debt, call your creditors and say so. Please note that a last minute girls' weekend to Aruba does not constitute a crisis. Don't lie to your creditors, but when you really can't pay them, you need to tell them so. Remember, these people lent you money because you agreed to pay them back, it's not fair to disappear on them.

February 11th – Keep the lines of credit open.
Never close cards with an existing balance. I know it might seem counter-intuitive when you're trying to get out of debt, but closing a card with an existing balance wrecks your credit score by sending your credit utilization (your available limit vs. your current debt) down, which drives down your credit score.

February 12th – Lighten the load.
Are you seriously in debt? I hope that's not the case, but for millions of Americans, the truth is they are one paycheck away from being homeless. If you are seriously that far in debt (or close to it), it may be time to lighten the load by liquidating your assets.

This is what I call "get real time." This is the time to think seriously about what you can sell off to raise some cash. It's time to be honest. Can you afford to drive that brand new car? If not, it's time to trade it in for something reliable, but a little less flashy. If you have a closet bursting with designer clothes, get the good stuff together and take it to a consignment shop. Start with big-ticket items that will raise some fast cash; a big screen TV, a Jacuzzi, an expensive stereo system. I know this sounds harsh, but desperate times call for desperate measures.

Even if you're not in such dire straits, look around your house and do a sweep of all the little items that you can live without, then, hold a yard sale! Remember, someone's trash is another man's treasure. Ridding your house of junk that you don't need not only helps you to make a few extra dollars, it helps you clear out the clutter and helps you enjoy your space with less stuff.

February 13th – Spend your tax refund wisely.

If you're seriously in debt, a hefty tax refund may be just the large chunk of change you need to pay off some debt and give you some breathing room.

If you aren't in debt, a hefty tax refund could go towards a nice vacation for your family, or a very special treat for yourself, like a spa day or some new clothes. Maybe you will use it to do some home improvements, or splurge for something special for the house like a big screen TV. Maybe you'll decide to put it away for Christmas presents later in the year, or, maybe you'll invest it.

It's your money, you can do with it what you'd like, but I urge you to spend it wisely. If you have no savings available for emergencies, a trip to Disney World may not be the best use of your cash, which we will talk about tomorrow.

February 14th – You need an emergency cash fund.

Credit cards are often where we turn when we have an unexpected and unplanned purchase, such as when the car or the water heater dies, but turning to your cards can result in undoing all the good work you've done to pay down your credit card debt.

You may have heard guidelines like, "have a three or six month salary reserve in savings for emergencies." This might be too steep for you, or you might have a hard time saving. If you need help getting into the savings mindset, try to do what I suggested earlier and try saving 20% of your income. Save it in a place that is not easy to access, and, set up automatic savings.

When I get my paycheck, I have my direct deposit set up so that a portion of my check goes right to my savings account. Because I don't really see the money, and because I have already worked it into my budget, I don't miss it. I will admit that sometimes it's tempting to dip in there and spend it, but, it's also fun to see the amount grow each month, and that makes it easier to leave it alone.

There are other easy and fun ways to put some money away. My first and last name both start with the letter K, so I save every dollar bill I get that has a K on it. My mom and dad used to call them "K Dollars," and I grew up thinking that they were special. Now, each time I get one, I put it away. I also got into the habit of saving every $10 bill I received. Maybe you just want to save fives, that's okay, or just certain ones; that's okay too. Whatever you decide, it makes saving a little more fun. I often get a healthy stack of tens and ones that add up to $100 or more. Let me tell you, that's a fun deposit to take to the bank!

February 15ᵗʰ – Don't reward yourself.

Are you feeling overwhelmed yet? I sure hope not! But if you are, it's time to take a break and breathe. And if you've been going through the steps and making progress, congratulate yourself, but don't reward yourself.

Once you start to take hold of your finances, you may be tempted to treat yourself to some CDs or a nice dinner out. DON'T DO IT! Just a few little splurges can put you back on the slippery slope to overspending. Want to treat yourself for all your hard work? Spend a little extra one week on groceries and cook a fabulous dinner for you and your friends, send the kids to grandma's house and have a spa night at home, go to the park with your favorite book and a picnic lunch and take in the beauty around you. Then, congratulate yourself again for showing some restraint and taking control of your spending.

February 16ᵗʰ – Perform a mid-month check in.
Have you been writing down everything you spend? If so, go back and look in your notebook and start to look for patterns. At the end of the month, I'm going to ask you to add up everything you spend to see where your money goes, but before we do that, now is a good time to see "why" your money goes.

What do I mean by that? Do you stop at a fast food place every Thursday night because you're tired and you don't want to cook? Do you find yourself ordering pizza every Friday night? Do you frequently go shopping on your lunch break when you've had a bad day at work? If you notice that you are establishing these patterns, it's time to take an honest look at what the patterns are, and how you can break them. If your boss ticks you off and your response is a $250 shopping spree, is that the best course of action? Could you take a (free) walk instead? Could you sit in the park and turn your face to the sun and breathe? Go back and look at your spending for the month so far.

February 17ᵗʰ – Retail therapy
How many times have you heard someone say that they needed "retail therapy?" Or maybe you've said it yourself at some time. Why does shopping make us feel good? It's not as mysterious as you might think.

The first thing about shopping is that it's a distraction. When you are worried about a problem, stressed about a situation, or dreading an upcoming unpleasant event or activity, you may look for something that distracts you from thinking about the problem at hand. Shopping is a pleasurable experience because it distracts you.

The next thing is that buying something new gives you a rush of endorphins. You feel good when you have something new in your

39

hand. It's fun to buy a new dress or new shoes or CDs or whatever it is that you buy. And retailers set you up for this! Stores are laid out in such a way that you feel good when you are there.

The next time you go shopping, pay attention to the atmosphere. You walk in, there are bright lights, pictures of people wearing cool clothes, laughing, dancing; they look happy. Many stores play upbeat music, the sales people are perky and smiling, and the slim mannequins are dressed in perfectly coordinated out-fits meant to entice you into buying. None of this is an accident! Retailers have gotten very savvy in the art of making you feel good to get you to buy.

Am I knocking shopping? Of course not! What I'm advocating though is shopping when you need something, not shopping for sport. Shopping is not a hobby. And it's important that we do not use shopping as a way to avoid dealing with issues that need our attention. If you need a new shirt, go shopping, if you need to get your life in order, go to therapy!

February 18th – Keep your eyes on the prize.
When you have a big savings goal, it's easy to get swayed off your savings path by instant gratification. It's hard to save a big chunk of money for a new car, or a vacation, or a wedding that's 18-months away. When you're saving for something specific, the lure of a 50% off sale, or a girls' weekend, or a new flat-screen TV, offers some-thing that your long-term item doesn't; instant gratification!

It's important when you have these moments of weakness to ad-dress them before you give in. Here's a few tips to help you:

1. Remind yourself of what you're saving for. If it's saving for a wedding, make a vision board and post pictures of the

venue, the flowers, the cake. Carry a picture of your dress in your wallet to remind you that the dress is worth more than the new jacket you're eyeing up at the mall.

2. Compromise! If you're longing for that new flat-screen TV, and you know it's not within your budget, take yourself out to a movie instead, or buy yourself a DVD or two that you can enjoy on your current TV.

3. Remove the temptation as much as you can. If you know you are saving for a new car, stop spending your weekends at the mall. You wouldn't take an alcoholic to a bar, so don't take a shopaholic to a shopping center. Now would be a great time to pick up a new hobby. Start walking or running, start scrapbooking, learn a language. Keep your eyes on the prize!

February 19th – It's time to come clean.

Last month, we talked about becoming like the five people we spend the most time with. If your group of five are spendthrifts, spending their weekends shopping and dining out at expensive restaurants, you need to be honest about whether or not you can afford to keep up with them.

For years I was embarrassed to admit to my friends that I didn't have the money to do the things that they were doing. I would go out with them for dinner and would often pick up the tab. Whenever we would out for dinner or drinks, I'd often agree to a restaurant that I knew was out of my budget, because I was too ashamed to speak up and tell my friends that it was out of my price range. How foolish I used to be.

When I first started my business, I scrimped and saved every penny I could. My "prize" was the opportunity to quit my nice, stable day job to live the life I really wanted. I could no longer afford to go out to lunch all week long, or go to expensive restaurants for happy hour. I couldn't afford to invite all my friends over and put out a lavish spread. It was time to fess up to my friends and tell them. And an amazing thing happened when I did...THEY DIDN'T CARE!

My true friends understood my desire to save and were trying to save just like I was! My cutting back prompted some of them to cut back as well, and we pooled our resources so we could all be thrifty together. We had Sunday night dinners at my house, many that were pot luck. We swapped services with each other, trading our talents to help each other out when we could. I hadn't become the leper of my social group, and you don't have to either.

And, if your friends love you more over an expensive dinner than they do over pizza and a $10 bottle of wine, maybe they're not really your friends.

February 20th – Know your credit score.

If you don't know your credit score, now is the time to find out. You can go to many reputable outlets to get your credit score (avoid those "free" credit score outlets with the dorky commercials). Your credit score is an important number! A good one can mean a better car or home loan with lower interest rates that can save you hundreds of dollars over time. Your credit score can even determine your future job and your future earnings. Many companies have begun to check the credit scores of potential employees.

A credit score over 720 used to be considered good, but now, 760 is the new 720; so the higher you can get your number, the better. There are lots of things you can do to boost your score, but the first step is to know where you currently are. So, stop reading and get online right now to check your score.

Start at www.equifax.com, www.experian.com, or www.transunion. com to get started.

February 21st – Boost your credit score.
Now that you've checked your credit score, it's time to boost it! Here are a few simple tips to put in place.

1. Pay your bills on time! If you have a hard time sitting down to pay your bills, or are inconsistent with them, set up automatic payments through your online banking provider. Just a few late payments can have an impact on your FICO score.
2. Resist the urge to open up a whole bunch of new credit card accounts to boost your credit. This will not work for you! The best way to boost your credit is to pay down what you currently have and pay consistently.
3. Avoid canceling your credit cards. Cancelling your cards may actually lower your score. Keeping an older account open and paid in full shows that you have a long track record of good credit.
4. I mentioned this before, but it bears repeating; if you are in trouble with your creditors, contact them! Hiding your head in the sand will not help you. Work out a payment plan that you can live with. As you make your payments consistently and ON TIME, you will start to re-establish a good track record.
5. Be patient. You don't build, boost, or destroy credit overnight. It takes time to get back on the right track.

February 22nd – Play the "cost-pay" game.
When I was younger and got my first job, I was in high school and like most high school girls I was into clothes! I remember going to

stores and eyeballing a cute top or skirt and thinking that come payday I would go back and get it.

Before I actually shopped for anything, I window shopped and then I played a game with myself. It was the "cost-pay" game. I decided what I thought was an acceptable price for each item and what I was willing to pay. I would look at that cute top and decide that it was worth $20. If I got into the store with my hard-earned paycheck and the top was $25, I wouldn't buy it. If the top was $15, SCORE, I'd snap it up. Sounds crazy, I know, but that helped me to avoid buyer's remorse more times than you can imagine.

In this way, nothing was really an "impulse buy." I knew what I wanted and what I was willing to pay for it. I used this strategy for many purchases, not just clothes. I decided what an acceptable price would be for my new car, my rent, the lamps in my living room. Go ahead and play the game! You have nothing to lose and everything to save!

February 23rd – Know what things cost.

This is a strategy that many bargain grocery shoppers will tell you about, and it works! Want to know if you are overpaying for an item? The only real way to know is to know what things generally cost. Retailers will give you the "sale price" of an item, but some-times, it's not really a bargain. Here's an example…The grocery store I normally shop at ran a special on cereal, two boxes for $6. That sounded like a great deal, and I snapped it up. But after I snapped it up I realized that the same box of cereal is normally $3.49 each, which means, I really only saved a dollar. A dollar is still a dollar, but it's not the big savings I thought I was getting. What's worse is that the grocery store across from my apartment sells the same cereal at the everyday price of $2.49, which means I not only didn't save, I actually overpaid by about a dollar.

Savvy grocery shoppers will look at the circulars and know what the items they buy generally cost; then, they know whether or not they are getting a good deal. Now, I'm not suggesting you drive to ten different stores, no one has time for that, and seriously, you burn up more gas money that way. But at least pay attention to what things cost so you can be sure you're getting a good deal on an item.

February 24th – Change your money mindset.

In the last few days of this month, I want you to start changing your money mindset. It's important to pay attention to your money, but not to obsess about it every minute of every day. I believe that where we focus our attention is important. When you are poor, the only thing you think about is money, but for many that are rich, the only thing they think about is money. The worry over money causes people to lose sleep, develop ulcers, or "hoard" money to the point where they no longer enjoy life. Let's get ready to change that.

February 25th – The flow of money.

As I've been researching more about money, there is one concept that has continued to come up and it's been very thought-provoking to me. It's the concept that money has a flow, like blood in your body. When you "hoard" your money (as mentioned yesterday) you create a blockage. No money is going out, but then again, no money is coming in either! When you hoard your money it sends a signal to the universe that you believe there will be no more money coming to you.

This is not to say that you should spend money you don't have and that you should empty out your savings account. This is just to say that you need to build a healthy relationship with money, just like you build a healthy relationship with food, or with other people. How? We'll talk about this tomorrow.

February 26th – Establishing your money relationship.

It's list time! Get out your journal and write down your top five priorities in life. Now, think about where your money goes. If you said that your family is your top priority; when was the last time you went on vacation together? You may say that your family is most important, but you don't have any money to take a vacation. However, if I look in your closet and see it overflowing with expensive designer clothes, that means your money priorities are not matching up to your life priorities. If you say that your health is a top priority, but you buy junk food and eat at fast food restaurants, your money priorities are not matching up to your life priorities.

See how this works? Now is the time to make an action plan that ensures that your finances are meeting your life priorities. If family is number one, work your budget to support that. Put some money away for a vacation, save your spare change and cash it in every other month and use that money to spend the day at a museum, or amusement park with the kids.

If your health is a top priority, organize your budget so you can afford to shop for good, fresh foods. You can't look like a million bucks if you're eating off the dollar menu!

It's time to take your budget to the next level by matching it up to your life priorities and life goals. Don't wait, sit down now with your journal and create your healthy relationship with money.

February 27th – Sit on it.

Money has the power to create a lot of stress in your life. Most stress is caused by lack or a feeling of lack, however, even those with money can stress about it. John D. Rockefeller is a name that is synonymous with wealth, however, he was so stressed out over money that he actually made himself sick over it!

It's rare that people stress about little expenses. The weekly shopping trip is usually not enough to send you into a panic, but when you have to make big decisions, your best option is to sit on it!

Unless there is water pouring into your basement or your roof has a hole in it and you need to act immediately, your best course of action is to pause and ask yourself the following questions:

1. What is the problem that I am facing?
2. Is spending money the only way to solve this problem?
3. What is the most expensive option to solve the problem?
4. What is the least expensive option to solve the problem?
5. Will waiting too long make the problem worse?
6. Based on all the information available, what is my best option?

Let's put this into practice. I'm going to use the leaky roof as my example.

1. **What is the problem that I am facing?** I have a leaky roof in my dining room.

2. **Is spending money the only way to solve this problem?** Perhaps you have a friend who is a roofer. If you offer to tutor his kid in math, maybe he will repair it for free. Maybe you are a phenomenal painter and you can swap painting services for a roof patch? Think creatively here! If you truly don't have this kind of hook up (I don't), then spending money is the only way to solve this problem.

3. **What is the most expensive option to solve the problem?** The most expensive option would be to replace the entire roof.

4. **What is the least expensive option to solve the problem?** The least expensive option may be to just have the roof patched.

5. **Will waiting too long make the problem worse?** In this case, probably so. You need to stop the leaking, and while you don't want to spend more than you have to, you probably don't have a week to go around getting multiple estimates. You should try to get at least three estimates (to be sure you aren't being taken advantage of), and then, you can make some decisions.

6. **Based on all the information available, what is my best option?** You've gotten some good estimates, you have a timeline for when each contractor is available, now you can decide what to do. People make the best decisions when they have the most information, so gather as much information as you can in the time available and then decide on your best option. Perhaps you have a roofer who will patch the roof now and give you a 20% discount on an entire roof replacement come spring.

The idea is that you make the best decisions you can with the information you have available to you. When you are thinking about spending a large chunk of money on anything, sit on it until you can ask these questions:

1. Is this something I need?
2. How am I going to pay for it?
3. What else could I be doing with this money?
4. Is this a need or a want?
5. Can I afford it?

February 28th – End of the month check in

We've made it through February! How do you feel so far? Have you done any of the things that I suggested for you? Go ahead and check off what you've done! You'll be proud of yourself, I promise!

February 29th – Bonus Day!

Hey! Is it February 29th? If it is, you've got a bonus day. I encourage you to do something really fun today. Do something crazy! Call out sick and go rock climbing. Serve the kids breakfast for dinner and let them watch a little extra TV. Send your mom flowers just because, call your boyfriend and tell him you need him to come fix your leaky kitchen sink, then when we gets there, take him straight to the bedroom! Perform a random act of kindness. Grab a bunch of $5 gift cards for a local coffee spot and give them to police officers patrolling in your neighborhood. Take a tray of cookies to a fire house and thank the firefighters (many of whom are volunteers) and tell them you appreciate them. Go to a woman's shelter and read to the kids there. Today is a special day, so do something special to commemorate it.

My February to-do list:

- ° I wrote down everything that I spent this month to see where my money is going
- ° I went through all my debts and know exactly what I owe
- ° I know what I owe on all of my credit cards
- ° I know what all of the interest rates are on my credit cards
- ° I set up my budget
- ° I focused on paying cash
- ° I budgeted enough to pay more than the minimum payment on my credit cards
- ° I made contact with my creditors*
- ° I started to identify items that I can sell off for extra money*
- ° I started my emergency cash fund
- ° I performed my mid-month check in
- ° I came clean to my friends about my financial position in an effort to stop overspending
- ° I know my credit score

If you are late on payments, or in financial trouble

MARCH – ORGANIZE YOUR HOME AND LIFE

Research has shown that there is a direct link between chaos and clutter in the home and chaos and clutter in the brain. When our homes are not in order, it can cause US not to be in order. I know I feel this in a big way, even when I'm not at home. When my house is a mess, even when I am away from home, I feel it. I feel out of balance and stressed out, and, for sure, this gets worse when I get home.

Home is the place that you should look forward to going to. Your home should be your sanctuary, where you can get away from the world and recharge, enjoy your family, your pets, and your items. But, when your house is a mess, when there's clutter everywhere and dirty dishes in the sink, and dirty socks on the floor, you may find it hard to feel relaxed.

It's not just organizing your home, you need to organize your life! If you went ahead and bought that planner back in January, you'll be thanking me, because you'll be able to organize and structure things much better now! So, welcome March! Let's get started.

March 1ˢᵗ – Get yourself in an organized mindset.

Before you go out and drop a bundle of money at your nearest Container Store, it's time to get yourself into the organizing mindset. Grab your journal and walk around the house with it. Jot down the "problem areas"; that spot by the door where shoes pile up, that one junk drawer that won't even close, that area on the kitchen counter that keeps filling up.

After you write down the problem spots, go back and write down what you really want each spot to be. Do you really want to keep shoes by the door? Should that junk drawer stay a junk drawer? It's important to identify how you want each area to function.

March 2ⁿᵈ – Let the clean out begin.

Pull out your planner and schedule a couple of days in a row when you can focus on a big clean. If you have a big house, or have a lot of spaces that need attention, you may want to add in a third day to get it all done. There is something very rewarding about getting a big clean done all at once, and taking the time to do this may help inspire you to keep it clean. Got kids? Schedule for them to be away during the clean up, if possible. Turn off the TV (you don't need the distraction), turn up the music, and get cleaning!

March 3ʳᵈ – Plan your attack.

It's best to start at the top and work your way down. If you live in an apartment or a ranch-style house, start at one end and work your way to the other. But before you do anything, write down some goals for yourself. You'll want to include things like:

1. Why do you want to organize your home?
2. What are the spaces that need the most attention?
3. What are some items that you can donate or throw away?
4. What are some things that you will want to bring in?
5. Are there any spaces that need a complete overhaul?

Once you've gotten in touch with your motivation for organizing, it will be easier to stay focused and get the job done.

March 4th – Bags, boxes, and bins...oh my!

When you begin your organizing journey be sure you have the right tools on hand:

- Trash bags for trash and soft items (toys, clothes, etc.) that will be donated
- Empty boxes for other items that will be donated or items (like out-of-season clothing) that need to be stored
- Cleaning supplies that you can easily carry from room to room (you can usually pick up a cheap plastic caddy with a handle at your local dollar store)
- A sharpie marker and some index cards to label storage boxes
- Your journal and a pen to make notes

As you go through each room and clear out the clutter, make a note in your journal of any items you may need to buy as a result of your clean out. While I don't suggest buying expensive organizing items if you don't need them, you may need a few nice baskets, hangers, storage boxes, etc. to keep yourself organized.

March 5ᵗʰ – The hanger trick

A good rule of thumb for cleaning out your closets is to discard any article of clothing that you haven't worn in six months. That means, if you pull out your summer clothes and realize that you didn't wear a particular item last summer, you probably don't need to keep it through this summer. For clothes that are hanging in your closet, a good way to keep track of what has been worn is to employ the hanger trick.

Put all your clothes in your closet with the hangers facing the same way. Once you've worn an article of clothing, and you put it back in the closet, turn the hanger. At the end of the season when you are packing up your clothes, look at each item hanging on an un-turned hanger. If you haven't worn it all season, it may be time to let it go!

March 6ᵗʰ – Set up stations.

If you find that certain areas of your house serve a specific pur-pose, it may be wise to set up the space so that it functions in the most efficient way. If you prefer that people remove their shoes upon entering your home, set up a shoe rack near the door. If mail gets habitually dropped on the coffee table, put a basket next to the front door to drop the mail into upon coming home. If you are an avid reader with stacks of books laying on the floor next to the bed, invest in a little bookcase that you can keep in the bedroom, close to the bed.

The idea is to set up stations and group "like" items, so your home functions in the way you need it to.

March 7ᵗʰ – Tame the paper.

Papers account for a good portion of the clutter we have in our homes. One reason for this is that we have it everywhere; our office, the kitchen, the living room, on the nightstand next to our beds; and it's hard to keep tabs on where everything is and how much there is.

Designate one spot in your home that will serve as the "inbox" for your papers, and commit to going through the papers once a week. Got mail? Put it in the inbox. Got school papers? Put them in the inbox. Receipts, warranties, notices? Put them in the inbox.

Once a week as you go through the inbox, decide what is to be dealt with (a bill to be paid) tossed, or filed. The rule though, is that anything you keep MUST have a place to go.

March 8th – Clear off the counters.

The goal is to get to a place where all of the flat spaces in your home are clear of clutter. Maybe you leave the toaster out because you use it every day, or maybe you have one candle, or one vase on your coffee table, but other than that, make it habit to clear off your surfaces.

Do you have a blender sitting out on your kitchen counter that you haven't used since jazzercise was all the rage? If it's not something that is used often, or something decorative that you love seeing every day, it's time to move it or remove it.

March 9th – Pare down your library.

I love books. I know many people like to read on their Kindles or iPads, but for me, there is nothing like reading an actual book. But, as much as I love books, I've learned (from more than a few moves) that I didn't need as many as I actually had. If you have a lot of books that are taking up space and gathering dust, it may be time to take a good, hard look at those books and donate those that you won't read again. Here's my criteria for books that get to stay:

1. Books that have sentimental value
2. Reference books that I know I will use again and again
3. Books that I know I will want to re-read at some point

Any books that don't meet that criteria get passed on to friends and family or donated. If you're thinking about purging your library, do it when you have time to sit down and really go through your books. Many of them are sentimental to people and it can be hard for them to part with, especially books they've had for a long time; but, I promise you, you'll free up lots of space and clutter and donating those books to someone else that can enjoy them is a nice thing to do. Just don't get rid of this book; okay?

March 10th – Play the pick five game.

Often, we hold onto items that no longer serve us. Sometimes, they no longer match our décor, or we have too many of the same item and no place to put them, or, we just leave items somewhere because we don't feel like looking for a place for them.

If you are feeling overwhelmed this month with all of the cleaning and de-cluttering, give yourself a break today and play the pick five game.

All you do, is go through the house and pick up five items in five minutes that don't belong where they are. Maybe you've got a vase on the kitchen counter that doesn't belong there; maybe you've got a clock on your nightstand that you don't really like, but you haven't dealt with it; maybe it's a pair of shoes that are laying out because they don't fit in the shoe holder.

Whatever it is, just spend five minutes and pick up five things. Once you've got your five things, either return them to their rightful place, find a place for them (if they didn't previously have a "home") or, box them up to be donated.

March 11th – Create a "maybe" box.

It can be very overwhelming to go through items and decide what to keep and what to toss. I was once helping a friend organize her basement, and she had a lot of items there that once belonged to her husband who had passed away. While she didn't need the items, it was heartbreaking for her to think about throwing them away, and I could tell that the stress of going through each item was starting to take a toll on her.

For some of the items that she just couldn't decide on, we made a "maybe" box. We wrote "maybe" on the side and put in all the items that she wasn't sure about. This helped us to move on and make decisions about other items and it helped her to alleviate the stress of having to decide right then and there about things.

The only caveat is that you don't want to have ten "maybe" boxes. Limit yourself to just one (if you can), and make a promise to yourself that you'll go back through the box again later and make firm decisions then.

March 12th – Be sure to donate your donations.

As you go through your home and decide on items that can be donated, make a plan to actually donate them. Don't laugh! I've been in many homes where there is a pile of stuff in the corner of a room, a closet, or the garage, that has been sitting there for many months waiting to be donated.

As soon as you have boxed and bagged up your items, commit to putting those items directly into your car and taking them to your nearest donation center. Make a commitment to take them within three days, and don't forget to save the receipt for when you file your taxes.

March 13ᵗʰ – Get close with your clothes.

As you are getting ready for work in the morning, or getting the kids ready for school, take a moment to look through your closet and take stock of things you no longer wear. It's said that we wear 20% of our wardrobe 80% of the time; that's a lot of clothes that aren't being worn for whatever reason.

If, while getting dressed, you put on a blazer that you just don't like any longer, the tendency is to just put it back on the hanger and pick another blazer. Instead of doing this, take the blazer and put it in a bag at the bottom of your closet. If you pull out an item that needs to be cleaned or repaired, commit to doing that by week's end. If you aren't willing to take the time to care for the item, discard it.

In the end, unless it is a special occasion or seasonal item, if it's an article of clothing you rarely wear, it's time to let it go.

March 14ᵗʰ – The case for minimalism

One of the problems with de-cluttering, is that once we have created space, we feel the need to fill that space up again, so we buy new items to replace the old ones. Once you have gotten a space cleared out, learn to appreciate the uncluttered look. Does anyone really need sixteen vases in their living room? Do we really need four different china sets? Does anyone? Living with less is not about deprivation, it's about learning to love the items you <u>do</u> have and focusing on the non-material things in life that are so much more important.

Instead of spending a Saturday or Sunday dusting rooms full of knick knacks and tchotchkes, imagine taking the kids to the park, going for a leisurely walk with your spouse, or just settling in and reading a good book.

March 15th – Tame your schedule.

Let's take a break from organizing your home and talk about organizing your life. What does that even mean to you? Grab your journal and answer the following questions:

1. What about your life currently stresses you out? Is it lack of time? Too many projects happening at once? A feeling that you have to be in ten places at once?
2. What are things you are currently doing in your life that you don't want to do?
3. What are things that you are currently NOT doing in your life that you would do, if only you had the time?
4. What are some tasks that you can delegate to others to help you reduce your stress?
5. What are the top three things that MUST be done every week, with no exception?

Time is the great equalizer. There are only 24 hours in a day. The richest man in the world cannot buy time. The greatest organizer in the world cannot organize their life to create more hours. The swiftest negotiator cannot bargain for more time. We all get the same amount.

In the end, it's not really how many hours you have, it's what you do with those hours. So let's take a look at what you wrote in your journal.

1. What is currently stressing you out? If it's your job, can you negotiate working less hours? Can you find a job that is less stressful for you? Can you negotiate working at home one or two days a week? What about feeling like you have too many projects? Are there some projects that you can delegate to someone else? Are there some you can "table" for the time being? What about projects that just need to be scrapped altogether?

2. What are things that you are doing that you don't want to do? Maybe you meet a friend every week for coffee, but meeting her leaves you feeling drained. It may be time to be honest and cancel that standing date. Certainly, you may not want to work, but that may not be an option if you've got bills to pay and a family to support, but can you work somewhere else? Do you take a yoga class three nights a week, but don't enjoy it anymore?

3. What are some of the things you wish you could do, if you only had the time? Maybe you've wanted to take an art class, but that weekly coffee date with your friend is eating up your time. Maybe you want to start running or take a kickboxing class, but that mounting pile of dishes isn't going to wash itself. Time is always a trade-off; because you can never get it back. An hour spent washing the dishes can never be spent reading a good book.

4. What tasks can you delegate to others? Can you hire someone to clean your house once a week so you can take a dance class? Can you ask a friend or neighbor to pick up the kids from school so you can go for a run after work? Would your spouse be open to cooking dinner a few times a week so you can work on your novel?

5. Now, for the top three things that must be done every week. Here are mine. I must sleep 8 hours a night; leaving me with 112 hours. I must work 45 hours a week to keep my job and pay my bills; that leaves me with 67 hours. And, I must keep up with my home (grocery shopping, cooking, and laundry) which usually takes about 5 hours a week, leaving me with 62 hours a week to do whatever else I want to do. If you factor in that I exercise regularly, run a business, write my book, and try to spend time with my friends, you'll see that 62 hours isn't that much time.

Now that you have an idea where your time is being spent, let's examine how you can rearrange some things.

March 16th – The Sunday night planning meeting

I have a weekly, standing meeting with myself every Sunday night that I absolutely refuse to give up on, no matter what else is happening in life. I call it my Sunday night planning meeting and it sets me up to have a productive and less stressful week.

The meeting only takes about a half hour to conduct and considering how much it helps me through the week, it is time well-spent.

On Sunday nights, I sit down with my planner and I look at the week ahead. I make note of any appointments that are already scheduled, and then I look at what pockets of time are open. If I say I want to run three days this week, I can instantly look at my calendar and know that realistically, there are really only two days that are open. If I can't rearrange my schedule to squeeze in that third day, so be it! I look at the remaining open days and times and write down which two days I will run.

I may decide that I want to visit my friends this week. Upon looking at my calendar though, I realize that there are just no openings where I can make that happen. Looking at the following weekend though, I realize I have no plans, so I make a note to call my friends this week to make plans for next weekend.

If I decide that I want to spend time writing this week, I actually block that time off on my calendar so nothing else gets scheduled. I've even gone as far as scheduling a relaxing bath on a weeknight. It's no different than scheduling an appointment to get your hair cut or have a manicure or pedicure. If I know I want that time, I have to schedule it, otherwise, I may be persuaded to stay late at work to finish a project, or have coffee with that friend that I'm not really interested in seeing.

Try the Sunday night (or any night that works for you) planning meeting and see how it can help you stay on schedule and keep your days more manageable.

March 17ᵗʰ – Purging people

Part of organizing, as you have probably seen in the past two weeks or so, means purging; that is, ridding yourself of things that no longer serve you, or that you no longer need. As harsh as this may sound, sometimes, that means purging some people from your life. It means purging "energy vampires." They are the people who:

1. Always have a frown on their face
2. Can never find anything nice to say

3. Are always embroiled in some kind of drama
4. Make you feel bad when you're with them
5. Squelch your dreams
6. Make every single thing all about them
7. Take more than they give in the relationship

I could go on and on, but if you've got an energy vampire in your life, you already know what I'm talking about.

Pull out your journal and make a list of the people that you spend your time with. Then, rank them in order from the person you spend the most amount of time with, to the person you spend the least amount of time with.

Look at your list. We already talked a few times about the five people you spend the most time with. If thinking about that makes you cringe, it's time to upgrade your people!

Now that you have your list, put a number from 1 – 5 next to each of them, with 1 being the most negative people you know, to 5 being the most positive, and then compare their level of negativity or positivity to the amount of time you spend with them. If you are spending a lot of time with number 1 people; you've got a problem.

March 18ᵗʰ – It's not me, it's you.

It is hard to cut people out of your life. Sometimes it's people that you have to interact with, such as a parent, your spouse, your siblings, or your children. Other times, there are people that have been in your life for so long, that thinking about cutting the cord seems scary.

I subscribe to the theory that people come into your life for a reason, a season, or a lifetime. And when a relationship is no longer serving you in a healthy, positive way, it's time to either make some changes, or, let people go.

There are a few ways you can let people go. No one is better than the other; it really just depends on the situation at hand. Here are three ways that I've seen work effectively in moving away and/or out of these types of relationships.

1. ***The evader*** – It's easy to start to distance yourself from some-one as a prelude to cytting them out of your life. You don't answer their text messages or phone calls as swiftly or as often; you don't initiate plans with them; you aren't readily available when they contact you to make plans. Sometimes, life just gets in the way, and people drift apart. You may have even been on the receiving end of this at one time or another. Evading is possibly the easiest way to get out of a toxic relationship.

2. ***The gentle let down*** – Some people are slow to get the hint when you're trying to pull off the evader move, and that may force you to have a conversation with the person in which you express how you're feeling about the relationship. This is not often easy for people. This is a good tactic to use if you don't want to cut someone out of your life forever and ever, but when you just need a break from them or are truly stressed out in life and they are adding to the stress.

   In this case, it's helpful to have a conversation, over coffee (it's quicker usually) at which time you tell your friend any number of things such as:

   a. "Life has gotten so hectic for me these days. I'm afraid I just don't have that much time to spend with you right now. I hope you understand that I need some space."

b. "I have decided to take some time to work on myself, so I'm really limiting my social life. That means I won't be able to hang out right now. I hope you understand."

c. "I've recently taken on a new project/new hobby/new class/insert-appropriate-activity-here, and I'm really trying to focus on that right now; which means I won't have time to spend with you for a while."

CAUTION!!!!

One word of caution here. If you and your energy vampire run in the same social circles, you need to be careful. You can't tell Patty that you are busy and cutting your social life down and then have drinks with Cathy on Thursday, and dinner with Paul and Brad on Friday. Your energy vampire may be a thorn in your side, but they're not stupid. Only use the gentle let down if you can do it without causing huge problems among your circle.

3. *The rip-off-the-Band-Aid technique*

Sometimes, relationships take such a turn, that your only course of action is to rip off the Band-Aid and end the relationship outright. As with the gentle let down technique, there is more than one way to do this. Much of it depends on your relationship, your regular mode of communication with the person, and your anticipated reaction from them.

If you have an extremely close relationship with the person, a face-to-face meeting is probably your best bet. However, if you normally don't talk to this person often, a thoughtfully written letter may be just as effective. This is also a good method if you think the person is going to have an aggressive response.

If you are letting go of a person that is not particularly close to you and you normally just exchange phone calls and texts (with the occasional coffee date thrown in) you may just send a well-crafted email explaining that you are no longer interested in continuing your relationship with them.

Harsh? It's not meant to be; it's meant to be realistic. As we established on March 15th, there are only so many hours in a day. Why spend those precious hours with people that make you feel bad?

March 19th – Make your life work for you.

There are reasons why we do what we do, why we spend time with who we spend time with, why we go the places we go, and spend money on what we spend money on. Sometimes the reasons are deeply rooted in tradition, or force of habit, or a comfort level. But, sometimes, we do things that are no longer healthy for us or things that we aren't really interested in any longer.

Continuing to hold onto these things means that you are not giving yourself the time and space to explore other things that may be more fulfilling for you at this time. It's important to make your life work for you by filling your time with people, activities, and experiences that enrich your life and help you enjoy it.

If you have been doing things out of habit, break those habits! You've got to start living your life on purpose. So many people slog through their day on auto-pilot and miss out on many enriching experiences.

Tradition is lovely, but always going to the same place for vacation, just because it's where you've always gone, robs you of the opportunity to go somewhere and experience something new.

Now is the time to take stock of your life and decide what types of experiences you want to have.

March 20th – Your bucket list

Get out your journal and find a quiet spot where you can write uninterrupted. Now is the time to make a bucket list for yourself of places you want to go, experiences you want to have, foods you want to try, and hobbies you want to try out. I want you to go big or go home with this list.

I want you to come up with 50 things that you want to do. They can be little things or big things, but please, don't limit yourself. If you want them to be big, then write them down that way. Don't limit yourself. Some items on my bucket list are:

1. Run the Marine Corps marathon
2. Learn to ride a bike
3. Compete in a mini-triathlon
4. Learn yoga
5. Write a best-selling book
6. Buy a beach house
7. Start a non-profit to give back to my community
8. Have a swanky apartment in New York City
9. Travel to Ireland
10. Travel to Australia
11. Travel to London
12. Carry the Olympic torch
13. Run the New York marathon

What will be on your bucket list?

March 21st – Bringing your dreams to life

Dreaming, bucket lists, wish lists, goals, etc. can be really fun to do, but if there is something you really want to accomplish, you've got to set your life up in a way that supports this. If one of your goals is to lose weight and get in shape, sitting around on the couch won't help you reach your goal. If your goal is to travel around the world, but you go on a shopping spree at the mall every weekend instead of saving, you won't reach your goal.

It's important to not just say "what?" or even just "how?" but to ask yourself "why?."

You've got to have a strong "why" to keep you committed to reaching your goals. If you say you want to lose weight, that's fine, but if your "why" is because you want to have enough energy to play with your kids, that's a strong "why." If you want to save money to travel, that's nice, but if your "why" is that you want to travel to visit your parents in India, who you haven't seen in several years, that's a strong "why."

A strong "why" will keep you motivated when you start to lose focus; a strong "why" makes the journey towards your goal feel "worth it."

March 22nd – Explore your "why."

Pull out your journal and look at the bucket list you created on March 20th. Pick out five of the things that are most important to you and the five that you feel most compelled to see through to completion.

Now look at those top five, and next to each one write down why you want them. If you have a compelling "why," it will help see you through those times when you want to throw in the towel. Here are some of my "whys":

1. Buy a beach house – WHY?…I dreamed of this as a little kid. I love the beach and actually feel like the sand and the sea are good for my soul. I feel so much better; physically, emotionally, and spiritually when I am at the beach. It would be so wonderful to feel that way every day.

2. Start a non-profit to give back to my community – WHY?...I have always felt like a philanthropist without money! I feel my best when I am giving back to others. Each time I've been in a position to help someone (financially or otherwise), I've felt so good about myself. There is so much need in my community, and the ability to help enrich the lives of others would enrich my life in immeasurable ways.

3. Run the Marine Corp marathon – WHY?...Running has always been a source of pride for me. Each time I've run a distance race, I've felt strong and powerful and it makes me believe that I could do anything that I really set my mind to. In that way, running is a metaphor for my entire life. As a former member of the military, it would be an honor to run the Marine Corps Marathon and feel the pride of finishing such a distinguished race.

My "whys" help shape the way I live my life. When I want to spend what I call "stupid money," I remind myself about the beach house sitting there waiting for me to move in. When I feel like giving up on my dreams to start and run a non-profit, I think of the people who need my help NOW! When it's cold, rainy, hot, snowy, or I'm just plain tired and I don't feel like running, I visualize crossing the finish line at the Marine Corps Marathon and force myself to lace up my sneakers and go.

March 23rd – Visualize your organized life.
Having your goals and dreams in writing is great, but having a visual of these things can be so powerful. I have two vision boards in my bedroom. I put them there because I knew I would see

them every morning when I wake up and every night before I go to sleep.

Having these powerful visuals of what I wanted my life to look like has helped me to keep after my goals and dreams. It is a constant reminder of why I work so hard and what I want to achieve in life.

I urge you to create a vision board that speaks to the things you want in your life. If you don't want the actual board hanging up, you can also make a vision book.

Get yourself a binder or a notebook and get ready to create your vision book!

March 24th – Your vision book realized

Grab yourself a stack of magazines that relate to the goals you have in mind. Want a beach house? Get the latest issue of *Coastal Living* magazine. Want to run a marathon? Pick up *Runner's World.* Want to become a successful businessperson? Pick up *Entrepreneur Magazine.*

You want to start this exercise when you have enough free time to really enjoy the process. If it's not today, that's okay, find another day when you have a few hours to sit and relax. Pour yourself a cup of tea or a glass of wine, enjoy a decadent snack and sit down with your binder or notebook, your stack of magazines, a pair of scissors and some tape or a glue stick.

As you thumb through the magazines, pick out pictures that "speak" to you; those are the pictures that inspire you towards your goals, the ones that look like the pictures you have in your mind's eye.

Make a separate section or page for each category of goals. You might have a section for your family and home life goals, a section for your business or financial goals, and yet another section for recreation and activity goals.

As you put your book together, allow yourself to really visualize your life looking like and becoming like those images.

March 25th – Create your "success corner."
With any luck, you spent the first part of March organizing your home and creating space. If that's the case, then, with any luck, you've created a cleaner, more organized home that works well with your life and your family's life.

Now is the time to create a success corner for yourself. This is where you will hang your vision board, store your book, hang achievements such as your diploma or certificates you've received, and where you'll keep your "feel good" file, which we'll talk about tomorrow. This is a place where you can relish past achievements while setting yourself up to achieve your future goals.

I live in an apartment by myself, so my entire apartment can serve as a success corner for me. I have vision boards in my bedroom, my planning wall and all my running medals are in the hall, certificates and diplomas hang in my office, and inspirational pictures and messages can be found on my fridge.

If you share your home with others, you may not want to have your items sprawled out in every room. Creating a success corner gives you a spot that is solely for you and you alone. You should feel free to retreat there when you need inspiration, or when you're having a day when you feel down about yourself.

Looking at past achievements and reminding yourself of all the good that's still to come is an excellent way to get through those days when you don't feel particularly good about yourself.

March 26th – The "feel good file"

I started one of these at home and at work years ago, and I've loved having them ever since! Whenever someone sends me a complimentary email or card, or writes something nice about me somewhere, I keep it and put it in my "feel good file." Once again, on those days when I don't feel particularly good about myself, I look in my "feel good file" and remind myself that I'm worth something, that I'm important, and that I matter.

My work file has copies of emails in which my boss or my colleagues have complimented me on work that I've done, and testimonials from happy clients that I have served. My home file has cards and notes from friends thanking me for something I've done to help them, or reminding me that I'm loved and cared for.

Your file does not need to be fancy. Just grab a file folder and write "feel good file" on it, then, start collecting those cards, letters, and emails and stick them in there as they come in. It's nice to look through it every so often.

March 27th – Check in.

We're less than a week away from the end of the month. How are you feeling about things so far? Have you gotten to all of the rooms in your house and organized them to your liking?

Grab your journal and go into each room of your home. Once there, take a moment to look around and write down one word about each room. Your entries might say something like:

Bedroom = Tranquil
Bathroom = Organized
Office = Inspiring
Kitchen = Functional
Living Room = Cozy

If any of the spaces in your home still need attention, grab your planner and decide when you'll tackle them. You need a specific date here. "Soon", "later", "in a while", and, "when I get to it" are not timelines! Make it a point to tackle any problem areas so your home can be exactly the way you want it.

March 28th – Getting your family on the organization train

If you live alone, this may not apply, but certainly if you share your living space, the other domestic dwellers in your camp may not be on board with your desire to keep your living spaces looking the way you like them.

It's important to make cleaning and organizing a family affair. If you are the only one committed to this, you will find that you are the only one spending time on it. You may be the only one picking up shoes off the floor, ensuring that dirty clothes make it to the hamper, instead of on the bedroom floor, or wiping up sticky messes from the kitchen counters.

If you can, get the family together for a family meeting where you'll decide on a division of labor for the chores. Get agreement from everyone that they will honor their part of the deal by being responsible for certain tasks. Create a chore chart that everyone in the household signs off on and hold people to their word!

March 29th – Look for ways to simplify.

Part of organizing both your home, and your life, is to find ways to simplify things. Simplifying is merely looking for ways to make things easier to do, automate some things, or stop doing things that you don't need to do.

Over the years I've figured out lots of ways to simplify my life, such as:

- Paying my bills online
- Paying recurring monthly bills through my bank's auto pay system
- Combining errands so that I'm not driving from one end of town to the other
- Finding a few really amazing "go to" recipes that are easy to make, and always come out tasting fantastic
- Delegating tasks that are easy to delegate to free up much-needed time to work on things that must be done by me
- Letting go of my need to have everything look perfect all the time. (Let's face it, Martha Stewart is NOT dropping by my apartment anytime soon!)
- Spending a little extra on pre-cut produce in the grocery store to reduce prep time when making healthy meals
- Swapping services with friends so we can each capitalize on what we do well
- Organizing my home so things are easy to reach, easy to clean, easy to find, etc.
- Paring down my wardrobe to items that are easy to care for, look great on, and are easy to mix and match

- Cutting out all the unnecessary things, like subscriptions to magazines I no longer read or enjoy, and cutting down expenses by not buying a lot of items I don't need
- Learning to enjoy the simple things in life; a walk in the park, cuddling with the cat, reading a good book, or watching a favorite TV show
- Simplifying my beauty routine by keeping my hair at a manageable length and style, and cutting down on the amount of beauty products I buy
- Learning to say no to things that stretch my time in an unhealthy way

March 29th – Where can you simplify your life?

Now it's your turn. Where can you simplify your life? Get out your journal and make a list of things you can do to help simplify things. Can you swap services with a neighbor? Maybe they can pick up the kids from school every day and in exchange you'll give them a date night two or three times a month?

Can you clean your friend's house in exchange for a week of home-cooked, ready-to-eat meals? Do you have a friend that is a handyman and will fix a few minor things around the house in exchange for you creating a custom piece of art?

What bills can you pay automatically? What payments can you combine? What errands can you combine? Can you write a few thank you notes while you are waiting for the kids to get done their soccer practice? Can you get all your groceries, health and beauty items, and pet items in one place instead of driving to three stores?

Spring is just around the corner, so now is a good time to look for ways to simplify and free up some time for yourself in the coming months.

March 30th – Organize your thoughts.

If your home and life are coming into shape, that's great, but before we get ready to close out the month, I want you to focus on organizing your thoughts.

> *"The most important conversation you will ever have*
> *in this life is the one that you have with yourself."*
> *~Karen Ann Kennedy*

When you engage in a lot of negative self-talk it erodes your sense of well-being in such a harmful way.

Think of all the times you say to yourself:

"Man, am I stupid!"
"What the hell was I thinking?"
"You idiot!"
"I suck at this stuff."
"I don't know where my brains are."

Or, anything that sounds remotely like any of these statements.

We've all been there. I have said things to myself, about myself, that I would never be cruel enough to say to another human being. I developed a seriously unhealthy pattern of treating other people much better than I treated myself.

I still have moments when I find myself engaging in negative self-talk. One technique that I've used that has really helped me is to say "CANCEL CANCEL" out loud as soon as I start going down a bad road in my head.

There's something about saying "CANCEL CANCEL" (as crazy as it may sound) that stops my brain in its tracks and allows me to let go of the "bad" thoughts and start fresh with healthier, more productive thoughts.

In the beginning, I found myself saying "CANCEL CANCEL" all day long. As I continued to practice this technique, I found myself saying "CANCEL CANCEL" less and less. Now, I hardly ever have to say it at all!

It's important to organize your thoughts in a way that is helpful, empowering, inspiring, and nurturing to yourself. Saying things like:

"I am so smart."
"I am so capable."
"I'm so proud of myself."
"Look how far I've come!"
"Look at what I just accomplished"
"I'm a good person."
"Even though I'm not exactly where I want to be, I'm working towards my goals."

If you can, stand in front of a mirror and say these things to yourself. It's a powerful exercise.

Organizing your thoughts is as simple as setting your thoughts up to support you. If you are trying to lose weight, calling yourself fat is not going to help, but acknowledging that you are working towards a healthier you is empowering.

If you're unemployed or underemployed, calling yourself stupid is counterproductive, but reminding yourself that you are working towards something bigger and better and that you are smart and capable is a way to feel good about where you are heading.

March 31st – End of the month check in

How do you feel about this past month? Grab your journal and make note of how things went. Were you able to get your home organized? Did you tackle those energy vampires head on and reduce or eliminate the negative drain they put on you? Have you strategized ways to simplify your life and organize your thoughts?

Congratulations for getting this far in the year. There's a lot more good stuff coming your way.

My March to-do list:

- I scheduled a whole home clean out
- I stocked up on organizing supplies like bags, boxes, bins, files, etc.
- I tried the hanger trick to organize my closet
- I set up stations around my house that work for each space
- I cleared off counters to create space
- I pared down my library
- I played the pick five game
- I created a "maybe" box (if needed)
- I donated items that were no longer wanted/needed
- I did the "tame your schedule" exercise
- I started holding regular Sunday night planning meetings
- I did the "energy vampire" exercise
- I created my bucket list
- I explored my "WHY"
- I created a vision board and/or book
- I created my success corner
- I created a "feel good file"
- I found ways to simplify my life

APRIL – DETOX YOUR LIFE

When people think of detoxing, they immediately think of drinking green juices and going to the spa for a colonic. But there are lots of ways to detox your life. Quitting smoking, cutting out toxins in your home, detoxing negative people from your life, and yes, detoxing your diet is part of it too!

Are you ready to clean up your act?

April 1st – This is no April fools joke!

Every day, your body and your life are exposed to harmful toxins; from second-hand smoke to car exhaust, chemicals in your household cleaning products and health and beauty products, and other environmental toxins all around.

It's so important to reduce the number of toxins in your life as much as you can. This month will be all about helping you detox your life; and avoiding the many toxins surrounding you will play a big part in that endeavor. While you certainly don't want to walk around town in a gas mask, there are many things you can do to clean up your home and your life. Get ready.

April 2nd – Quit smoking.

According to the Centers for Disease Control, tobacco use remains the single largest preventable cause of death and disease in the United States. Cigarette smoking kills more than 480,000 Americans each year, with more than 41,000 of these deaths from exposure to secondhand smoke. In fact, nonsmokers who are exposed to secondhand smoke increase their risk of lung cancer by 20 – 30%. These numbers should scare you!

Quitting smoking is one of the hardest things a person can ever do. I've never smoked, but my mother has been smoking since she was twelve years old. She has no desire to quit, even though she coughs uncontrollably all day long, and knows how unhealthy her habit is.

Last month when we talked about goals, we talked about having a strong WHY. When you're attempting something as daunting as quitting smoking, you definitely need a strong "WHY." Maybe yours is:

- Living a long and healthy life to see your children grow up
- Living a long and healthy life to see your grandchildren being born
- Not suffering through the myriad of diseases caused by smoking

And, get help! I've talked to many people who have tried to quit smoking, and almost all of them report that having help; the patch, the gum, a support group, etc. was helpful in keeping them on track.

You can start with a number of online resources such as:

www.smokefree.gov
www.cdc.gov
www.heart.org
www.lung.org

Please make the decision to quit and do whatever you can to stick with it. You know your life depends on it; that right there should be a big enough WHY for you!

April 3rd – Stifle the secondhand smoke.

If you're not a smoker, that's great for you! But in reading the statistics from yesterday, you know that secondhand smoke is nothing to mess with either. Are there people in your life that smoke? Urge them to quit! While they are going on their quitting journey, you need to limit your exposure. Here are a few ways I've dodged the secondhand smoke bullet over the years:

1. DO NOT allow anyone to smoke in your home! It doesn't matter if the windows are open or they lean out the door. DO NOT allow it! The smoke will linger long after the offender has gone. Smoke lingers in the curtains, rugs, furniture, and even clings to the walls. You've got to be firm on your no smoking rule.

2. DO NOT allow anyone to smoke in your car. Same thing applies as above. Don't let them pull the, "but the windows are open" line. Stay firm.

3. Most places now are smoke free, but there are still some bars and other establishments that allow smoking. Don't frequent these places.

4. If you have friends that smoke, limit your visits to their homes. Again, smoke gets trapped inside a home no matter how often people try to "air out."

5. Even if you are outside, if people are smoking, and you can smell it, insist that they move away from your proximity, or ask them to put their cigarettes out! If you're smelling smoke, it doesn't matter that you're outside, you're still being exposed.

You have to protect yourself. Maybe you'll hurt someone's feelings by employing the tactics above; but, so what? This is your life we're talking about here! If your friends don't care about your health and well-being, maybe it's time to upgrade to some new friends.

April 4th – Detox your beauty products.

Quick quiz! Do you know what the largest organ of the body is? The answer; your SKIN! No, it wasn't a trick question! Notice I didn't ask about the largest organ IN your body, I asked about the largest organ OF your body. Your skin is your largest organ with a total area of about twenty square feet. The skin has a very important job; it protects us from germs and toxins, regulates our body temperature, and is responsible for us being able to experience the sensation of touch.

It's important to know that what goes <u>on</u> your body, goes <u>in</u> your body, so if you're currently slathering on lotions, potions, and creams containing chemicals, those chemicals are going into your body.

A good place to start in cleaning up your skincare and beauty routine is to start by eliminating products containing the following chemicals:

- BHA and BHT
- Coal tar dyes
- DEA ingredients
- Formaldehyde-releasing preservatives such as methenamine and quarternium 15
- Parabens
- Parfum - aka fragrance
- Petroleum
- Sodium lauryl sulfate
- Triclosan

Remember, you need to be just as choosy with your health and beauty products as you are with your food choices.

April 5th – Choose the right products.

Now that you are ridding your home of unhealthy beauty and skincare products, you'll need to restock with some more all-natural choices. There are so many companies out there now offering organic and all-natural products. A quick Google search will give you a list of sites where you can go. Or, you can just check out some of my favorite companies below:

1. 100% Pure
2. Bare Minerals
3. Ecco Bella
4. J.R. Watkins (try their lemon hand soap)
5. Kiss My Face (the coconut lotion is so decadent)
6. Nature's Gate (I am in love with their aloe vera shampoo)
7. Origins
8. Physicians Formula
9. Piper Wai (the best deodorant on the planet)
10. Seventh Generation
11. Suki
12. Tracie Martyn

April 6th – Make your own!

You may not know it, but you have an entire beauty lab in your kitchen! Making your own beauty products is:

1. Economical
2. Eco-friendly
3. And, just plain fun

For example, did you know that just one mashed banana applied to your hair for fifteen minutes can repair your hair and make it smooth and shiny?

How about an avocado hair mask?

Or, a face mask made with mayonnaise?

I'm going to share with you some of my favorite kitchen cabinet beauty recipes, but before I do, I want to encourage you to do some browsing on line to see what you find and might like for yourself.

The best thing about making your own products is that even if you don't end up liking what you've made, if you're using all-natural ingredients from your kitchen, it won't hurt you, and, you won't have made a huge investment in some off-the-shelf product!

Grab your journal and a pen and jot down recipes that you find interesting, then get ready to head to the kitchen!

April 7th – It's all about the hair
Below are some of my favorite homemade hair care recipes. Of course, keep in mind, that you don't always need to whip up something complicated; that mashed banana does the trick every time!

For limp hair:
Mix ½ cup flat beer with 1 teaspoon of canola oil and 1 raw egg. Apply to hair and let sit for fifteen minutes, then rinse.

For dry hair:
Mix ½ cup honey with 2 tablespoons of olive oil. Apply to hair and let sit for fifteen minutes, then rinse.

For sun-damaged hair:
Mix ½ cup honey with ½ an avocado. Apply to hair and let sit for fifteen minutes, then rinse.

To combat residue build up:
Mix 2 tablespoons of baking soda with enough water to make a thick paste. Apply directly to scalp and let sit for fifteen minutes, then rinse.

April 8th – Homemade skincare
We've already established that the skin is your largest organ, so it's super important to take care of it! Your skin is porous, meaning, it "drinks" in what you put on it. Try mixing up some these fun skincare concoctions in your kitchen.

Lemon/Lime Sugar Scrub:
Mix the juice of one lemon and the juice of one lime with ½ cup raw sugar. Massage gently over damp skin, rinse, finish with moisturizer.

Sea Salt & Tea Tree Oil Foot Soak:
Mix ¼ cup sea salt and ten drops of tea tree oil in a basin of warm water. Soak feet for 15 to 20 minutes. Tea tree oil is a natural antiseptic that will help with foot odor, should that be an issue for you.

Detoxifying Bath Soak:
Mix ½ cup Epsom salt with ½ cup baking soda in tub of warm water. Add a few drops of your favorite essential oil (I use lavender for help with sleep). Soak and enjoy!

Cuticle Repair:
Mix 1 teaspoon of honey with 1 teaspoon of olive oil in a small bowl. Dip fingers into the mixture and massage into cuticles. For best results, put on right before bed, then put on a pair of light gloves.

April 9th – Detox your home cleaning products.

Most everyone wants a clean home. There's few things nicer than walking in the door after a long day to a clean, fresh-smelling, well-organized home. But what you clean your home with could actually be harmful to you! Most commercial cleaning products are loaded with chemicals and toxins; some of which are banned in other countries! Even some of the "green" products on the market have been scrutinized by watchdog groups like the EWG (Environmental Working Group).

Today's assignment; get rid of the chemicals. Go ahead and get a roundup of all your cleaning supplies, then, get to work on reading those labels. You'll want to toss any products that contain:

- Borax and boric acid
- Chlorinated phenols
- Diethylene glycol
- Formaldehyde
- Petroleum solvents
- Phenols
- Triclosan

April 10th – Upgrade your cleaning supplies.

Just like the variety of all-natural beauty products available, you can find a fair number of companies also manufacturing healthier homecare products. Check out these folks:

1. Citra-solv
2. Dr. Bronner's (I love the 18-in-1 hemp pure castile soap in peppermint)
3. Earth Friendly
4. Ecover
5. Green Shield
6. The Honest Company

7. Mrs. Meyers (just try everything, seriously, I love everything they make!)
8. Planet
9. Seventh Generation (they make terrific dishwasher pacs)
10. Zum Clean

April 11th – DIY to the rescue

You knew I was going here; didn't you? I must say that making your own cleaning products is easy and affordable. Since I've been cleaning with vinegar and baking soda, I've saved hundreds of dollars on commercial cleaning supplies; and my house has never looked or felt better! I like knowing that I can live without the chemicals and toxins while still enjoying a clean and sparkling home.

Below are some of my very favorite tips!

Tub Scrub:
Mix ½ cup baking soda with ½ cup dishwashing liquid, and ¼ cup white vinegar. I use this as a scrub for my bathtub and I must say it cleans better than any commercial product I've ever tried.

Toilet Bowl "Foamie":
I pour about a ½ cup of baking soda into the toilet and then pour in about a cup of white vinegar. No need to measure; you're not making a cake! I let the mixture sit in the toilet and let it "foam," then I scrub with a toilet bowl brush. Works like a charm!

Countertop Cleaner:
Whenever I need countertop cleaner I peel some grapefruit, oranges, lemons, or limes; whatever kind of citrus you like, and I put the peels in a glass jar. I pour white vinegar over the peels and let it sit in a cool, dry, dark place for about a month or two. When I'm

ready to use, I strain out the peels and put the liquid in a squirt bottle. This cleans my countertops beautifully.

"Let the Sun Shine In" Window Cleaner:
Seriously, nothing will clean your windows better than a mix of half white vinegar and half water in a squirt bottle, wiped down with newspaper. Newspaper wipes off clean (no paper towel fuzz leftover) and the vinegar will leave your windows looking absolutely clear!

Fresh Air-Air Freshener:
For a very small investment at my local craft store I bought a few ceramic lamp rings. The rings have a small groove in them to hold liquid essential oil. I just put a few drops of whatever oil I like into the lamp ring and set it on the lamp over the base of the light bulb to release the scent. No more commercial air freshener for me!

Refreshing Carpet Refresher:
When I want a little something extra for my rugs, I put some baking soda in a bowl and add a few drops of essential oil. I sprinkle the mix on my carpet and let it sit for fifteen minutes before vacuuming it up. Leaves my home smelling GREAT!

April 12th – Detox your diet.
Okay kids, hold onto your hats and DON'T PANIC! Cleaning up your diet is going to take you more than one day. We're not even halfway through the month so we have plenty of time to work on this and you may be surprised at how easy this can actually be.

What if I told you that there is one simple strategy you can employ today that would dramatically change your diet and your life forever? I'm talking about something that can help you lose weight, sleep better, calm your nerves, and look younger and healthier than ever before? Would you do it?

Do you want to know what it is?
Are you ready?

The simplest strategy you can employ is to stop eating processed foods! Basically cut out the CRAP:

C – Carbonated sodas and drinks
R – Refined sugars
A – Artificial ingredients
P – Processed foods

If a food product has ingredients you can't pronounce, walk away. If you don't know what it is, your body won't know what it is either, and it won't know how to process it.

Food doesn't HAVE ingredients, food IS ingredients. When you eat a banana, do you know what's in it? Of course; BANANA!

Not ready to give up processed foods? Okay, at least wean yourself off them, and if you have to choose items in cans, boxes, and bags, try to stick to items with five or less ingredients and things that you can identify.

April 13th – Kiss your sweet tooth goodbye.

There have been a lot of studies out lately that suggest that sugar is as addictive as heroin. Now, when I first heard this, I thought, "Okay, that makes for a sexy headline, but it's also a little misleading. I mean, you can go to your local grocery store and buy a 5-pound bag of sugar; you can't go to the grocery store and check out with heroin!" But, then I dug in deeper on the research and

I saw a series of brain scans done on people who were addicted to heroin and people who were addicted to sugar. Guess what? The scans looked exactly the same! That gave me pause.

Kicking sugar is not a matter of willpower. Sugar is highly addictive and fuels every cell in your brain. Your brain also sees sugar as a reward, which makes you want more and more of it!

There are lots of techniques to help you break the cycle of sugar addiction. Some people suggest weaning yourself off slowly while others will tell you that the "cold turkey" approach is the way to go.

When I work with individual health coaching clients, I spend some time really analyzing them before I make my recommendations. For some people, cold turkey is the way to go, for others, it's too much for them, so a step-down approach works better. Since I don't know you, I can't tell you what's best for you as an individual, but I can at least share with you a few general tips that may help you avoid the sugar bowl.

1. Start saying no to obvious sugar choices. Passing up donuts, cookies, cakes, sugary drinks like soda, and other obviously sugar-laden foods.

2. Start to reduce the amount of added sugar you put in things like coffee and tea. For coffee lovers, the step-down approach has worked great for me and others. Over time, you won't even miss the sugar in your daily cup of Joe.

3. Start to appreciate the sweetness in fruit. A bowl of berries won't taste very sweet next to a pint of sugary ice cream, but once you wean yourself off of added sugar, that same bowl of berries will taste wonderfully sweet and fresh.

4. Be committed to doing a sugar detox. Start with three days, seven if you can do it, ten if you can really do it; and work your way up from there.

5. Limit your intake of "natural sugars." Agave nectar, honey, stevia, and the like are still sugar, and your body will process it as such. If you have to use something, it's best to opt for a less processed, less refined sugar, but you still need to limit your intake.

6. Learn to be a world-champion label reader. Sugar hides in all kinds of food, including things you wouldn't think of, like ketchup and sauces. Start to weed out these products.

7. Be wary of artificial sweeteners. Some studies suggest that the sweet taste of artificial sweeteners will actually leave you craving more and more sweet stuff. I wouldn't use those artificial sweeteners anyway; they're nothing but chemicals!

8. Eat fat! That's not a typo! Aim for healthy fats like coconut oil, olive oil, and avocados. The fat will fill you up and will help you with your sugar cravings.

9. Manage stress. It's no accident that the cartoon with the stressed out woman eating a pint of ice cream exists. Stress can cause you to crave comfort foods, and for many of us, comfort foods = sugary foods. Take a walk, count to ten, practice deep breathing; just do something to help calm you down and keep you from reaching for sugar.

10. Some studies suggest that taking a vitamin B complex supplement, as well as 1,000 mg of chromium picolinate a day,

will help reduce sugar cravings. I have personally used the chromium supplement with really great results.

11. Start your day with protein! Protein will help keep you full and satisfied. This will help you steer clear of sugary foods.

12. Watch your carbohydrate consumption. When people eat foods containing carbohydrates, the digestive system breaks down the digestible carbs into sugar.

13. Beware of social triggers. The kids are begging you to take them for ice cream, it's your co-workers birthday and you don't want to seem rude by turning down cake; you've got to plan and prepare. If you're truly committed to beating your sugar addiction, you're going to need to come up with coping tools to get past these times. Ice cream and birthday cake are never going to go away!

14. Eat regularly. Skipping meals will only leave you hungry, or hangry, as I call it. Have you not heard of hangry? It's when you get angry from being hungry! When you are hungry and feel like you could eat anything, you just might, and that might include the very sugary foods you're working to eliminate.

15. In the end, know that there is really only one "cure" for sugar addiction, and that is to get rid of it completely from your diet.

April 14th – Figure out your food issues.

One of the best ways to detox your diet is to figure out what foods cause an issue for you. You don't have to have full-blown food allergies; you could simply have a food intolerance or sensitivity. I did an elimination diet that revealed a sensitivity to gluten. I don't have Celiac disease, but I have found that eliminating gluten from my diet has done wonders for both my physical and mental health.

An elimination diet is not easy for some people, but if you can stick it out, it can help you feel better than you've ever felt before.

A lot of people keep a food journal where they write down what they weigh and everything they eat. If you're doing that, it's fine, but if that's all you're doing, you're missing a critical part of the equation.

It's far more useful to not only write down what you eat, but when, how much, and how you felt after you ate. When you write down how you feel, don't just write down how you physically feel (bloated, gassy, stomach cramps), you also want to write down how you emotionally feel (disappointed, mad at yourself, disgusted).

In the next few days, we're going to start prepping you to tackle the elimination diet. The length of the elimination diet can vary depending on your age and severity of any gut issues you might be experiencing. Most adults do well with an elimination diet that lasts at least 3 weeks.

I'm going to walk you through step by step in the next few days. For now, let's get ready.

April 15th – Clean out the junk.
If you want to be successful with the elimination diet, you want to start to get rid of the foods you won't be eating. If you aren't ready to throw things away, or, if you share your home with others that

will not be eliminating with you, at least hide "contraband" food out of sight and out of reach.

A good elimination diet will remove the following items:

- Gluten
- Dairy
- Soy
- Eggs
- Corn
- Pork
- Beef
- Chicken
- Beans
- Lentils
- Coffee
- Citrus fruits
- Nuts
- Nightshade vegetables (such as tomatoes, eggplant, and potatoes)

I know that sounds like a lot, but there's plenty of things you can still have, primarily rice, meat (turkey, fish, lamb), most fruit, and most types of vegetables.

*Please Note...*This can be a VERY difficult undertaking for vegetarian/vegan types. Because there are no beans, lentils, or soy, many vegetarian/vegan soy-based substitutes won't be allowed. I follow a mostly vegan diet, but do sometimes eat fish, which helped me get through a little, but after a week of eating mostly rice and vegetables, I was feeling a little discouraged. If you follow a similar diet as I do, please try it for at least one week; if I can do it, you can do it too!

April 16th – Add in the good stuff.

The following chart may be helpful for you in taking a trip to the grocery store to stock up for your elimination.

	What to Include	What to Avoid
Fruits	Almost all fresh fruit	Citrus fruits; orange, grapefruit, lemon, lime, etc.
Vegetables	Almost all fresh, raw, steamed, sautéed, or roasted vegetables	Tomatoes, eggplant, potatoes (sweet potato and yams are okay)
Starch	Rice*, buckwheat*	Wheat, corn, barley, spelt, kamut, rye, oats, and all products that contain gluten
Legumes	None	Soybeans, tofu, tempeh, soy milk, and all beans, peas, and lentils
Nuts and Seeds	None	All nuts and seeds
Meat and Fish	Fish, turkey, lamb, wild game	Beef, chicken, pork, cold cuts, bacon, hotdogs, canned meat, sausage, shellfish, and meat substitutes made from soy
Dairy Products and Milk Substitutes	Unsweetened rice milk*, almond milk, coconut milk	Milk, cheese, cottage cheese, cream, yogurt, butter, ice cream, non-dairy creamers, and eggs

99

Fats	Olive oil, flaxseed oil, coconut oil	Margarine, butter, processed and hydrogenated oils, and mayonnaise
Beverages	Drink plenty of fresh water and herbal teas such as rooibos and peppermint	Alcohol and caffeine, such as coffee, black tea, green tea, and soda
Spices and Condiments	Sea salt, fresh pepper, fresh herbs and spices, such as garlic, cumin, dill, ginger, oregano, parsley, rosemary, thyme, and turmeric	Chocolate, ketchup, mustard, relish, chutney, soy sauce, barbeque sauce, and vinegar
Sweeteners	None	White or brown sugar, honey, maple syrup, stevia, artificial sweeteners, corn syrup, high fructose corn syrup

May also be removed if you suspect a sensitivity to grains.

April 17th – Don't get too serious.

As I said, this is a very restrictive diet. If you find it too hard to do, at least work on eliminating what you can. Pay attention to things you eat every day. If you have coconut milk every day, or broccoli every day, you may find that you've become intolerant to one of your daily staples, just because you're eating it so much.

Follow the diet as closely as you can to what's above. If you aren't able to fully follow it, that's okay, but keep in mind that the more you remove, the more likely you are to figure out what does and does not work for you.

And please, I'm begging you, make sure you drink enough water on the elimination diet!

April 18th – Tips for success.

- Have the foods you need on hand and know how to cook them. If you know how to cook, it will make this much easier. After all, no one wants to eat raw vegetables for three weeks! That same boring cauliflower can be a superstar in the elimination diet if you roast it one day, saute it the next, and then "rice" it on the third day!

- Don't skip the step of cleaning out your kitchen before you start the elimination diet. Willpower is not your friend here. You can't eat chocolate chip cookies if there are no chocolate chip cookies to eat!

- Don't skip the food journal. The whole point of doing this diet is to figure out what foods work best for your body. If you aren't writing things down and keeping track, you're missing the most crucial step in the process.

April 19th – Detox the air.

Who here likes plants? I love plants! They make my home look lively and colorful on a very reasonable budget, but even more important, plants can clean the air in your home. Plants are good at absorbing gases through surface pores on their leaves (hey, like your skin!) An indoor plant's ability to remove harmful VOCs (volatile organic compounds) is an example of phytoremediation.

While most plants will help clean the air, the following types of plants have been shown to have the best air-purifying qualities*:

- Bamboo palm
- Boston fern
- Chinese evergreen
- Golden pothos
- English ivy
- Heartleaf philodendron
- Lady palm
- Peace lily
- Red-edged dracaena
- Rubber plant
- Snake plant
- Spider plant
- Wax begonia
- Weeping fig

Pet Parents…Please note; just because these plants are good for the air, they may NOT be good for your fur babies! Some plants are dangerous, even toxic to pets! Please research all plants before introducing them to your home if you have pets.

April 20th – Detoxing Debbie Downers

Last month we talked about purging people, and we're going to talk about that a little more this month.

Ridding your life of toxic people is so important to your well-being. It's time to let the Debbie Downers, the Negative Nellies, and the Bad Attitude Betty's go.

If you went through last month's exercises for ridding people from your life, I'm proud of you. If you haven't, ask yourself why.

Could it be that you are holding onto people out of fear, loyalty, guilt, a sense of responsibility, or because of habit? You need to understand why you are holding on to people that are no longer healthy for you.

Grab your journal and try this exercise:

1. Make a list of all the negative people in your life.

2. Next to each person's name, write down EXACTLY what it is that they do that got them on the list.

3. Write down how much time you normally spend with each person every week and every month.

4. Now, write down all the things that you want to do but don't have time to do.

5. See if you can substitute the time you spend with your energy vampires for some of the hobbies and activities you'd like to do.

April 21st – Listen to your heart.

If you're still resistant to the idea of cutting out the NEDs (Negative Energy Drains), try this exercise out.

1. Schedule a coffee or lunch date with your NED.

2. As you spend time together, play close attention to how you feel. Do you feel anxious or angry? Are you fidgeting, looking at your watch, or wishing you were somewhere else? Is your NED spending the whole time talking about themselves? Is the talk positive or a lot of whining?

3. As soon as you've broken free from your NED, grab your journal and write down everything that happened and how you felt. It's important to do this ASAP after you've had your meeting. If you wait until the next day, or even until you get home, you'll start to minimize how you really felt. Don't do that to yourself.

4. Once you have everything recorded, assign the "date" a number from 1 – 5, with 5 being, the best time you've ever had, and 1 being, the worst time you've ever had.

You know where I'm going with this! If your number is anything that's a 3 or below, you need to think carefully about whether this is really how you want to spend your precious, and, most likely, limited time.

April 22nd – Detox your social media.

Almost every person I've met, every client I've coached, every business owner I've networked with, has reported being caught up in information and technology overload! I know I am! I manage my website, two blogs, three email addresses, a monthly newsletter, four social media accounts, and I answer two separate voicemails.

Whew!

While you're in detox mode, this is an excellent time to think about detoxing some of your social media. Cutting down on the information coming in to you can help you to feel less pressured to keep up with things and may actually buy you some precious time!

Follow these steps to help you unplug and detach from the crushing weight of information overload:

1. Scale down your Facebook friend list. Ask yourself if these people are really your friends. If you pass by their name and don't immediately know who they are, you might think about letting them go. They won't get a notification that they've been cyber-dumped, and chances are, they are going through information overload as well, and they may not even notice that you've gone away.

2. Pare down to just three email addresses if you can. One address should be for work (likely the one your employer provides you if you work for someone else), one address should be for personal email from close friends and family, and the third should be for junk mail.

3. Unsubscribe to automated emails that you no longer read/want. Unless you have time and an interest in reading special offers, newsletters, and other related items, unsubscribe yourself from incoming email. Most information that you want you'll be able to find by going to a company's website. Unsubscribing means less stuff coming in to your mailbox and into your world.

4. Establish blackout periods for yourself. Make a deal with yourself and your family that there will be no electronics after a certain time at night. No email, no Facebook, no Twitter, no nothing! Use that time to decompress and reconnect with your loved ones. Have a real face-to-face conversation, play a game, or take a walk. Live alone? You should still give yourself some time to unplug and unwind.

5. Get over FOMO. Have you heard of FOMO? FOMO stands for Fear Of Missing Out. Many people "troll" Facebook because they feel that they will miss something if they aren't on there constantly. Please remember that people post only what they want you to know/hear about. Facebook jealousy is a real thing that happens when people get caught up in envy for the lives of others. Vacation pictures, declarations of the "world's greatest husband," and check-ins at the city's hottest restaurants can make you feel pretty crappy if you're spending your Saturday night at home alone in your pajamas. I guarantee that if you unplug for a while, you won't miss anything urgent. Facebook will always be there.

April 23rd – Detox your social life.

Just like taking a break from social media can help you relax and recharge your batteries, so can taking a break from too many social gatherings, happy hours, and lunches with people that you aren't really interested in seeing. It's great to spend time with other people. Humans are social beings and we need to feel connected, but sometimes, too much connectivity with others drowns out our own inner voice and our need to be alone to unwind.

If you're finding that your dance card is always full, pull out your planner and schedule at least four days next month that you can take for yourself. That's only one day per week! Write it in your schedule and stick to it like you do all your other important appointments. Schedule a massage, or a walk in the park. Schedule an afternoon to watch your favorite TV show that no one else in your family wants to watch. Whatever you do doesn't have to cost a lot (or anything) and doesn't have to take a lot of time.

Scheduling even one hour for yourself will help you feel more grounded and in touch with what you really like and really want. Go get that planner and put those dates in NOW!

April 24th – How's that elimination diet going?

Have you tried the elimination diet yet? Have you at least cut out the sugar and CRAP that we talked about earlier this month? If you've decided to try this, take out your journal and look back on the last week to see how you've been feeling. Do you notice any patterns yet? Is there anything so far that has surprised you? Notice your energy levels. Do you have more energy? Are you having any headaches? How has your sleep been? It's important to pay attention to all the clues that your body is giving you.

April 25th – Reach for a healthier snack.

Snacks are not necessarily a bad thing, in fact, healthy snacking can keep you from overeating at mealtime and keep you from getting so hungry that you make poor choices. While you don't want to eat all day long, a snack or two between meals (if you're hungry) is A-Okay!

The problem with snacks is when we choose unhealthy things, like junk food from the vending machine, sugar-laden coffee drinks that can pack in a whole day's worth of calories in one cup, or, even healthy snacks in portion sizes that are equal to the size of a full meal.

One of the best snack combinations I've found are snacks that pair protein and fiber. These tend to keep me fuller longer and keep my energy levels steady. Think of things like:

Peanut butter and an apple
Greek yogurt and berries

Hummus and veggies (my favorite)
String cheese and an orange
Lentil or bean chips with salsa

Snack on, my friends!

April 26th – Reach for healthier fats.

Fat does not make you fat! Fat has gotten a bad rap over the years on the diet scene, but, healthy fat is not the enemy, in fact, your body needs some fat! What you want to detox out of your diet are all the unhealthy fats like saturated fats found in:

- High fat meats such as beef, lamb and pork
- Butter
- Cheese
- Ice Cream
- Palm oil
- Lard

Trans fats, such as those found in:
- Pastries such as cookies, donuts, muffins, and cakes
- Packaged snacks like crackers and chips
- Margarine
- Vegetable shortening
- Fried foods such as French fries, fried chicken, and breaded fish

Start adding in good, healthy monounsaturated fats like those in:
- Olive oil
- Sesame oil
- Avocadoes
- Olives
- Nuts

YOUR BEST YEAR YET!

Polyunsaturated fats like:
- Flaxseed
- Fatty fish, such as salmon, tuna, mackerel, and sardines
- Tofu

April 27th – Let go of your "supposed to be."

Life is funny sometimes. We often miss the amazing moments in life because what is happening to us is not what is "supposed to be" happening. We get so caught up in thinking that our life is supposed to go a certain way, and when it doesn't go that way, we get angry, bitter, or confused. Life does not come with a set of instructions or a play book, and sometimes what we think "ought to be" happening, isn't happening, and may never happen.

This does not mean that I think you should wander through life aimlessly with no plan and no direction. What I am suggesting is that you give up a little of the controlling "supposed to be" thinking and learn to appreciate your life for what it is, where it is.

I am always striving for constant improvement in my life. I always want to do the best that I can, do things that I can be proud of, and always do what I can to help others on their journey through life.

In building my business, and my life, and even in writing this book, I found myself caught up in wallowing over what I thought was supposed to happen. I had a very clear vision in my head of what everything was supposed to look like, and when it didn't look that way, I got discouraged, even angry. Getting caught up in the "supposed to be" was robbing me of enjoying what actually was.

Starting today, learn to be grateful for where you are in life and what you have. Even if you are not exactly where you want to be or are still working towards a bigger goal or striving for something greater, take some pressure off yourself by not getting caught up in what is "supposed to be." Trust that what is happening is what should be happening and anything that is meant to be in your life will be.

April 28th – Let food truly be your fuel.

Food should taste good and be enjoyable, however, we should never forget the true purpose of why we eat; we eat to fuel our bodies. When we go through something like an elimination diet or even when we just consciously try to cut out sugar or junk food, it's a good time to remind ourselves that what we eat is fueling our bodies to give us the energy, strength, and stamina to do all the things we need and want to do.

Hippocrates said it best when he said:

"Let food by thy medicine and medicine be thy food"

The food that we eat plays a critical role in our overall health and well-being. We literally are what we eat! We've all heard that phrase before, but researchers have shown that it is absolutely true. The foods that we eat make up our cells, bone marrow, blood, and hormones. The average adult loses about 300 billion cells every day and must replace them. Our bodies are literally created out of the food we eat!

What are you made of? Are you made of greasy French fries and other fast food items? Are you made of pizza and beer? Are you made of organic fruits and vegetables?

As we are winding down this month of detoxing it's important to keep in mind the impact that food consumption has on your body.

As you continue to go through this life-changing year, keep detoxing unhealthy things from your life (including unhealthy foods) and get back to fueling your magnificent machine with the right foods for your body.

April 29th – Learn to let go.

I am a perfectionist. Being one has caused me to struggle often with things in my life. And, just like we talked about letting go of your "supposed to be," sometimes, you have to let go of your need to perfect things.

I can't tell you how many times in my life I've gone through "analysis paralysis," meaning that I analyze a situation so long, that by the time I'm ready to make a leap, the window of opportunity has passed.

In the immortal words of Matthew Broderick in one of my all-time favorite movies *Ferris Bueller's Day Off:*

> *"Life moves pretty fast. If you don't stop and look around once in a while, you could miss it."*
> *~Ferris Bueller*

Don't let yourself miss the little things while obsessing over whether or not it's perfect. I've missed so many opportunities, big and small, because I was waiting for the perfect time. THERE IS NO PERFECT TIME! The only time you have is right now. The situation may never be "perfect!"

Learn to let go of the need for perfection in your life and embrace what you have right now. Learn to love the lopsided birthday cake, the jacket with the missing button, your favorite book with the torn acknowledgements page, your favorite tea cup with the chip out of it, and the tiny scar on your forehead from that biking accident when you were ten.

"Things don't have to be perfect to be perfectly wonderful."
~ Karen Ann Kennedy

April 30th – Detox that "one thing."

It's soul searching time, so get out that journal, find a quiet spot and let's end the month with this…

We all have that "one thing." It's the thing that has power and control over us. It's the thing that we know we don't need and know we should detox out of our lives, but for some reason, we just can't seem to do it. We all have that one thing that is getting in the way of us living our best lives, moving forward, and feeling great about ourselves.

Maybe your one thing is an abusive relationship, a needy friend who takes way more than she gives, an addiction to something like caffeine or nicotine that keeps you from reaching your health goals.

Perhaps your one thing is not being able to stand up for yourself, not finishing your degree, staying up too late, eating too much, or your constant need to be right.

Whatever your one thing is, it's time to face it head on, and slay the dragon.

In your journal, I want you to write a letter to your thing. I want you to tell your one thing that you are breaking up with it; that it is no longer serving you, and that you need to let it go. Your letter might end up looking something like this:

Dear Caffeine,

I am writing today to tell you that I am letting you go. You have been an unhealthy feature in my life for a long time, but up until now, I've never been strong enough to tell you to get out. You have had control over my life for way too long and I need you to go away. Starting today, you are no longer welcome in my life. By letting you go, I will be able to take back control of my life. No more running to the coffee shop two or three times a day, spending money I don't have, and obsessing about you when I don't have you around. I'll be able to sleep better, and hydrate my body with enough water to stop my constant headaches. So, caffeine, take note that today, I'm saying goodbye. I no longer need you in my life.

Karen

Maybe your letter will be longer, or shorter. There's no right way to do it. But I encourage you to really do this exercise, even if you feel a little silly at first. You can keep it in your journal (if you don't want anyone to see it) or hang it in a spot where you can see it easily (if you need to be constantly reminded of it).

It's time to detox that one thing so you can open yourself up to lots of other things!

My April to-do list:

- ° I took steps to quit smoking (if applicable)
- ° I took steps to reduce my exposure to second-hand smoke
- ° I detoxed my beauty products
- ° I researched/bought new beauty products
- ° I tried my hand at making my own beauty products at home
- ° I detoxed my home cleaning supplies
- ° I tried some of the DIY home cleaning recipes
- ° I consciously cut down on my sugar consumption
- ° I cleaned the junk food out of my kitchen
- ° I tried the elimination diet
- ° I bought some plants for my home and/or office
- ° I detoxed the Debbie Downers out of my life
- ° I talked to at least one NED
- ° I detoxed from social media
- ° I scheduled my four "me" days for May
- ° I upgraded my snacks to more healthier options
- ° I swapped out the unhealthy fats for healthy fats
- ° I wrote a letter to my "one thing"

MAY – GET STARTED ON A HEALTHY EATING PLAN

We're five months into the New Year, so why wait until now to get started on a healthy eating plan? May is a great time to start cleaning up your diet. In most parts of the world the weather is getting warmer and more of the healthy fruits and vegetables that we like are back in season.

As the warmer weather moves in, I tend to ditch the traditional "comfort foods" that kept me satiated through the winter, in favor of lighter foods that keep me cool and hydrated.

May is all about getting started on a healthier way of eating. It's not about a DIET; it's about making little changes in the way you eat, so you can improve your health and upgrade the foods you use to fuel your body.

Get excited, we're about to get our eat on!

May 1ˢᵗ – It's May Day!

May 1ˢᵗ is traditionally known as May Day, but this year, we're putting it out as a mayday! If you haven't been eating healthy foods, your body will be sending out an SOS, begging for you to pay attention to what you're feeding it.

Your body may be sending you an SOS if you're suffering from any of the following symptoms:

- Unexplained weight loss or weight gain
- Frequent headaches
- Fatigue
- Lack of concentration
- Sore joints
- Gastrointestinal issues such as constipation, diarrhea, or stomach pain
- Skin issues such as acne

Now's the time to get serious about the food you eat.

May 2ⁿᵈ – Eliminate, eliminate, eliminate!

If you tried your hand at the elimination diet that we reviewed last month; good for you! If you didn't embark on the journey, I urge you to think about trying it now.

Although it is tough to do, an elimination diet will give you a really solid sense of what foods are working for you and what foods are not. Even if you cannot commit to doing the elimination diet in its entirety, at least consider giving up foods that you suspect may be giving you trouble and give them up for at least a week.

It's important as you go through this food exploration that you keep notes in your journal about what you ate and how you felt, so you can get the most out of the experiment.

May 3rd – Bio-individuality

As I was going through school to obtain my Health Coach certification, a consistent concept kept coming up in my studies; the concept of bio-individuality. This is just a fancy way of saying that what works for one person may not work for someone else.

Has this ever happened to you?

Your friend goes on the latest fad diet (there's a new one every week) and she quickly drops forty pounds and looks great. You run out and buy the same diet book, follow the same plan, and lose ten pounds? You're angry and frustrated. After all, you did everything the book said, and still, your results are not nearly as good.

It's not you that's wrong, it may not even necessarily be the book that is wrong, it's just that that particular diet plan was not right for your body.

Now, I don't know you, so I can't practice bio-individuality with you this month, but what I can give you are some tried and true tips that GENERALLY work for MOST people. This is where you want to consult your physician about any changes you plan to make to your eating plan. It's important that you recognize what works well for you and what may not work well based on your unique DNA.

As we dive into the rest of May, I'll be sharing with you my top tips for getting started on a healthy eating plan. Some of these may work for you, some may not. The key is to know your body and pay attention to which things feel good to you.

May 4th – Add more vegetables.

This is the single best thing you can do for your body; add more vegetables. Fruits are important too, and we'll certainly be talking about them this month, but fruits have sugar, so you want to watch your portion sizes. With vegetables, forget portion sizes; eat as much as you want! And eat from the rainbow...no...not Skittles! Eating a variety of colors will help you get the most from your vegetable consumption as different colors have different nutrients.

Green vegetables contain lutein, an antioxidant that helps improve vision. They also have potassium, vitamin C, vitamin K, and folic acid, an important nutrient for healthy pregnancy.

Orange vegetables are rich in beta carotene and vitamin C, which promote healthy skin and support a strong immune system.

Red veggies are rich in phytochemicals like lycopene that improve heart health and have been shown to reduce the risk of cancer.

Consuming purple vegetables can help with anti-aging because of their antioxidant and phytochemical properties. These nutrients can help fight cancer while supporting mental clarity and function.

White vegetables also have phytochemicals, as well as potassium, and can help reduce overall cholesterol levels, lower blood pressure, and help stave off diabetes.

Think of ways to sneak vegetables in whenever you can. Add some onions and peppers to your morning omelet, throw some vegetables in with your pasta, enjoy a salad before your evening meal.

May 5th – Consume a variety of foods.

Different foods provide different nutrients, so it's important to eat a variety of foods to get all the nutrients your body needs.

Certainly, if you have chosen to cut out an entire category of food, because of health, religious, or moral beliefs, e.g. a vegan or vegetarian lifestyle, you'll have to be extra vigilant about getting in the nutrients your body needs, but it can be done!

As a vegan, I always hear, "How do you get your protein?" My fellow vegans out there are likely rolling their eyes right now. There are plenty of foods besides meat that are rich in protein. The trick is to research and seek them out. If you are on a restrictive diet, please take the time to research alternative ways to get all the nutrients your body needs.

If you are not on a restrictive diet, do a little research anyway. Know what foods are rich in what nutritional properties and talk with your doctor about what to eat to ensure you are taking in a balanced, nutrient-dense diet.

May 6th – Learn to read food labels.

Am I the only one confused by food labels? You have to learn to read the label and not just the claims on the front of the packaging. There are plenty of misleading catch phrases out there, "vitamin enriched," "low-fat," "calcium enriched," and the like. This does not mean that these foods are healthy for you. On the contrary, they may just be some of the worst foods on the market.

Get in the habit of reading food labels, and, look for these four things:

1. Serving size – The first thing to check is the serving size. That "healthy" bottle of juice at just 120 calories might

actually contain two servings, which is a whopping 240 cal-ories! Always look at the serving size to know exactly how much food you get for your caloric buck.

2. Fats – Look for products with zero trans fat and low satu-rated fat.

3. Sodium – Americans consume far too much sodium. Even if high blood pressure and heart disease are not a factor for you, keeping your sodium intake at reasonable levels is an important step in staying healthy. Full meals should contain no more than 600 mg of salt, and snacks should come in under 180 mg.

4. Sugar – Some people will tell you to limit your sugar to 25 grams or less a day; that's about 6 teaspoons. I think that's still way too much sugar. At any rate, if you are trying to cut down on sugar, and use the 25 grams as your guide, make sure you read the labels and know how much sugar is in your food.

May 7th – Steer clear of "red flag" ingredients.

If you don't know what an ingredient is, guess what; your body won't know what it is either.

> *"The problem is we are not eating food any-more, we are eating food like products."*
> ~Dr. Alejandro Junger

Most of the processed foods on store shelves today weren't around 80 – 85 years ago. I can assure you that your grandparents and great-grandparents were not eating Twinkies and squeeze cheese from a can.

One of the best things you can do is to stop eating processed foods altogether. Not ready to take that leap? Try eating foods that have five or less ingredients. If that's still too extreme for you, at least steer clear of the following "red flag" ingredients:

- Artificial sweeteners – Look for words like aspartame, glycerol, isomalt, saccharin, sorbitol, and sucralose; they're all bad news.
- High fructose corn syrup – don't let the fact that it comes from corn make you think it's healthy; it's not.
- MSG – used as a flavor enhancer in many processed foods
- Trans fat – an artificial, unsaturated fat
- Food dyes – particularly red dye #3
- Sodium nitrate – found in processed meats. I swore to my mom as a kid that hot dogs gave me a headache; I wasn't lying.

May 8th – Stop using food as a reward.

The problem with treats is that they are no longer treats, they are part of our everyday diet! When I was a kid, I can tell you that we had birthday cake twice a year; once on my birthday, and once on my sister's birthday, unless we were lucky enough to get invited to some other kid's birthday party, where we'd no doubt have cake there, too!

It's okay to treat yourself occasionally to something decadent. When I say decadent, think high-quality, like a piece of really good dark chocolate, an exquisitely crafted French pastry, or a hand-churned frozen treat, not a Twinkie or a Snickers bar.

What's not okay is eating treats as meals, or using treats as a reward for every little victory.

Johnny scored the winning goal at soccer, ice cream for everyone! Heather aced her math test, pizza and soda for the whole family! I knocked that presentation out of the park, three glasses of wine for me!

We have to stop using food as a reward. I look at many of my health coaching clients and I see the unhealthy relationships they have with food, many of which are rooted in their childhoods.

When you want to reward yourself or your family, get in the habit of turning to non-food rewards. Maybe let Johnny pick the next movie for the family, take Heather and her friends to a local water park and let them spend the day, get yourself a new blouse or a new pair of shoes to celebrate your rock-star status.

May 9th – Practice "crowding out."

Another quite interesting concept I learned in nutrition school was the concept of crowding out. This means, not giving up anything, but, actually adding more stuff in.

I can see that look on your face from here. Trust me, when I tell my clients that I actually want them to eat more food, they usually start asking me for a refund on their program.

When you practice crowding out, you start bringing in more healthy foods, and eventually you "crowd out" the bad stuff.

As David Wolfe puts it in the groundbreaking film *Hungry for Change:*

> *"The best strategy we've got is to just add in the good stuff! Eventually it's going to crowd out the bad stuff."*

Here are some of the best "crowding out" techniques I've developed for myself and for my clients.

- If I want chocolate, I'm allowed to have it...but I have to eat the chocolate with lots of healthy, vibrant berries
- If I want cookies, I am allowed to have them...but I have to eat a piece of fruit first
- If I'm going out to eat and I want pizza, French fries, or some other greasy food, I MUST eat a salad as my main meal and eat the other item as a side dish
- For every piece of candy I eat, I am required to add in one additional cup of vegetables that day. If I'm having a rough day and eat two mini peppermint patties, that's two cups of broccoli come dinnertime!

Today, practice crowding out when you eat. Consciously think about adding in more and more of the good stuff.

May 10th – Try a meatless Monday.
DISCLAIMER – I don't eat meat...I am not forcing you to stop eating meat. My reasons for giving up meat are not dietary reasons, they are moral reasons; I simply cannot eat an animal.

By no means am I suggesting that you should stop eating meat, too! I have lots of clients who are omnivores and I pride myself on not being a "judgy vegan!" But, I do want to encourage you to try cutting back on meat to experience the benefits that a plant-based diet has to offer. If you haven't yet heard of the Meatless Monday movement, it's basically picking one day per week to abstain from eating animal products.

It doesn't have to be a Monday; you can have meatless Wednesday or meatless Saturday if you want. Cutting back on your animal consumption can yield many health benefits such as:

- A reduction in your intake of saturated fats
- A reduction in cholesterol intake
- A potential reduction in the risk for heart disease, cancer, and diabetes
- Increased energy
- Healthy, glowing skin

As you plan your meals for the week, try going meatless at least one day in the week. Set yourself up for success by checking out recipes online, or visit my blog *Carrots Don't Scream When You Boil Them* for lots of great meatless recipes.

May 11th – Focus on eating for health, not weight loss.

A funny thing happened to me when I stopped trying to lose weight; I lost weight! Why? One of the biggest mistakes I see people make is that they obsess about food when they're dieting. They measure their food, count their calories, plan their meals, and write down everything they eat. What this means is that they are literally spending all their waking hours THINKING ABOUT FOOD!

They also rely heavily on diet food products, which are nothing but chemical-laden, manufactured "food-like" products.

When I stopped eating for weight loss and focused on eating for health I actually started to shed pounds. My simple rule was to eat when I was hungry, stop when I was full, and eat real food with ingredients I could pronounce. Not only did I lose weight, but it made my life so much easier. There was no more agonizing at the grocery store, reading labels, and counting every calorie. I just knew that if food had a longer shelf life than me, I wouldn't buy it, and, when I was hungry, I ate, and when I was full, I stopped. That's it!

Here's your activity for today. Each time you think about eating something, I want you to rate your hunger on a scale from 1 to 10. If your hunger is at a five or less, ask yourself if you're really hungry, or, are you feeling something else; loneliness, boredom, etc. If your hunger is a six or above, go ahead and eat something, but pay attention while you are eating, eat slowly, and stop when you're full. Don't let your hunger get above an eight or nine; that's usually when you get so hungry that you may find it difficult to make smart choices.

May 12th – Watch your portion sizes.
Even healthy food has calories, so you'll want to watch your portion sizes as you get on your healthy eating plan.

If you haven't ever tried the dinner plate trick; give it a go, it really does work. I never eat my meals using regular-sized dinner plates or bowls. I always fill up a salad bowl and small plate. When you pile your food onto a smaller plate, it gives the illusion of there being more food than there actually is. I have found that this smaller portion is really more than enough for me.

When I use a full-sized dinner plate, I feel cheated if it's not filled to the edges. This means that I end up eating more than I want or need. The same goes with bowls. I don't need a giant bowl for cereal or pasta. A small bowl that looks overflowing makes me feel like I'm getting more food than I actually am.

It's important to pay attention to not only what you eat, but also how much you eat. Use the handy portion size guidelines below to help you out.

- Protein – A serving size of protein should be about six ounces, about the size of a deck of cards
- Starch – A serving of starch (rice, potatoes, etc.) should be a cup, roughly the size of a tennis ball
- Cheese – Limit your serving size of cheese to just an ounce, that's about the size of the tip of your thumb
- "Loose" snacks – (think nuts, popcorn, etc.) should be one to two ounces, or just enough to fit in the palm of your hand
- A pancake should be about the size of a DVD
- When using salad dressings, keep the serving size to about an ounce, which is the amount that will fit in a shot glass

May 13ᵗʰ – Don't drink your calories.
Let's look at a day's worth of calories in your beverages:

- You start off the day with a "healthy" eight-ounce glass of orange juice; that's 110 calories.
- On your way to work you stop and get a medium-sized mocha coffee drink; that's 400 calories.
- You have a 20-ounce soda with your lunch; that's 280 calories.
- After lunch, you hit the mid-afternoon slump and reach for another soda; that's another 280 calories.
- You have a 16-ounce sweet tea with dinner; that's 200 calories.
- After dinner, you kick your feet up and enjoy a 12-ounce beer for an additional150 calories.

That's 1,420 calories and you haven't even factored in your food!

The average coffee drink in America is 340 calories! Let's look at three of the worst offenders.

A large frozen cappuccino at Dunkin Donuts is 610 calories, with eight grams of fat and 105 grams of sugar. A venti white chocolate mocha at Starbucks is 580 calories with 22 grams of fat and 75 grams of sugar. A large mocha at McDonald's is 400 calories with 14 grams of fat and 49 grams of sugar.

Whew! A 12-ounce can of Coca Cola clocks in at 140 calories, while the same size can of Pepsi comes in at 150 calories; the same size Sunkist orange soda has 170 calories.

A 16-ounce can of Rockstar Energy Drink packs in a whopping 280 calories and 62 grams of sugar; that's the sugar equivalent of six Krispy Kreme donuts!

What you want to look for is nutrient-dense foods that help you feel full. Chances are, once you down that sugary coffee drink in the morning, you're still going to be hungry! Few people I know drink that coffee drink as a meal replacement, most are having it **in addition** to their morning meal.

Want to cut the calories and sugar? Stick to water! Don't like plain water? Jazz it up with some slices of lemon, lime, or orange, or try some fresh mint.

May 14th – Stick to a schedule.
You want to get in a habit of eating regular meals at regular intervals to keep your blood sugar stabilized and keep you from getting

hangry when you haven't eaten for a long period. Remember hangry? It's when you get hungry and angry: hangry! I laughed when I heard that term, but only for a minute, because I realized that is totally me when I'm hungry! Steer clear of me if I haven't eaten for a while!

You should certainly eat when you're hungry and not by the clock, but you shouldn't let yourself get to the point of starvation before you put something in your stomach. If you can, try to eat three solid meals a day, with no more than two healthy snacks in between.

Eat breakfast within an hour or two of waking, be sure to eat lunch, and eat dinner at a reasonable time of day. You want to try to refrain from eating 2 – 3 hours before bedtime, if you can.

May 15th – Aim for two cups of fruit each day.
There are many health benefits to fruit, but, fruit also contains sugar, so while you want to get your fill of vegetables, you want to be mindful of how much fruit you are consuming.

Just like vegetables, fruit has terrific health benefits.

Apples – help your body fight infection
Bananas – give you great energy
Blueberries – protect your heart
Cherries – help calm your nervous system
Grapes – relax your blood vessels
Kiwis – increase bone mass
Oranges – help maintain great skin
Peaches – are rich in potassium and iron
Strawberries – have been shown to help with aging
Watermelon – helps control your heart rate

Many of these amazing fruits are in season in the month of May!

Fruit is like nature's candy; eat up!

May 16th – Stay hydrated.

We've already talked about not drinking your calories, and while water is certainly your best non-calorie drink, the health benefits go far beyond calorie content.

Drinking water helps keep you energized and alert; promotes weight loss, flushes out toxins, and improves your complexion.

Drinking water also helps prevent headaches, as well as migraines and back and joint pain, which are commonly caused by dehydration.

Keep in mind that your body is composed of about 60% water. The water in your body helps with digestion, circulation, transportation of nutrients throughout the body, and maintenance of your body temperature; this is not something to mess with!

When your body starts to run low on fluids, you start to feel thirsty. Many experts in the health community will tell you that when you feel thirsty, you're already dehydrated, so it's best to get in enough water before you feel the thirst signal.

Although there isn't a lot of hard evidence that drinking at least eight, 8-ounce glasses of water a day should be the norm, it's a popular piece of advice because it's easy to remember. Just keep in mind that you may need more water if:

- You are exercising intensely and sweating
- You are in a hot climate

- You are sick with the flu or have diarrhea (which may cause dehydration)
- You have frequent urinary tract infections
- You are pregnant or breast-feeding

Your best rule of thumb is to drink water throughout the day to avoid feeling thirsty.

Your assignment for today is to go get yourself a slick, cool water bottle to keep at the office, and one to keep at home. Look for a BPA-free water bottle such as a Nalgene, www.nalgene-outdoor. com; Camelbak, www.camelbak.com; Intak by Thermos, www. thermos.com; or Contigo, www.gocontigo.com.

Remember to keep your bottles full and drink from them often throughout the day.

Don't like plain water? You can invest in an infuser water bottle and make your own fruit water with jazzy combinations like:

Blackberry sage
Blueberry lavender
Orange, lemon, and lime
Pineapple mint
Raspberry lime
Strawberry, lemon, and basil
Watermelon mint

Drink up!

May 17th – Know why you eat.
While we have already established that we need to get back to the basics of why we eat; for fuel, not for entertainment, many people

do eat for lots of reasons other than satiety and fuel. Eating is how we celebrate, how we mourn, and how we socialize.

I want to share with you the four questions to ask yourself before you eat. Copy them and tape them to your fridge, and get in the habit, starting today, with asking yourself these four things before you eat <u>anything</u>.

1. **What am I eating?**
   This is not a perfunctory question! To say, "I'm eating a Twinkie," is not enough. You have to know what's in the Twinkie. When you ask yourself what you're eating, you need to really think about the answer. If what you're eating is full of chemicals that you can't pronounce, chances are, you shouldn't be eating it. This is why reading food labels is so important.

2. **Where did it come from?**
   Did your food come from a farmer that lovingly cared for his crops or did it come from a factory where some guy in a chemical suit pushed it down a conveyor belt? If you buy into the notion that your food carries certain energy in it, then you'll likely want to pay attention to this question. Even if you don't subscribe to this particular way of thinking, it's still smart to know the answer. Chances are, the food that came from the farmer is healthier for you than the food that came from the factory. Don't believe me? Refer back to question one.

3. **Why am I eating it?**
   This is a big question! Are you eating because you are craving something specific? Are you craving salt, sugar, or carbs? Are you eating because you are bored, lonely, sad, or angry? Are you eating to fuel up for a workout? It's important to

pinpoint why you are eating because doing so helps you identify issues with emotional eating.

We often eat for reasons other than hunger. Eating is how we celebrate, mourn and socialize. We go out to eat to celebrate birthdays; the family goes out for ice cream when the kids get good report cards; when there's a death in the family, we hold a luncheon to honor the departed; and it's not often you hear, "Let's meet for a walk in the park," but we often hear, "Let's meet for coffee!" The idea here is to get to a place where you are eating only to fuel your body or satisfy physical hunger.

4. **How will I feel after I eat this?**
Before you eat, think about how you will feel afterwards. Not just how you will physically feel, but how you'll emotionally feel as well. Will you feel guilty, angry or annoyed with yourself? Will you feel bloated? Will you have gas? Is this food item going to give you a headache? A stomachache? Will too much of this food keep you up all night?

I know lots of people that keep a food journal and write down everything they eat, but, if you're only writing down the item and not how the food makes you feel, you're missing an important part of the equation. Paying attention to what your food does to you will help you figure out if you have any food allergies or sensitivities. It will also help you to identify triggers that cause you to overeat or eat the wrong things.

May 18th – Watch how you prepare your food.
Even if you have changed what you eat, you still have to be mindful of HOW you eat it! One medium grilled chicken breast has about

98 calories, but that same medium piece of chicken has about 320 calories when fried! That's a whopping 222 calorie difference!

It's not just grilling that can help you save those calories. You can also try employing some of these other healthy cooking techniques.

Baking – Done in the oven, usually without the introduction of additional fats.

Braising – Usually done with meats, involves searing the meat first in a pan on top of the stove then slowly cooking it in a small amount of liquid (usually broth or water).

Broiling – Done in the oven just below the broiler. This method allows fat to drip away from food.

Poaching – Similar to braising, poaching allows a food to gently simmer in water or another liquid such as broth or even wine. Poaching fruits, such as pears, makes a flavorful, and healthy dessert option.

Sautéing – Can be done in a non-stick pan, or with just a light coating of a healthy oil, such as coconut oil.

Steaming – A lovely way to cook vegetables with no added fats. Can be done right on the stove top with a steamer basket over boiling water.

May 19ᵗʰ – Make healthy "swaps".
It can be overwhelming, and depressing, to give up foods that you love. That's why if you plan to stick to a long-term healthy way of eating, it's important to swap out some of your favorites for healthier versions. This is not the same as "crowding out" which is basically eating more and more healthy things and ridding yourself completely of unhealthy choices. This is more about still allowing

yourself to have treats that you enjoy, but finding healthier versions of them. Think frozen yogurt instead of full-fat ice cream.

Here are some of my favorite healthy swaps. Today, pick two or three that appeal to you and in the coming weeks, work them into your eating plan.

Banana "ice cream" – I keep bananas in my freezer (a great way to use them when they start to get soft). When I want ice cream, I put the bananas in a food processor with a little lime juice, honey, and cinnamon and pulse it until it is the consistency of ice cream. If I'm feeling really naughty, I'll put some chocolate syrup on it!

Fruit freezer pops – There is nothing more refreshing on a hot summer day than a frozen treat, but most commercial fruit pops are loaded with sugar and artificial colors and flavors. I chop up whatever fruit I have, berries, kiwi, melon, etc. and pop them in small paper cups. I pour coconut water over the fruit and pop them in the freezer. As they start to take shape, I stick a Popsicle stick in the middle and after freezing for a few hours, I have healthy and delicious frozen fruit pops.

The cheese and cracker switcheroo – Who doesn't love cheese and crackers? Well, I don't…I don't eat cheese! But everyone else I know loves it! Crackers can add up to a lot of calories, fat, and sodium, so I swap out the crackers for apple slices. There is something elegant and decadent about fruit and cheese, so when my guests come over to visit, I lay out a beautiful cheese board with apple slices, grapes, and a selection of cheeses; no one ever misses the crackers.

Black cherry "soda" – I don't drink soda any more, but sometimes I do miss the fizz. I put a tablespoon or two of black cherry concentrate (you can get it at places like the Vitamin Shoppe) in a glass and add a squeeze of lime juice and some seltzer water for my healthy version of black cherry soda.

Carrot chips – When I'm craving something crunchy, I no longer reach for chips or even pretzels; I reach for carrot chips. You can actually get carrots at your grocery store that are cut like crinkle cut chips! I'll often eat them just plain as a side snack, or if I need something a little more substantial, I'll dip them in hummus.

May 20th – Limit your sugar intake.

As a Certified Health Coach, the biggest question I get from people is about sugar. People want to know what the healthiest sugars are and what they should be eating instead of white table sugar.

The bad news that I have to break to all of you is that while there are certainly less processed sugars out there on the market, sugar is still sugar and your body really doesn't know the difference.

Instead of focusing on sugar substitutes, trying focusing on reducing your overall intake of sugar. Here's a few tips to help you.

- Do not use artificial sweeteners. Besides the fact that they're nothing but chemicals, their sweet taste will not help you kick the sugar cravings.

- Eat regularly. We already talked about the importance of eating regularly, and another good reason to do this is to stabilize your blood sugar levels so you aren't reaching for the nearest sweet treat in the vending machine.

- Get off the processed foods. Most processed foods are loaded with sugar, even foods you wouldn't think of, like salad dressings and even ketchup.

- Learn to rely on spices like cinnamon, nutmeg, cardamom, and cloves to sweeten your foods.

- Try to incorporate protein at every meal.

May 21ˢᵗ – Shop Smart.

"You win the war at the grocery store!"
~ Karen Ann Kennedy

Today's tip should be easy for you, as it's really only three words you have to remember and live by...

DON'T BUY IT!

When it comes to getting on a healthy eating plan, willpower is not the answer. If you do not have double fudge stuffed cookies in your house, then you cannot eat double fudge stuffed cookies. If you do not have chunky chocolate cookie dough and peanut butter cup ice cream in the freezer, then you cannot eat chunky chocolate cookie dough and peanut butter ice cream.

You win the war at the grocery store! You do not win the war at 11:00 at night when you are stressed out and can't sleep and that ice cream is calling your name. You do not win the war when you are PMSing and crying at Hallmark commercials and there is a sleeve of Girl Scout cookies in the cupboard.

The easiest way to avoid eating junk, is to not buy the junk in the first place. Below are my tried and true methods to help you shop smarter at the grocery store. Are they new? No! Are they my original ideas? No! Do they work? Absolutely!

1. Do not shop when you are hungry! I know you've all heard this before, yet many of you still do it! Shopping when you are hungry means that everything, and I mean everything, in the store looks good to you. I've been so hungry that a donut dropped in the parking lot looked good! Be sure to eat before you go to the store so you are not tempted to buy what you don't need.

2. Make a list and stick with it! Know what you need before you go to the store. Make your meal plan and buy only what is on your list. If Pop Tarts are on sale two for five dollars, that's great for the people buying Pop Tarts, but if Pop Tarts are not on your list (and they shouldn't be), then buying them is not a deal. Not only do you not need to spend the money, but you don't need to bring unhealthy items into your home. It's not really a deal if it's wrecking your health.

3. Shop the perimeter of the store. Stick to the produce, dairy, meat, and seafood aisles. This is where you will find the least processed items in the grocery store. It will also help you stick to buying only what you need, should you fall short of the number two goal above. One note, while you're shopping the perimeter, beware of "end caps" in the store. These are the displays at the end of each aisle with "special deals." Sometimes, these items are no cheaper than they are any other day, and, they are usually a pre-packaged item.

May 22nd – Watch your weekends.

If I had a dime for every time a client has told me, "I do really well Monday through Friday, but then when the weekends come…" I'd be rich and I could quit my health coaching practice.

The issue is not the day of the week, the issue is structure! Most people do well during the week because they are on a schedule, a routine that gives them very little room for error. But, when the weekends come, it seems that all bets are off!

If you are like most people and work outside the home at a Monday through Friday job, you likely get up at the same time each morning, have an established routine for getting yourself out of the house; you may eat breakfast, lunch, and dinner around the same time every day, and you may even find time for a workout or two.

Saturday and Sunday give us flexibility and free time and we often do not use that free time in healthy ways. We get up a little later, head to the kitchen and make a big breakfast (usually something carb-loaded and unhealthy). We scarf down some fast food with the kids in between errands. We plop ourselves down in front of the TV and go into full out sloth mode. We go out to dinner with friends and eat foods we don't normally eat, in portions that we definitely don't need, and we wash it all down with drinks that we probably don't need to be drinking.

If this sounds familiar, take comfort in knowing that you're not alone; and get out that planner.

One of the best ways to keep your weekends from going off the rails is to make sure that you pencil in one healthy activity each day of the weekend. It could be going to the gym, shopping at the farmer's market, making a healthy meal, taking the dog for a long walk, playing ball with the kids at the park, or going to a karate class together as a family.

Just penciling that in and knowing what you're going to do will go a long way in helping to keep you motivated to stick with a healthy routine. I'm not suggesting that you can't go out to dinner, have a glass of wine on the back patio, or sleep in a little later, you just don't want to go from health-conscious working girl to sloth level weekend warrior!

So whether your weekend falls on Saturday and Sunday, or Wednesday and Thursday, or whatever days it falls on, grab your planner and fill in a healthy activity for your next two weekends. Try that and see if you can keep the streak going well into June and the second half of the year.

May 23rd – Spice things up.

Now that we have totally dissed sugar and salt, let's talk about some healthy herbs and spices that you can add into your healthy eating plan.

Food is meant to taste good. I said that a few weeks back and I meant it. There are a variety of healthy and tasty herbs and spices that you can be using in your cooking that will give new life to some of your old favorites. Don't be afraid to experiment to find the combinations that you like. Here's a few of my favorites to get you started.

Anise – Anise seeds have a sweet taste that is similar to black licorice. Anise has been shown to help calm upset stomachs and help tame symptoms of the common cold.

Cilantro – Cilantro is high in vitamin K which has been shown to improve bone strength and help your blood clot. And hey...it's awesome in Mexico food, one of my favorites!

Cinnamon – I recommend cinnamon to all of my clients for its anti-inflammatory properties that may help alleviate the pain of arthritis. I know that it has worked for me. Plus, cinnamon has a sweet taste that can help you kick that sugar addiction; you know who you are!

Ginger – Ginger is well-known as a remedy for an upset stomach. This is also a spice that I recommend for people with arthritis and joint pain. I add fresh ginger to my tea often for its pungent taste and to help when my tummy doesn't feel quite right.

Turmeric – Turmeric has been used to treat everything from depression to liver disease to skin ailments. I use it specifically for arthritis, in fact, I take turmeric capsules to make sure I get enough. For those of you starting out with turmeric, try adding it to curries, stews, and rice dishes.

May 24th – Add those healthy fats.
The low-fat craze that swept the nation in the late 70's/early 80's put us on a disastrous path of buying into a myriad of low-fat products that were designed (so "they" said) to help us slim down. Numerous research studies have shown that the obesity rate actually went up with the introduction of all these low-fat products. SUGAR, it turned out, was the real enemy.

Your body needs fat for the proper function of:

- Bones (to assimilate calcium)
- Cell membranes
- Heart
- Hormones
- Immune system
- Liver

- Lungs
- Satiety (reducing hunger)

The good news is that you can get those healthy fats by incorporating some of the following foods into your diet:

- Avocados
- Butter
- Coconuts and coconut oil
- Grass-fed meats
- Organic egg yolks
- Raw nuts, such as almonds, macadamia nuts, pecans, walnuts, and seeds

So, on your next shopping trip, skip the fake margarine and buy some real butter, and throw a couple of extra avocados in your cart for smoothies and salads.

May 25th – Eat when you're hungry.

This may sound like the ultimate "no-brainer," but, many people do not follow this simple rule when it comes to eating. I have often said that diets don't work, and one of the reasons why is because diets are rooted in guilt and deprivation. Just following this one simple tip has helped many of my clients become more aware of their eating, and shed a few pounds in the process.

Food is all around us, as we established earlier in the month, and food is very social for many of us. We tend to eat for reasons other than hunger. In fact, when I was on my own weight loss journey, I spent two weeks tracking this and was able to confirm for myself that most of the time I ate when I wasn't truly hungry.

I know we discussed this earlier in the month, but today, I have an exercise I want you to work on; I call it the "social cues" exercise. Grab that journal! For the next seven days, I want you to write down:

- What you ate
- What time you ate
- Where were you when you ate
- Who were you with when you ate
- How did you feel when you were eating (stressed, bored, entertained)
- How hungry were you when you ate (using the 1 – 10 scale)

The key is to start looking for patterns over the next week. Maybe you always have tea and cookies when your mother comes over, because maybe you feel anxious. Maybe you eat a burger and fries with your coworkers because they always do, and you don't want to feel left out. Once you know why you are eating, you want to change your habits to only eat when you're truly hungry. If you know that you will be socializing with friends later in the day, eat a smaller meal earlier in the day, or eat a snack before you go out to prevent you from loading up on unhealthy stuff.

Eat when you're hungry, stop when you're full!

May 26th – Barbeque to-do
Memorial Day (and the rest of the summer) is barbeque season in most places I've been. Time to fire up the grill and relax with friends and family. As a vegetarian, barbeques are always tricky territory for me. At the last barbeque I attended, I ate pickles and potatoes; super fun! Whether you are a meat eater, a vegan, gluten-free, watching your calories, or, whatever; there is usually a lot of room to improve your summer barbeques.

So, please step away from the pre-packaged hot dogs, the gallons of beer, and the pints of ice cream with all the fixin's. I'm going to show you how to "healthy up" your summer barbeque routine with these few simple to-do's:

Kabob me – You know you have to get in your daily veggie intake, so why not make kabobs for the grill! Alternate a few pieces of healthy chicken or lean beef with hearty vegetables that will stand up to the grill. Think onions, peppers, thick slices of tomato, and zucchini.

Swim with the fishes – Swap out your meat from time-to-time in favor of fish. Try this marinade on tilapia, swordfish, or salmon at your next barbeque for an instant hit!

¼ cup olive oil
3 cloves garlic
1 teaspoon paprika
1 teaspoon ginger
1 teaspoon black pepper
1 teaspoon oregano
1 teaspoon chili powder
1 tablespoon Dijon mustard

Marinate fish for one hour before cooking.

No chugging – I'm not suggesting that you abstain from alcohol all together, but, I am suggesting that you sip, not chug, your beverage. Here's your alcohol plan:

1. Upon arriving at the barbeque, drink a glass of water first. Most barbeques I've been to happen outdoors, so this is a good way to hydrate yourself before you add in any booze.

2. Drink a glass of water between each alcoholic beverage. Again, you need to stay hydrated, plus, this will help you cut down on how much alcohol you are taking in.

3. Focus on the food and the conversation instead of the alcohol.

4. Lighten up your drinks whenever you can. Instead of downing a glass of red wine, make a spritzer by combining the wine with some seltzer water. Make yourself a glass of refreshing sangria, and load it with chunks of real fruit.

5. Look for the signs that you've had too much. You start to feel groggy, overheated, slurring your speech; don't wait until your friends have to cut you off, that's a sure-fire way to get yourself uninvited from the rest of the barbeques this summer.

Don't drown in desserts – Grilling fruit is a lovely way to cap off a barbeque! Grilled peaches, nectarines, pineapple, and even strawberries are a healthy and flavorful end to a meal. Grilled peaches with a little scoop of ice cream (emphasis on the <u>little</u>) make an awesome dessert. Plus, they are easy to prepare and relatively inexpensive, if you're feeding a larger crowd. And honestly, they couldn't be simpler to make!

Grilled Peaches
- Heat your grill to medium-low
- Halve the peaches, take out the pits, and brush the cut sides with butter and a little honey
- Put the peaches on the grill, cut side down, cover grill, and cook until peaches are charred about 4 to 5 minutes.

There you go! You're already on your way to lightening up your summer barbeque season!

May 27th – Watch your alcohol consumption.

Although we touched on alcohol yesterday, this is a really important message that I want to talk about. I find that people I know drink more when they are out with friends, socializing, out to dinner, and visiting at each other's houses. This is probably not an issue if you are imbibing every once in a while, but if you find yourself drinking to the point of getting drunk, not only is this detrimental to your waist line, it can have a serious effect on the rest of your body and your overall health as well.

When you drink, a portion of the alcohol is absorbed right away into the bloodstream, while the rest is absorbed while it is processing through the gastrointestinal tract. Alcohol consumption has been shown to affect everything from reflexes and coordination to your ability to think clearly and make good decisions.

Long term use of alcohol has been linked to fatty liver, which can lead to hepatitis. It can also cause cirrhosis of the liver when liver cells become so damaged that they cannot regenerate. Excessive drinking has also been linked to several kinds of cancer, such as breast and pancreatic cancer.

Alcohol can irritate the lining of the stomach, which can lead to ulcers.

So how much is too much alcohol?

Both the CDC and the USDA recommend that women have no more than one drink per day, and men, no more than two drinks per day. This equates to twelve ounces of beer, eight ounces of malt liquor, five ounces of wine, or one and a half ounces of distilled liquor.

One more reason to watch your alcohol intake? Studies have shown that when you drink, you lose your inhibitions and tend to make bad decisions. That's why, at the bar, you're more likely to chow down on fried mozzarella and buffalo wings. People tend to make unhealthier food choices and eat more than usual when under the influence.

If you or someone you know has a problem with alcohol, I urge you to get help! There are plenty of resources out there.

Check out Alcoholics Anonymous at www.aa.org, or www. quitalcohol.com, for more information.

May 28th – Embrace protein.
When looking to lose weight, one rule of thumb that I learned from my nutrition classes at the Institute for Integrative Nutrition, was to aim to take in half your body weight in grams of protein per day. So a 140 pound woman would take in 70 grams of protein. While that may seem like a lot, consider this:

- A cup of Greek yogurt is 18 grams
- Two eggs are 13 grams
- Two ounces of lean poultry has about 25 grams
- A medium-sized piece of fish is about 22 grams
- A cup of black beans is 39 grams
- A cup of lentils gives you 18 grams
- A small handful of almonds is 6 grams

Even if you're not a meat eater, you can see from the list above that you have other alternatives. You can also get your protein from some vegetables, such as:

- Artichokes
- Beets

- Broccoli
- Peppers
- Spinach

And fruit, such as:

- Banana
- Cherries
- Mango
- Melon
- Papaya

Of course, if you are going the vegan/vegetarian route, you can always get meat substitutes such as:

- Seitan
- Soy burgers
- Tempeh
- Tofu

Just be sure to read the packages, and try not to rely too heavily on these products as they are processed!

May 29th – **Choose food over supplements.**

If you look at the Webster's Dictionary definition of the world supplement, you'll see that it means:

Supplement - noun – something that is added to something else in order to make it complete.

This means that supplements are supposed to be in addition to healthy eating, not in lieu of it!

I have met countless people on my journey that eat like crap, but, tell me that it's okay because they take their daily multi-vitamin.

The best way to get the vitamins and nutrients your body needs is through real, whole foods. Supplements work well for people that aren't getting enough of a particular vitamin or mineral due to their diet or a medical condition diagnosed by a medical professional.

Below are some popular vitamins, minerals, and nutrients, and the whole foods where you can find them.

Calcium – Dairy, non-dairy alternatives such as soy milk, yogurt, and dark green, leafy vegetables

Fiber – Oatmeal, lentils, peas, beans, fruits, and vegetables

Iron – Fortified cereals, beans, lentils, beef, turkey, soy beans, and spinach

Magnesium – Dark green, leafy vegetables, nuts, dairy, soybeans, potatoes, and quinoa

Potassium – Potatoes, bananas, yogurt, milk, and soybeans

Vitamin A – Sweet potatoes, carrots, spinach, and fortified cereals

Vitamin B1 (thiamine) – Whole grain breads and cereals

Vitamin B2 (riboflavin) – Milk, breads, and fortified cereals

Vitamin B3 (niacin) – Meat, fish, poultry, and enriched whole grain breads

Vitamin B12 – Fish, poultry, meat, and dairy products

Vitamin C – Red and green peppers, kiwis, citrus fruits such as oranges, lemons, and limes, strawberries, broccoli, and tomatoes

Vitamin D – Fish, fortified milk products, and fortified cereals

Vitamin E – Sunflower seeds, almonds, and peanut butter

Vitamin K – Spinach, collard greens, broccoli, Brussel sprouts, and cabbage

Zinc – Red meats and some seafood

There you have it. If you abstain from eating a particular food group, you may need to use supplements to get what your body needs. As with all medications, you should tell your doctor about any supplements you take. People often forget to do that, but it's important for your doctor to know what you're taking.

May 30th – Learn to say no to food pushers.
I hate these people! You know the ones, "C'mon, one little piece of cake isn't going to kill you." "Oh please, you're so skinny; what's one bite of ice cream going to do?" "It's just a candy bar, you can go to the gym later and work it off."

UGH!

Around Thanksgiving, I wrote a blog about food pushers. They are the annoying people that continue to shove food in your direction, even when you've made it perfectly clear that you don't want any.

Sometimes they are well-meaning people, like your grandma, or your mother, who thinks that you're too skinny.

Other times they are saboteurs that want to derail your progress so they can feel better about themselves.

Whatever their motives, you've got to help these people learn that no means no! Here's the thing, when I say I don't want something, it could be for any number of reasons including:

    a. I'm not hungry
    b. I'm really full and I couldn't eat another bite
    c. Your food sucks and I don't want to say so and hurt your feelings
    d. I can't eat a particular type of food (gluten, sugar, etc.)
    e. I really just don't want it

So how do you stand up to a food pusher? The easiest way I've found to turn down something I don't want is just to say, "No thank you," and then continue on with the conversation. Most of the time, they won't notice and they'll keep it rolling.

If you're dealing with a hard-core food pusher, they may not let up, in which case, I follow up with a more stern, "No, really, I don't want any, thank you."

Now, if you've got a food pusher who is like a dog with a bone they may ask, "Why?", to which I simply respond, "I just don't want any," and that's usually enough to kill the conversation. Sometimes I have to raise an eyebrow or make a face when using that last statement, but, if I'm persistent, I can usually get the food pusher to back off.

The important thing is to eat only what you want to eat and only when you're hungry (as we said earlier). It's not grandma that will have to go to the gym to work off the extra slice of pie you ate; it's not Aunt Gina that will be in the bathroom with gas all night due to the gluten in the biscuits; that's all you! So don't be afraid to put food pushers in their place!

May 31st – Eat without distraction.

We made it to the end of the month, my friends. I hope that you've picked up lots of healthy eating tips and real, practical information that you can incorporate into your daily life.

I want to leave you with just one more healthy eating tip. This one has been tough for me over the years, but I want to point it out to you in hopes that you can start to work on it as we move into the second half of the year.

One of the surest ways to overeat is to eat while distracted. In our busy world of multi-tasking like it's an Olympic sport, it's important that when you are eating, just eat! That means, no TV, reading the newspaper or a magazine, surfing the internet, or doing work. I can almost guarantee that your Facebook friends can do without you for an hour while you sit down to eat dinner.

The only activity I encourage during meals is the activity of sitting down in fellowship with your friends and family and enjoying good conversation and each other's company.

It's very easy to mindlessly overeat while watching television. Once, while watching a movie, I ate an entire sleeve of Oreo cookies without realizing it! When you focus on the act of eating, you'll notice a few immediate benefits. One, is that you'll eat less because you'll be paying attention to your body and you'll notice that you're full. Two, is that you'll actually enjoy your food so much more.

Take the time to savor each bite. Chew your food. Think about the flavor and the texture. Let the food sit on your tongue for a second before you chew it. Make eating a ritual. Don't stand in front of the fridge and scarf down cold leftovers. Take the time to set the table, use the good china, sit down and relax before you eat.

Cutting out the distractions will allow you to focus on and enjoy your food, and pay attention to the cues from your body that tell you when you've had enough.

So please step away from the TV; your dinner is calling you!

My May to-do list:

- I tried the elimination diet
- I started a food journal
- I added more vegetables into my diet
- I focused on choosing a variety of foods
- I started reading food labels
- I consciously avoided "red flag" ingredients
- I stopped using food as a reward
- I practiced "crowding out"
- I went meatless at least one Monday this month
- I practiced ranking my hunger from 1 to10
- I paid attention to my portion sizes
- I stopped drinking my calories
- I tried sticking to a regular eating schedule
- I ate only when I was truly hungry
- I ate two cups of fruit each day
- I increased my water intake
- I asked myself the four questions before I ate
- I practiced healthy cooking techniques such as baking, broiling, and steaming
- I tried at least one of the healthy swaps
- I practiced limiting my sugar intake
- I paid particular attention to my food habits on the weekends
- I tried at least one new spice
- I added in some healthy fats
- I did the "social cues" exercise for seven days
- I paid attention to my alcohol consumption
- I incorporated more protein into my diet
- I practiced eating without distractions

JUNE – FOCUS ON FITNESS

You may be wondering why it's taken me so long to get to the fitness portion of the year. Well, wonder no more. Research has shown time and time again that your overall health has more to do with diet than exercise (although both are important). Some studies suggest that your health is 80% diet and 20% exercise.

Getting you started on a healthy eating plan was the beginning of helping you with your overall physical health; now it's time to get moving.

June 1ˢᵗ – Get a checkup.

I can't stress this to you enough. If you're about to embark on an exercise plan, it's important to get a checkup first. I want you to pull out your planner, right now, I'll wait, and make an appointment to see your General Practitioner (GP).

It's especially important to do this if you have a chronic condition, are coming off of an illness or injury, if you are pregnant, or, if you haven't been physically active in a long time.

If nothing else, a check in with your GP will help give you peace of mind that you're physically fit and ready for exercise. Please do not skip this step.

June 2ⁿᵈ – Assess your fitness level.

One of the best ways to be able to chart your progress is to get a baseline of where your current fitness level is. While you probably have some idea of how physically fit you are, you can start off by writing down the following:

- Your pulse rate before and after you walk one mile
- How long it takes you to walk one mile
- How many pushups you can do at one time
- How far you can reach forward while sitting on the floor with your legs out straight in front of you
- The circumference of your waist. (You want to measure around your bare abdomen just near your hipbone)
- Your mass index or BMI*
- Your current weight

- Your blood pressure (you can learn this at the doctor's office or you can go to your local drug store to see if they have a blood pressure screening machine)

*To calculate your BMI, divide your weight in pounds by your height in inches squared and multiply that by 703.

Take this example.

Colleen is 5'5" and weighs 150 pounds.
Colleen's height in inches is 65

First, she calculates her height squared (65 x 65), which equals 4,225
Next, she divides her weight, 150 by 4,225, which equals .0355
And finally, she multiplies that number by 703, which equals 24.9585
The resulting number is rounded to 24.96, which is Colleen's BMI

If your BMI below 18.5 you are considered underweight
If your BMI is between 18.5 and 24.9 you are considered normal weight
If your BMI is between 25.0 and 29.9 you are considered overweight
If your BMI is 30.0 and above you are considered obese

So grab that calculator and grab your journal and write down your pulse rate, your blood pressure, your weight, your BMI, etc. Now you have a starting point to work from.

June 3rd – Research your options.
The best way to stick with a workout routine is to find an activity you love to do. No one I know is inclined to run a marathon when they hate running; no one I know drags themselves to the gym at five o'clock in the morning when they hate weight training. If you don't find an activity that you enjoy, you won't be likely to stick with it.

Now is the time to research the different activities available to you. You can choose anything from walking in the park, to hitting the weights at the gym, to swimming, to martial arts. Here's a list of a few suggestions to get you started:

- Boot camp classes
- Bowling
- Cycling
- Dancing
- Golfing
- Martial arts
- Roller blading
- Running
- Skiing
- Softball
- Step classes
- Swimming
- Walking
- Weight lifting
- Yoga
- Zumba

Today, I want you to pull out your journal and make a list of at least four to five activities that you think you might enjoy, are physically able to do, have the right equipment for, and can fit into your busy schedule.

June 4th – Write it down.

Scheduling your fitness is critical to actually getting out there and doing it. You must schedule in your workouts and keep your commitment to doing them. Starting the week hoping that you'll find time to go to the gym is not nearly as effective as looking at the week ahead and filling in the exact times on your calendar when you'll go.

One of the best ways that I have made this work is by making my workout times a priority and building the rest of my schedule around the remaining time. Now, to be sure, work is always the priority (gotta make that money) but, then I schedule my workouts next. The time that is left over is used for other activities.

Another tactic I've used successfully, is to sign up for a class that occurs at the same day and time every week. This way, I know that time is already spoken for and I know other people are expecting to see me. I take karate on Tuesday and Thursday evenings, and because I know that class is already scheduled, I guard that time. Unless there's something really, REALLY important taking place on a Tuesday or Thursday evening, you can be sure you'll see me at the dojo working out!

So grab your planner and start looking at where you can get your exercise in. If you can stick with a consistent schedule, that's great, but if you're just starting out, at least look at the next two weeks and write in when you'll work out. Then, stick to it!

June 5th – Utilize a variety of motivators.

For many people, exercise is a motivator to lose weight. But, people that I've worked with who had goals other than just weight loss tend to do better. Remember back in March when we talked about having a strong "why"? This is one of those times that having a strong "why" will work really well for you.

I want you to grab your journal and write down the top ten reasons why you want to start working out. This list will become your motivation to stick with it when you feel like quitting. My list looks like this:

1. I want to lose weight.
2. I want to see some actual muscles.
3. I want to look lean.
4. I want to look good in my clothes.
5. I want to have lots of energy.
6. I want to have lots of stamina (endurance).
7. I want to keep myself healthy.
8. I want to look good for my age.
9. I want to be able to continue running.
10. I want to be proud of myself.

Your list might look similar, or completely different, but, hey, it's your list! Once you have it done, make a couple of copies. Put one on your fridge, one on your desk, keep one near your gym bag, or by the front door. Keep your motivators at the top of your mind by reviewing them often and reminding yourself why you are embarking on this journey.

June 6th – Use a variety of reminders.

Most people I know don't need to be reminded to exercise, but some do. More often than not though, what they really need is a PUSH! There are a number of tools and techniques you can employ to help you get out there when you need to. You can try:

- Telling your family, friends, and coworkers that you have a workout scheduled and ask them to remind you to go, or to ask you about it when it's over.
- Set a reminder on your smartphone to go off a half hour before you are scheduled for your work out.

- Sign up for an app or website that gives you points or rewards for working out; you might try www.sparkpeople.com or apps like Charity Miles or Nexercise.
- Schedule your work out in your online calendar and set a pop-up reminder for when it's time to go.
- Keep your workout clothes, gym bag, workout gear, etc. in a spot where you can see it regularly as a reminder to use it!

June 7th – Start with the basics.

It's great to have long range fitness goals but remember:

> *"A journey of a thousand miles begins with a single step."*
> *~Lao-tzu*

No one I know got up one day and decided to get in shape and ran a marathon. It's important to start off slowly and gradually so your body can get acclimated to the new routine, and, so you can avoid injury by going out too hard, too soon.

If you're still researching what kinds of activities are out there for you, that's great! Continue to see what appeals to you, and while you are checking out the options, start out with the basics.

- Aim to get in thirty minutes of brisk walking each day. Can't find thirty minutes all at once? No problem! Do fifteen minutes at lunchtime and fifteen minutes at the end of the day. Your thirty minutes do not have to be consecutive.

- Try stretching. When you're sitting at home watching TV, try to do a few stretches. You don't need a lot, just 15 to 20 minutes of light stretching will do the trick.

- Add in a few pushups and sit ups when you can. Later in the month, we're going to play the commercial game that incorporates a set of exercises each time a particular type of commercial comes on. To get ready for that, just try alternating some pushups and sit ups during the commercial breaks of your favorite shows.

- Play! This is a big one. If you have a dog, take him/her out back and play fetch, take the kids to the park or to the pool, put on some music you like and dance around your living room. Play is the BEST kind of exercise, because it doesn't feel like exercise! Don't be afraid to have fun.

June 8th – Replace a bad habit with a good one.
Being physically active is a great habit to get into, but with limited time on your hands, you may need to replace a bad habit (watching too much TV) with a good habit (going for a walk after dinner).

Today, I want you to start noticing where your time goes and see where you can make some healthier choices. Just like we did last month with our food choices, you can make healthy swaps with your fitness routine. Try:

- Going for a walk after dinner instead of watching TV
- Dancing around in the living room instead of snacking after dinner
- Taking the kids to the park to play ball instead of to the movies
- Walking around the entire mall instead of getting ice cream at the food court
- Logging off Facebook, Twitter, Myspace, or whatever other social media site you are hooked on, and go for a short run

In life, it's all about the choices we make. When it comes to your time, you get 24 hours each day to make a series of choices that end up defining how healthy (or unhealthy) you will be. Choose wisely.

June 9th – Track your measurements.

Just like giving yourself a baseline of your fitness level, giving yourself a baseline of your measurements will help you to track changes in quantifiable terms. The best way to do this is to take pictures of yourself (front view and side view) and take your measurements.

The measurements you want to take are:

Bust – Place the tape measure across your nipples and measure around the largest part of your chest.

Calves – Measure around the largest part of each calf.

Chest – Place the tape measure under your breasts/pecs and measure around your torso.

Hips – Place the measuring tape across the widest part of your hips.

Thighs – Measure around the largest part of each thigh.

Upper arm – Measure around the largest part of each arm above the elbow.

Record your measurements in your journal. We'll look back at them at the end of the month to see if there's been any change.

June 10th – Find a workout buddy.

Sometimes the best way to stay motivated and keep going is to find a workout buddy who will hold you accountable and keep you getting out there. Not only is a workout buddy good for accountability, but you'll also have someone to commiserate with and celebrate with along the way.

It's a lot harder to skip your early morning workout when you know your friend will be waiting for you at the gym.

When choosing a workout buddy, try to find someone who is close to your fitness level. It can be very discouraging when you're just starting out and your workout buddy is on their fifth marathon. Also, choose someone who is generally positive about the workout sessions. While one or both of you might whine from time-to-time, someone who is constantly whining will make the workouts really unpleasant.

If you can, find someone who is in close proximity to you so that you don't have to factor a lot of travel time into your workouts, and choose a workout buddy who will push you. While you don't want someone who is way ahead of you physically, you don't want someone who will allow you to be a slug. Make sure that you are both encouraging each other and pushing each other to be your best.

Who can you choose to be your workout buddy?

June 11th – Invest in the proper gear.

Depending on what activities you choose, you may or may not need to invest in a lot of equipment. At the very least, you'll probably need a good pair of shoes.

When thinking about what activities you'll get involved in, it's important to think about the financial impact. If you're joining a gym, you'll need to pay the gym membership fee, and you'll probably need a good pair of cross trainers, a good sports bra (for the ladies), some decent socks, and some comfortable tops and shorts.

If you plan to take up biking, you'll need to get the right kind of bike, a helmet, possibly some knee and elbow pads.

Even if you'll just be walking, you'll still want to get a good pair of walking shoes, good socks, and comfortable clothing. You may also want to invest in a visor, a pedometer, a good water bottle, and some sunscreen.

Take some time to figure out what you need, how much you'll want to spend, and then, have fun gathering your equipment. There is nothing more exciting for me than to get a gift card for my favorite running store for my birthday or Christmas and walking around the store exploring all the fun and colorful gear.

Sometimes, knowing that I am getting something new is also a motivator for me to keep going!

June 12th – Listen to your body.
While you definitely want to push yourself, there is a big difference between soreness and pain.

When you're sore from a good, hard workout, that's different than having pain that limits your activities and leaves you feeling terrible. I don't mind the morning after a good karate class when my muscles are achy and I know that I got a good workout! But, pain is an entirely different thing to deal with.

If you wake up with a sore throat, headache, sore ears, and a rumbling stomach, that might not be the best day to go out for a run. If you're up to it, maybe you'll want to do some light stretching at home. But even if that seems like it's too much, skip the workout and get some rest.

So what's the difference between soreness and pain?

	Muscle Soreness	Pain
Type of discomfort:	Tender when touching muscles, tired or burning feeling while exercising, dull ache, tight and achy feeling at rest	Ache, sharp pain at rest or when exercising
Onset:	During exercise or 24 – 72 hours after activity	During exercise or within 24 hours of activity
Duration:	2 – 3 days	May linger if not addressed
Location:	Muscles	Muscles and/or joints
Improves with:	Stretching, following movement	Ice, rest
Worsens with:	Sitting still	Continued activity
Appropriate action:	Resume offending activity once soreness subsides	Consult with your doctor if pain is unbearable or lasts over 1 week

If you experience any type of pain that causes you to have to limit your activities or pain that interferes with your daily living, you need to consult your doctor. Continuing to push yourself may actually worsen the situation and can sideline you for even longer.

June 13th – Set some goals for yourself.

Just like it's helpful to have a few different motivators, having a few different goals will help keep you energized. Maybe you want to train for a neighborhood 5K? Lose a certain number of pounds or inches? Maybe your goal is to be able to run for ten minutes or walk for an hour without stopping.

Sit down today with your journal and spend a few minutes writing down some fitness goals for yourself. There's no right or wrong answer, just make sure they are goals that stretch you some, but are achievable. You don't want to set yourself up for disappointment by choosing goals that are too far off the mark for you to achieve, but pick goals that are enough of a stretch that you'll be proud of yourself for accomplishing them.

Choose a few. It's good to have three to four goals that you can accomplish over the next six weeks. Make a vision board and write your goals on there. Attach pictures that inspire you to continue on your journey. Look at your vision board often. Once you've reached a goal, put a big check mark next to it and write the date of completion. You can always save your board and look back on it when you need to remind yourself of how awesome you are.

June 14th – Learn what exercises do what.

If you have fitness goals that revolve around your physical features, it's important to know what exercises do what. If you want sculpted abs, you've got to spend time doing exercises that work your core. If you want to increase your endurance, you'll need to do cardio work.

Pushups, dips, dumbbell curls, and barbell front raises will work your upper body. Squats, lunges, calf raises, and leg raises will all work your lower body. Crunches and sit ups will help work your core.

If you're unsure about what exercises to incorporate into your workout routine, see if you can book a session with a personal trainer. Most gym franchises have a personal trainer on staff and some will even give you a session or two for free. Tell the trainer what you want to work on and ask them to suggest some exercises that are appropriate for what you're trying to achieve.

PAY ATTENTION to the correct way to perform these moves to avoid injury! Focus on quality of your moves, not quantity. Most people get hurt when they start to get tired and their form starts to get sloppy. Make sure you find out the correct way to do each move and focus on proper execution to avoid unnecessary injury.

June 15th – Build in rest days.

We're halfway through the month! It's time for your mid-month check-in. How are you feeling about your fitness plans? Have you started working out yet, or are you still in the fact-finding stage? Do you have a workout buddy? Did you come up with some goals for yourself?

If you're like a lot of people I know, you're probably really gung-ho at this point to continue on with your fitness routine and continue to see good results. While it's important to stay consistent with your workouts, it's equally important to build in some rest days.

Unless you are a movie star who has a personal trainer, a chef, a nutritionist, a stylist, and a whole host of other people whose sole job it is to make you look good, you probably don't have time to work out every day anyway. Even if you do, it's important to make sure that you build in rest days to give your body a chance to recuperate and recover.

Rest days are important because:

- Working out too much can cause your weight loss to plateau.
- Overtraining can cause your hormones to go haywire.
- Overtraining can wreak havoc with your sleep; either sleeping excessively, or being unable to sleep are both signs that you may be training too much.
- Working out too much can cause you to feel anxious or "amped up" all the time.
- Working out too much can lead to burnout and make you want to stop altogether.
- Overtraining can cause you to miss out on play time, fun time, and relaxation with your family and friends.

As you schedule your next two weeks of workouts (yes, pull out your planner and do that now) be sure to build in some time to rest and relax. If you find you are having trouble doing this, schedule something that forces you to relax, like a pedicure, a massage, or a movie date.

Rest days are just as important as workout days, so don't skip them! Your body will be thankful for them!

June 16th – Give yourself a shout out.

Nothing made my weight loss journey easier for me then when a co-worker or friend would point out my weight loss or make comments like, "You look terrific," or, "Are you losing weight?" I was noticing the changes in myself; my clothes were fitting better and I looked better naked. When others started to take notice, it was a jolt of energy that made me want to continue.

Sometimes you'll need to create that buzz yourself by giving yourself a shout out and letting people know that you've been working out and doing well. This creates some accountability for you by telling people what you've been doing (they'll likely ask you in passing how your workouts are going) and it helps you feel less alone in your training (if you don't have a workout buddy).

Plus, it's okay to be proud of yourself! Really! And, it's okay to brag about it to others. While you don't want to dominate every conversation with, "Guess how many miles I ran yesterday?" It's nice to be able to share your accomplishments with others.

June 17th – Start your onsite fitness research.
By now, you should have had ample time to poke around and find some activities you think you might like. Before "paralysis analysis" sets in though, it's time to start trying some of these out.

If you've decided that you'd like to take dance classes, do a quick Google search for dance schools in your area. If you've thought about martial arts, find some karate schools. If you've been thinking about joining a softball league, look around your neighborhood or ask friends that might play.

Many gyms will let you try out the equipment one day for free. Many karate schools will allow you to sample a class and see what it's all about. Even the dance schools I've seen in my local area will let you try a class or two to see if it's your cup of tea.

"You never know until you try."

~Unknown

You may find that you have quite a knack for salsa dancing, or that you're a natural on skis, but unless you try it out, you'll never know for sure. Don't be afraid to get out there and sample what's available, and to be honest about what isn't working for you.

Your friends may rave about Zumba, but if you're anything like me (completely uncoordinated), you may hate it! Boot camp classes where some big, burly guy is hollering at you for forty five minutes might make you anxious and uncomfortable, but a 45-minute yoga class in a quiet studio with soft music might be just what the doctor ordered!

Pull out your journal and go back to the list you made on June 3rd. Start trying out the four to five activities you listed as potential contenders. Choose only the ones that you really enjoy. You'll be much more likely to stick with your fitness regimen if you find something that you really look forward to doing.

June 18th – DIY your workout routine

Don't be afraid to tailor your workouts to fit your own needs. In a while, I'm going to share with you the "commercial break" workout, but in the meantime, feel free to experiment with whatever works for you.

I've seen this done often at my karate school. We have a number of black belt instructors who put together fitness routines that work for their own individual needs (remember bio-individuality?) They are also very good at tailoring workouts to meet the needs of the students. Some of our students are older, some come with physical disabilities, some come with lingering injuries; and what works for one person does not always work for another.

It's important that your workouts give you the fitness results you need while also working with your own preferences and/or limitations. The good news is that you can "borrow" moves from other fitness routines without committing to that style altogether.

My morning stretching routine has elements of martial arts, Pilates, yoga, and dance incorporated into it. There are parts of Pilates that I love, and parts that I hate, so I take out the parts that I hate and I add in some yoga moves that I really enjoy.

I find some yoga moves impossible for me to do, so I take those out and I add some strength training or ab work instead.

The point is to feel free to customize your workout routine so you can get the results that you're really after.

June 19th – Bulk up your "stick with it" muscles.

For my clients that haven't worked out in a long time, they often see fast results and that gets them very pumped up to keep going. But, after a while, when weight loss starts to slow or they hit a plateau, their motivation starts to wane. They start to cut their workouts short, skip a few extra days, or give less than their best effort.

These are the times when you need to bulk up your "stick with it" muscles!

This is the time to:

- Pull out your list of goals and recommit yourself to achieving them
- Buy yourself a new piece of gear to motivate and reward yourself
- Download some new music or an audio book to entice you to stay focused

- Take a few minutes to write down your accomplishments so far (weight loss, clothes feel better, more energy, etc.)
- Re-examine your "why" to ensure that it's still enough to keep you motivated
- Set some new goals for yourself to give you new challenges to work towards
- Be sure you are still having fun

If you're not still having fun, it's time to perform CPR on your workout routine.

- **Change**
- **Prioritize**
- **Recommit**

Change up your routine to stave off boredom. Try working out at night instead of in the morning. Take a different route with your daily walk. Try out a different yoga studio. Try running on the beach instead of on the sidewalk.

Prioritize. This is important if you aren't sticking with your workouts due to feeling overwhelmed. You can try cutting back to just one activity (if you are taking on multiple disciplines) or letting go of some of your goals for a while in favor of just purely having fun.

Recommit yourself to the reasons why you started working out in the first place. Don't forget to look back on your accomplishments, give yourself a shout out, and be proud of what you've been doing. Recommitting sometimes means taking a week off from your workouts so that you can come back with a renewed sense of purpose.

June 20th – Tap into the power of music.

Music can be an awesome motivator when you're working out. I mean; who doesn't get pumped up when they hear the Rocky theme music?

If you're walking, biking, running, or even doing yoga or Pilates at home, music can keep you entertained and keep you feeling energized.

CAUTION!!!!

Always use good common sense when listening to music, especially when using headphones. Always be aware of your surroundings, don't have your music turned up so loud that you can't hear what's going on around you, be alert to traffic, people on bikes, people walking dogs, etc. I've read many a cautionary tale about people who were injured or even killed because they were not in tune with their surroundings.

I cannot imagine running without music. It's my companion, my motivator, and my entertainment. You can download lots of work-out apps that incorporate music, or, feel free to create your own playlist, based on songs that you like. I have three criteria when I choose songs for my running playlist.

1. They have to have a really solid beat.
2. They have to be inspirational/motivational, or,
3. They have to tell a good story.

Here are some of my favorites, but you should feel free to pick your own:

- *Ain't Going Down (Till the Sun Comes Up) by Garth Brooks*
- *Amazing by Aerosmith*

- *Baba O'Riley by The Who*
- *Beautiful Day by U2*
- *Family Affair by Mary J. Blige*
- *Fergalicious by Fergie*
- *Flagpole Sitta by Harvey Danger*
- *Glamorous by Fergie*
- *Goody Two Shoes by Adam Ant*
- *Hey Ya by OutKast*
- *I Gotta Feeling by the Black Eyed Peas*
- *Imma Be by the Black Eyed Peas*
- *The Jean Genie by David Bowie*
- *Lose Yourself by Eminem*
- *Moves Like Jagger by Maroon 5*
- *My Songs Know What You Did in the Dark by Fall Out Boy*
- *Pork and Beans by Weezer*
- *Rock & Roll Part 2 by Gary Glitter*
- *Save Me, San Francisco by Train*
- *She's the One by Bruce Springsteen*
- *Sk8er Boi by Avril Lavigne*
- *So What by P!nk*
- *Spiderwebs by No Doubt*
- *Sweet Caroline by Neil Diamond*
- *Tessie by the Dropkick Murphys*
- *Thrift Shop by Macklemore & Ryan Lewis*
- *Use Somebody by Kings of Leon*
- *Wake Up Call by Maroon 5*
- *Whiskey's Gone by the Zac Brown Band*
- *Without Me by Eminem*
- *Yeah! by Usher*

As you can see, that's a pretty diverse list of artists. Go ahead and make a plan to sit down and put together your own list of workout music. Tailor the music to your discipline and have fun with it.

YOUR BEST YEAR YET!

June 21st – Don't be afraid to switch it up.

If you've heard or read anything about cross training, then you'll know that it simply means engaging in more than one training activity.

There are lots of benefits to cross training including:

- Switching up your routine to keep boredom from setting in
- Preventing injury by giving a break to the muscles you use regularly
- Increasing overall fitness by engaging your entire body
- Increasing enjoyment by mastering new skills and learning new disciplines

One of the most effective ways to cross train is to vary your activities between aerobic conditioning, strength training, endurance, and balance. I know several runners that practice yoga (there are even yoga classes out there specifically for runners). I know lots of weight lifters that remember the importance of getting in a good cardio workout as well.

> *"Variety is the spice of life!"*
> *~Unknown*

Look at your current workout routine and think of where you might add in a good cross training activity. If you're an avid walker, try yoga; if you're a Pilates master, throw in a Zumba class for cardio. Don't be afraid to switch it up!

June 22nd – Use visualization.

Many athletes will tell you that they use visualization as an important training tool. Indeed, when I was training for my first marathon, I used visualization techniques to help get me to the finish line.

I didn't just visualize the finish. I visualized getting out of bed that morning, sitting down to eat my breakfast. I visualized what I would wear, the route I would drive to the race; how I would fuel and hydrate throughout. In my mind's eye I saw each individual mile marker pass by, and thought about how my body would physically feel. And, of course, I visualized crossing the finish line.

Visualization basically gives you a dress rehearsal for the actual moment. Walking through each step in my mind helped me to prepare for the day. It also helped me problem solve ahead of time (what if the roads are closed on my usual route?)

Visualizing yourself successfully completing a workout or an exercise challenge will help you feel confident. It will also help keep you motivated as you visualize yourself being successful.

Before you head out for your next workout, take a few minutes to mentally walk yourself through the exercise. If you're a swimmer, visualize putting on your suit, dipping your toe in the water, stretching on the sidelines, jumping in, and finishing your laps.

If you're a softball player, visualize yourself at bat, how you will hit the ball, the run to first base, then second base, then third base, and finally, visualize sliding into home plate and scoring the winning run.

While visualization does not take the place of actual physical training, it is a powerful tool in helping you achieve your goals.

June 23rd – Make it stick.
By now you probably know that consistency is key. You won't reap long lasting benefits by working out like the Hulk for six days straight and then laying low for three weeks.

While you may have some short term goals, like running a 5K or besting your spouse at tennis, your overall goal should be to incorporate exercise into your schedule as a way to stay fit and healthy for life.

Therefore, it's important to stick with exercising to continue to see the health benefits that come along with it.

> *"People often say that motivation doesn't last. Well, neither does bathing – that's why we recommend it daily."*
> ~*Zig Ziglar*

Commit yourself to making fitness a part of your overall plan for lifelong health and wellness. Never stop improving!

June 24th – Why so serious?

There is enough drudgery in the world; taxes, bills, your job, the in-laws, long lines at the grocery store. Don't make your exercise routine one of them!

The moment that you stop having fun is the moment when you'll want to give up, throw in the towel, trade in your yoga pants for sweatpants, and trade in your dumbbells for a pint of Chunky Monkey ice cream.

However you can, as often as you can, infuse a little fun into your workout routine. Don't be afraid to laugh and play and enjoy what you're doing.

Remember the popular 90's sitcom *Friends*? There was a great episode where Rachel didn't want to go running with Phoebe because Phoebe had this odd way of running where she would basically flail around laughing and being silly.

One day, Rachel tried it and lo and behold, she loved it! When she let go of trying to look like a "serious runner", she found the joy that was running and letting your body just move.

Stop worrying so much about what you look like. Although I have a black belt in Tae Kwon Do, I have no delusions that I look like Bruce Lee in the dojo. I know there are certain moves that leave me looking as graceful as a giraffe on ice, but I do them anyway because they're fun and I know if I continue to do them, I'll improve.

Stop taking your workouts so seriously. Unless you're an Olympic athlete and training is your job, let loose and enjoy. Have fun, laugh while you're working out, don't worry if you don't know all the moves at Zumba, or your have two left feet in step class. If you're enjoying what you're doing, KEEP DOING IT; that's the best piece of fitness advice I can give you.

June 25th – Try the "Commercial Break" Workout

As promised, we're at the day to start the commercial break workout. Here's how it works. As much as I want to give up TV watching (I have cut down a lot), I still like to indulge every now and then. Hey, I have to see *Modern Family*!

One way that I cut the guilt from my TV watching is to exercise when the commercials come on. To make it fun, I base the exercises I do on the type of commercial that is airing. I didn't invent this, by the way, I just tailored it to stuff that I like; you can do the same thing. Try doing the exercise for the entire duration of the commercial. If you aren't quite there yet, start with a set amount like ten or twenty repetitions.

Below is my commercial break workout. You can feel free to change up the exercises to suit your own tastes. Have fun!

Commercial for Baby Products	Plank
Commercial for Beauty Products	Russian Twists
Car Commercial	Crunches
Cell Phone Commercial	Flutter Kicks
Commercial for Diet Products	Jumping Jacks
Drug Commercial	Squats
Electronics Commercial	Arm Circles
Fashion/Clothing Commercial	Jog in Place
Fast Food Commercial	Push Ups
Feminine Hygiene Commercial	Sit Ups
Insurance Commercial	Wall Sit
Jewelry Commercial	Burpees
Men's Health Commercial	High Knees
Miscellaneous	Drink Water
Movie Trailer	Bicycles
Pet Product Commercial	Leg Lifts
Public Service Announcement	Hip Raises
Restaurant Commercial	Lunges
Shampoo Commercial	Bicep Curls
Travel Commercial	Leg Scissors
Commercial for a TV Show	Toe Touches
Vitamin Commercial	Butterfly Stretch

June 26th – Stretch Yourself.

There is a double entendre to today. First we're going to talk about stretching yourself by stretching what you're doing, and then we're going to talk about the importance of actual stretching.

181

Stretching yourself means challenging yourself; pushing yourself to go farther, longer, harder, faster. Only you know your body and your limitations, so it's important that you do what you can without hurting yourself. When we talked earlier about finding a workout buddy, we talked about finding someone who would push you a little past your comfort zone, however, you've got to be realistic about what you can do.

Years ago, I signed on with a personal trainer at my gym. Looking back, I knew at the first session that he wasn't right for me, but because I worked out early in the morning, there weren't a lot of trainers to choose from.

He was always pushing me to do more, lift more weight, do more reps, etc. What he failed to realize was that I was about twice his age and I had some physical challenges to get past. What I saw as smart and calculated moves he saw as me being lazy.

You can imagine our "relationship" didn't last long. I quickly hated going to the gym and would dread my alarm clock going off in the morning. That's when I knew I had to respect my body and my health and break up with my trainer.

I want to encourage you to reach a little further than you normally do, but respect your limitations and your own natural boundaries.

Now let's talk about <u>actual</u> stretching. Believe it or not, you want to warm up a little bit before you stretch. This is important because stretching your muscles when they're "cold" can lead to injury. It's a good idea to do some jumping jacks or jog in place to get your body warmed up and then employ your stretching techniques. You can find lots of good stretches on the internet (again, choose the ones that work for you). Some of my favorites include:

- Arm circle
- Butterfly stretch
- Pulling your knees to your chest
- Reaching back with your hands in the air
- Stretching from side to side while standing
- Toe touches

Find some stretches that you enjoy and stretches that work the muscles you need to work. Stretching can help you with flexibility and blood flow and can also help reduce stress and tension, so stretch away!

June 27th – Gradually increase.

A common theme you may have noticed this month is the concept of taking your time, not doing too much too soon, and listening to your body to avoid injury.

As your workouts become easier for you, you'll want to start to gradually increase so you can continue to challenge yourself and avoid the dreaded plateau that occurs when your body gets used to what you're doing.

As you gradually add to your workouts, an extra mile, a few extra reps, some added weight, it's important to continue to pay attention to your body. If you feel pain, excessive fatigue, soreness, or tiredness that sidelines you for a few days, dial back for a few weeks until you start to feel better.

June 28th – Monitor your progress.

Grab your journal and look back at the beginning of the month where you assessed your fitness level and look at your measurements. Now it's time to see what type of progress you've made.

One caveat here; you can't expect that in just a little over three weeks, you're going to be an entirely different person. It's important to remember that even if you've only lost a pound or a few inches, that's better than putting on a pound or a few inches!

Don't get caught up with just the numbers! Rate your total fitness, too. If you started out the month only being able to do five pushups, and now you can do fifteen, that's quite an accomplishment!

Be sure to write down your new measurements and new fitness level. Going forward, you may want to update these benchmarks every three months or so. Looking back at where you started will help you appreciate how far you've come.

June 29th – Build in good rewards.

As you reach your goals and continue to create new ones, it's important to reward yourself. Maybe you treat yourself to new running shoes after you complete your first 5K. Get yourself a cool training watch or download a new training app when you've walked for thirty consecutive days. Buy a new workout outfit when you go to the gym at least fifteen days in a month.

Giving yourself fun treats will give you something to look forward to and serve as a nice reward for exercising those "stick to it" muscles.

Pull out your journal and make a list of ten treats that you can buy/do for yourself to keep you motivated and help you feel good about what you're doing.

Here's my list:

1. New running shoes
2. New workout wear
3. A pedicure
4. A massage
5. A TV-watching marathon of my favorite show
6. New song downloads for my running playlist
7. A fun new exercise DVD
8. A funky new nail polish for my toes
9. A new book
10. A picnic lunch in the park

As you can see, the list isn't made up of crazy stuff, in fact, some of the items are actually FREE, and the items don't have to be work-out related.

As I'm on the last mile of my run, I think about how good that pedicure is going to feel. When I'm pushing to finish up my last fifteen minutes at the dojo, I think about stopping at the bookstore over the weekend to pick up something I've been wanting to read.

These little treats just make me really happy! What's on your list?

June 30th – Celebrate yourself.

June is done; the year is half over! How did you do this month? I want you to take some time today to celebrate yourself. If you wish to include your family and friends, host a BBQ and make it known that the purpose of the gathering is to celebrate your successes over the past month.

If you choose to celebrate alone, pack yourself a healthy, but decadent picnic, and head to the park with a good book. Or, stay home and cook yourself a fabulous dinner, put your feet up, and relax. Go get a massage or a new haircut; just do something for the express purpose of celebrating yourself and all that you've accomplished.

Go you!

My June to-do list:

- ° I got a checkup with my doctor
- ° I assessed my fitness level
- ° I research my exercise options
- ° I scheduled my workouts on my calendar
- ° I wrote down my top ten reasons for wanting to exercise
- ° I started walking more frequently
- ° I wrote down my measurements at the beginning of the month
- ° I found a workout buddy
- ° I bought the proper gear needed for my sport/activity
- ° I set some goals for myself
- ° I built some rest days into my schedule
- ° I tried a few new classes or activities
- ° I performed "CPR" on my exercise routine
- ° I explored some fun new music options for my workouts
- ° I utilized the power of visualization
- ° I tried the "commercial break" workout
- ° I incorporated stretching into my workout routine
- ° I began to gradually increase my workouts
- ° I created my rewards list

JULY – NURTURE YOUR RELATIONSHIPS

I could probably write an entire book on just this subject alone! In our fast-paced, tech-reliant society, being able to connect and reconnect with the people in our lives is more important now than ever.

But why do it in the summer? During the summer months the pace of life just seems to slow down. People take vacations (often with others) and spend more time outdoors away from the TV and other electronic distractions.

So this month, I want you to think about nurturing the relationships in your life. Not just romantic ones or ones with your family, but your relationships with your friends, your co-workers, your neighbors, and most importantly, with yourself.

July 1ˢᵗ – Always be kind.
Webster's dictionary defines nurture as "to help (something or someone) to grow, develop, or succeed; to take care of (someone or something that is growing or developing) by providing food, protection, a place to live, etc.

One of the easiest ways to help someone grow, develop, or succeed, or to take care of someone, is approach everything you do with kindness.

> *"My religion is very simple. My religion is kindness."*
> *~His Holiness the Dalai Lama*

Kindness is a universal language and it can be shown in a million different ways. It could be something as simple as a smile or as complex as caring for someone who is terminally ill. When you practice kindness, a wonderful shift begins to happen within yourself. The act of kindness not only benefits the recipient, it benefits the person bestowing the kindness as well.

It's simply impossible to be angry, resentful, bitter, or mean when you're walking around practicing kindness every day.

Don't forget that kindness starts with being kind to yourself, and to those around you. We tend to be nice to people we work with or people we meet on the street, and forget to be kind to the people closest to us.

Don't forget to practice the simple things with those that are close to you. Say "please" and "thank you," show appreciation for things that they do for you, and do nice things for them in return.

Starting today, and for the rest of the month (and the rest of the year if you can make it a habit), start each day in a spirit of kindness. Use the mantra below (or find another one that speaks to you) and say it each morning before you get out of bed. Focus on infusing all of your interactions with kindness.

"For today, I will practice kindness, I will embody kindness, I will work to bring kindness into every interaction. I am kindness personified."
~Karen Ann Kennedy

July 2nd – Always be honest.
Being honest, telling the truth, and living your life with the integrity to be truthful and forthcoming in your dealings with others is not always an easy thing to do; but it's always the right thing to do.

"If you tell the truth you don't have to remember anything."
~Mark Twain

People lie for lots of reasons. Sometimes, we tell a lie to spare someone's feelings, sometimes we lie to get ourselves out of a jam. Sometimes we lie because we aren't strong enough to say what needs to be said. That last reason is called "taking the easy way out," and while it is easy in the short run, it has the potential to go really wrong in the long run.

Now that we've spent the last six months together (and because we're talking about honesty,) I will tell you that I haven't always told the truth. In the last few years, as I examined my life more closely, I realized that the person I have lied to the most in my life is myself. I have also lied to other people around me and in the past several years, I've started to make amends with people that I feel I have "wronged."

You've probably heard the old adage, "honesty is the best policy," and it's true. Honesty protects your reputation and upholds your integrity, which are two things that are hard to repair once they've been damaged.

The best way to begin to be honest with others is to be honest with yourself. Take a deep breath and have the courage to be honest about what you like and don't like, what's working in your life and what's not working, and where you aren't being the best version of yourself.

July 3rd – Speak up!

One of the most important aspects to having a healthy relationship with others is the ability to speak up. This concept of speaking up is an extension of being honest by telling people what you need or want.

You are not a mind reader, and neither are the people around you. The only way that people will know what you want and need is if you tell them. That's not to say that you're always going to get everything you want from other people, but you have a much better chance if you are willing to speak up.

If nothing but a pair of diamond earrings will make you happy for your birthday, but you don't tell your husband that's what you want, then you can't be upset when you open a waffle iron or a new tennis racket instead.

The most sure-fire way I know to be disappointed in life is to not speak up!

So, you guessed it, starting today, you need to marry honesty with your ability to speak up. When someone upsets you, does something that is in direct conflict with your values, or says something that makes you angry, you need to practice speaking up about it.

That doesn't mean that you have to be rude or degrading; you can still be very polite and respectful. You may try phrases like:

"I just want you to know that when you said that, it really hurt my feelings."

"I need you to know how much that comment hurt my feelings."

"I just have to tell you that it really bothers me when you say things like that."

Do not be afraid to speak up and say what's on your mind. It's an important foundation for strong, healthy relationships.

July 4th – Free yourself from grudges.
HAPPY INDEPENDENCE DAY! Today, I want you to free yourself – from grudges that you are holding against others.

> *"Holding onto anger is like drinking poison and expecting the other person to die."*
> *~Buddha*

The quote above is one of my favorite quotes of all time! It gets down to the heart of what really happens when you hold onto anger or hold a grudge; it doesn't hurt the other person, but it continues to hurt you.

Being angry robs yourself of peace and joy in your life. Man cannot be simultaneously angry and happy, resentful and at peace, bitter and joyful.

I learned this lesson many years ago in a very hard way. I was terribly angry at a classmate of mine who I thought was my friend, but turned out not to be. I felt so betrayed by her and when it all finally came to a head, after lots of screaming, yelling, and crying, I walked away from the relationship feeling hurt and angry.

I held onto that anger and bitterness for many years. Looking back, I realized how it clouded my judgment and affected my future relationships.

Years later, I ran into her, randomly, at the bank. I decided that I could continue to be resentful and bitter, or, I could forgive her for what she had done and close that chapter. I approached and told her that I was sorry about our falling out and that I hoped she was doing well. I told her that I forgave her for what had happened and that I wished her nothing but the best.

She responded with…

"I'm sorry, do I know you?"

All those years of holding a grudge and she didn't even remember me!

> *"Hanging onto resentment is letting someone*
> *live rent-free in your head."*
> ~*Esther Lederer*

195

All this time, I let someone live rent-free in my head; taking up space that would have been better used over the years.

Today, I want you to claim your independence from the joy-stealing, time-wasting, poison-inducing grudges that you are holding onto. Let them go!

July 5th – Be a giraffe.

I teach a corporate training program on communication and conflict resolution, and in that program, one of the concepts I teach is "giraffe language." Giraffe language is all about compassionate communication.

One of the core principles that I tell participants when they are practicing giraffe language is to remember that giraffes are "willing to stick their necks out."

Whenever we reach out to another human being, there is an inherent vulnerability in the act. We may be rejected, laughed at, made fun of; we may even be misunderstood.

When communicating with others we are always sticking our necks out in hopes that we will make a positive connection; but it doesn't always work out that way. One of the most important (and most difficult) times that we stick our necks out is when we are working to resolve conflict with someone.

When you've had a fight with your spouse, when your best friend has said something unkind, when you have a falling out with your boss, it's human nature to want to retreat, to lick your wounds, and to repair the damage that has been done.

But, progress will never be made if both parties retreat and neither one is willing to stick their neck out, or, extend the olive branch.

"Blessed are the peacemakers, for they will be called children of God."
~The Bible, Matthew 5:9

When faced with conflict, be a peacemaker, practice being a giraffe, stick your neck out, and work to resolve the issues and move forward. If, for no other reason, be a giraffe to protect your own peace of mind and joy. Be a giraffe that brings peace to yourself.

July 6th – Be authentic.

Just recently, I wrote an article for The Huffington Post titled, *The Freedom Not to Care.* The article was about the freedom I felt when I finally let go of worrying about what everyone else thought of me. I spent a lot of my early years trying to fit in, trying to be like everyone else, and suffocating the authentic me so I would be accepted.

A funny thing happened to me when I stopped all of that and starting being my authentic self; I started attracting the right people for me; I found my tribe.

In order to have healthy relationships with others, you first have to have a healthy relationship with yourself (we're going to talk about that more as the month goes on). Before you can have a healthy relationship with yourself, you have to know who you are.

It sounds crazy to say this, but I know lots of people (I was one of them) who don't really know who they are. They don't really know what they like, they don't really understand what makes them tick.

As we get older, we start to self-identify with our outside relationships, "I'm Timmy's mom," "I'm John's wife," or, we identify with what we do, "I'm a banker," "I'm a lawyer," "I work at XYZ Company."

Go grab your planner, because today, I want you to schedule a very important date – with yourself! No one else is allowed to go with you. If you can schedule a whole day, that's awesome. If you can schedule an entire weekend getaway, that's even better! Even if all you can spare is just one afternoon or evening, get it on the books now!

I want you to plan your date with the same care and consideration you would use if you were planning an outing with your spouse, your children, or your best friend. Make a list of all the things you like to do, your favorite foods, your favorite color, things that make you happy, and I want you to spend your date doing those things that you love, those things that feed your soul.

Maybe your date will be going to the beach with a good book and reading all day, then going out for a fabulous seafood dinner at night, all the while wearing your favorite color.

Maybe your date will be kicking everyone out of the house, grabbing your oil paints and an easel, and painting all day to the sounds of Mozart or Beethoven, while drinking wine and eating fresh peaches.

Perhaps you will take yourself to the farmer's market in the morning and notice all the vibrant colors and smells as you walk through each merchant's stall, then spend the afternoon at your favorite museum looking at the things that YOU want to look at and not feeling rushed by an impatient spouse or a hungry toddler.

Get in touch with who you are and don't be afraid to let your authentic self come through. Doing so may give others the courage to be who they were meant to be as well.

July 7th – Disagree without demonizing.

There are plenty of times in life when the people you love and care about will do things that you don't agree with.

Anyone out there who is raising, or has raised a teenage child, can probably identify with this statement very well.

When someone does something or says something that you don't agree with, it's okay to disagree with them. It's even okay to tell them so (speak up)! Remember to disagree with the action, not with the person.

While there is much debate about who to credit with the quote, "Hate the sin, love the sinner," it is certainly an appropriate sentiment for what we're talking about today.

You aren't always going to see eye-to-eye all the time with everyone in your life. The ability to disagree with someone and still love and respect them is an important component to nurturing those healthy relationships.

When you find yourself in a disagreement with someone, I have a simple trick you can employ. Take a deep breath, think about three quick things you like about this person, and then, compliment them.

Yes, you read that right, compliment them. In the midst of the disagreement, just stop and say, "You know, I really love the way you take care of the people around you." This will accomplish two things.

1. It will instantly diffuse the situation. It's pretty hard to be angry at someone who just said something nice about you.

2. It shifts the focus away from the issue and back onto what really matters – the people.

Try it next time you're in a disagreement with someone, and see how it works for you!

July 8th – If you can't say something nice…
Words have the power to hurt or heal and once something is said, it can't be "unsaid," so choose your words wisely.

It's easy to get caught up in the heat of the moment when you're arguing with someone and you feel hurt, betrayed, or disrespected. The natural response to that is to lash out and try to hurt them back.

Sometimes, we lash out first as a kind of pre-emptive strike, "get them before they get me."

While I am not able to recall all of the times when someone has said something kind or flattering about me, I seem to always remember almost every time someone has said something cruel to me.

I remember unkind things that were said as far back as kindergarten. Taunts on the playground, unflattering remarks from a teacher, things my mom said when she was mad at me. These things are so easy to recall; why?

Dr. Phil once said, on his popular daytime TV show, "It takes 1,000 'Atta boys' to erase one, 'You're an idiot'!"

We are our own worst critics. We are tougher on ourselves than anyone else could ever be. That's why it's so easy to believe people when they tell us that we're fat, ugly, stupid, worthless, useless, or any number of other words that are meant to bring us down and make us feel bad about ourselves.

Close your eyes for a moment and think back to a time when someone said something mean to you. Think about what they said, and think about how it made you feel.

Now imagine how it feels for someone else when you say unkind things to them.

The next time you are in a verbal exchange with someone and your instinct is to say something unkind, stop speaking and walk away. If you can muster up the energy to say, "I need a minute," do so, but, remove yourself from the exchange as soon as possible.

Find a quiet place where you can focus on your breathing for ten minutes. While you breathe, repeat a soothing mantra in your head. I've used things like, "I'm better than this," "I'm stronger than this," "This too shall pass."

Do not re-engage with this person until you are confident that you can do so without saying something you might regret.

Words have the power to hurt or heal; choose wisely!

July 9th – Practice compassion.

"Remember that everyone you meet is afraid of some-
thing, loves something, and has lost something."
~H. Jackson Brown, Jr.

How wise was our friend H. Jackson Brown, when he said the above quote! It is true that everyone you meet is struggling with something. Some folks may even have it tougher than you do!

Practicing compassion means understanding that everyone has struggles, problems, and issues, and that we're all just going through life trying to do the best we can with what we've got.

Life does not come with an instruction manual; at least mine didn't! I have screwed up more times than I care to admit, and continue to screw up – more times than I care to admit!

When you practice compassion, when you feel empathy for others and what they are going through, it is a way to nurture and care for people. It is a way to move through your relationships with a spirit of kindness and connection with others.

We must learn to give people the benefit of the doubt. When someone isn't particularly nice to you, it may not be about you at all. The cashier that isn't smiling from ear to ear may be working a second job to take care of her dying mother; the person on the bus that doesn't move over to make room for you may be trapped in his own head thinking about how to provide for his family after losing his job.

I'm not excusing rude behavior here, I'm merely suggesting that we practice compassion at every turn, regardless of how others are behaving.

> *"Be kind to unkind people. They need it the most."*
> *~ Ashleigh Brilliant*

July 10th – Find the good in others.

In the training program that I referenced earlier this week, I talk about how to engage in healthy conflict. One of the cornerstones of this is learning to find the good in others; to focus on just one thing that is good about someone, even when you don't particularly like them.

In my role as a Human Resources Director for a large non-profit organization, I have some interaction with nearly everyone that works at the company. If I'm being honest (and I need to be after the talk I gave you on the 2nd), I don't like everyone I work with. Now, to be sure, I have no delusion that everyone likes me either!

My job is to take care of people and make sure they get everything that they need and are entitled to as an employee of the company, and at every turn, no matter how much someone gets under my skin, I am always able to find one thing about them that is good. Even if the only thing I can think of is that they work hard for the company, I always focus on that one thing.

Just about every person you meet has some redeeming quality to them and it's important to understand that even if someone isn't your particular "cup of tea," they are still a human being with thoughts and feelings and fears and desires, just like you and me.

Finding the good in others means finding common ground and that can help you create healthy relationships with the people around you. Try it out today with one or two people that you aren't very fond of. See if it changes your thinking about them.

July 11ᵗʰ – Practice generosity.
When you read the word generosity, did your mind immediately go to money? Most people think of monetary gifts when they hear the word generosity, but you can be generous in many other ways with the people around you.

You can be generous with your:

- Time
- Attention
- Skills and/or talents
- Affection
- Expertise
- Connections
- Patience

And, of course, you can be financially generous if you're able.

Your time is the ultimate gift you can give because once you've given it away, you can never get it back. Spending time with people that need human interaction can make a big difference in someone's life.

Think of an elderly neighbor that lives alone and might enjoy a visit. Think of your friend that just had a baby and could use some help around the house. Think of a coworker that just had surgery; could you take some groceries or some pre-cooked meals to them?

Starting today, and for the rest of this month, I want you to practice one act of generosity each day. It doesn't have to be anything big, and it doesn't have to cost any money, just start off each day thinking that you're going to do something nice for someone.

You may:

- Let someone get in line in front of you at the store
- Buy a cup of coffee for a police officer in line at the coffee shop
- Send a card to a friend that you haven't seen in a while
- Send an email to a co-worker, just to thank them for doing a good job
- Drop off dog and/or cat treats at your local animal shelter
- Invite a neighbor over for tea
- Take a friend without a car out to run errands
- Leave a little box of chocolates on your co-worker's chair
- Babysit for a family member so they can go out on a date with their spouse

With each day that you conduct a generous act, pay attention to how it makes you feel. I can almost guarantee that you'll get out more than you put in.

July 12th – There's an app for that.

Seems there is an app for everything these days, and while I have enjoyed connecting with old friends and faraway friends over Facebook, there is no app that can replace the joy of unplugging and spending real time, in person, with the people that you love.

When spending time with your friends and family, resist the urge to spend that time with your face buried in your iPhone.

One of the saddest things I've ever seen happened at a baseball game a few summers ago. I'm not a big baseball fan, but I got a few free tickets through my work and I took a coworker with me as a nice afternoon out to thank him for a job well done.

Sitting a few rows over was a man with his young son. The father spent the entire game on his cell phone. His son was frantically trying to get his dad's attention. When one of the players on the home team hit a home run, he was jumping up and down, and begging his father to watch the replay on the big screen.

Eventually, the son gave up and sat down, defeated. I couldn't tell if he was crying or not, but he sat with his arms crossed and his head down for the remainder of the game.

I felt so bad for this little boy who only wanted to spend some time bonding with his dad over America's favorite pastime. What a missed opportunity for this man to create a lovely memory with his son and spend quality time with him.

If you want to truly connect with those around you, you have to be fully present in the moment. That means you're not checking your work email while you're at the park with your kids; you're not texting your friends when you and your spouse are having a date night, and you're not checking your latest eBay bid when you're having lunch with a friend.

Unplug and be present with those around you to establish a healthy bond with those you love.

July 13th – Reconnect.
Life just seems to be getting more and more hectic with each passing day. There never seems to be enough hours in the day to do all

the things that need to be done. Between running the kids back and forth to school, laundry, housework, meal preparation, and going to your actual job, there seems little time to unwind and reconnect with people.

Time moves really fast and one day you wake up and your six-year old is thirteen and she wants you to drop her off a block from the mall. One day you're a newlywed on your honeymoon, then you blink and you're going on ten years of marriage and you can't remember the last time you and your spouse went out without the kids.

Reconnecting doesn't have to be an epic endeavor like a trip to Disney World for the whole family. You can reconnect in simple ways a little bit every day.

One of my favorite things to do with the people close to me is ask them two questions at the end of each day:

1. What was the peak of your day?
2. What was the pit of your day?

This is a good way to connect with people and let them know that you care about what's happening with them. If you have kids at home, this is a nice exercise to do with your family around the dinner table. Take turns asking each other those two questions to spark conversation, catch up, and learn about what's happening in each other's lives.

In the hustle and bustle of life, it's critical not to lose sight of what's important; the people in your life that love you and are there to support you. Take the time to reconnect with them today.

July 14th – Practice good listening skills.

I have learned through years of corporate training, employee relations, and mediation, that there are three levels of listening.

1. *Level One Listening* is when you are waiting for the other person to stop talking and are already thinking about what you're going to say.

2. *Level Two Listening* is when you listen to the words that are being said. When you ask a question or make a statement, your question or statement is directly related to what is being said to you.

3. *Level Three Listening* is when you hear all the words, when questions or comments are directly related to what is being said, and, you are paying attention to the person's body language and demeanor; hearing above what's being said.

One of the fastest ways to erode your relationships is to be so self-absorbed that you don't listen to what others are saying. Take the two questions we talked about yesterday. It does no good to ask the questions and then not listen to the answers.

People want to be heard. Listening is a form of respect and validation of others. When you give someone your undivided attention, you are sending the message to them that there is nothing else that's more important than them in that moment.

Today, as you go through your interactions with others, try practicing Level Two Listening. As this level of listening becomes a habit for you, try taking your listening to the next level by practicing Level Three Listening.

Through the development of these good listening skills, you'll build a reputation for being a thoughtful and caring person that others will feel naturally connected to.

July 15ᵗʰ – Be realistic.

As you move through relationships with the people in your life it's important to be realistic about what you expect from these relationships.

I learned this one the hard way.

When I got married, I assumed that life would be perfect, that my husband would take care of everything that needed taking care of, and I could just let go, relax, and ride the wave.

I'm divorced now. It is any wonder why? What a huge amount of pressure I put on my husband!

No one is perfect. You aren't, I'm not, your boss isn't; even your children, whom you love and adore and would do anything for, are not perfect!

Loving someone doesn't mean that they will never get on your nerves. It doesn't mean that you will never have an argument, or that sometimes, you won't even just hate the sight of each other.

> *"You cannot spend any significant amount of time with someone and not get on each other's nerves."*
> *~Karen Ann Kennedy*

This quote was born out of a tumultuous time I was having with my boss, who I actually love dearly, respect, and admire. We were spending an enormous amount of time together and were getting on each other's last nerve. It got to the point where I couldn't stand the sight of him, and I'm pretty sure he felt the same way about me.

I realized though, that part of the reason why he was dancing on my last nerve was because I wasn't being realistic about our relationship. We had enjoyed a much-envied working relationship over many years; the kind of working relationship where, even though he was the boss, I could be honest about how I was feeling and "tell it like it was."

But the truth was, he was still the boss, and within that relationship there were inherent boundaries that still needed to be observed.

I also realized that it was because I loved, respected, and admired him that I was annoyed by him. People that you don't care about don't have the power to make you angry, sad, or hurt. Their opinion of you doesn't rattle you because you don't feel a connection to them.

It's when you truly care about a person and your relationship with them that you can get frustrated and angry when things don't go the way you think they should.

Take the pressure off yourself and those around you by being realistic about your relationships with them.

July 16th – Write a letter.
If there's someone that you have lost touch with that you want to reconnect with, or someone that you have a strained relationship with, you may find healing and repair of your relationship by writing them a letter.

I have often told people that I'm "better in writing;" perhaps that's why I wanted to become a writer. When I get flustered, angry, or upset, I find it hard to articulate what's going on in my heart and in my head. For me, the best way to tell someone how I'm feeling is to write it down.

Today, carve out some time to sit down, uninterrupted, and write a letter to someone that you've lost touch with, or someone that you're currently having a tough time with. There is something profound about a handwritten letter, a real letter on real paper, not typed on the computer, and not an email.

You may have heard about the exercise where you write a letter to someone but never send it. This is not that exercise. The goal here is to nurture a relationship, so the letter you write today is one you're going to want to send to someone as a way to reestablish your relationship.

Don't have anyone that fits the description above? Great! Use the time today to write a letter to someone special to you. Invest in some pretty paper and a fancy envelope and tell this person in your own words and in your own writing how much they mean to you and how important they are in your life.

The act of writing down how you're feeling, expressing gratitude, or articulating pain can be a very cathartic experience for the author, and can be a powerful communication piece or keepsake for the receiver.

July 17th – Be bold enough to admit your mistakes.
Since we've already established that no one is perfect, you have no doubt had some missteps or made some mistakes in your relationships with others.

> *"The truly great person is not one that never makes mistakes, but the one who is willing to admit to them."*
> *~Karen Ann Kennedy*

A powerful way to endear yourself to others is to admit when you have done something wrong. The quicker you can own up to something you've done, the quicker you can move past it and shift the focus to the future.

There's no real exercise or action step here other than to just be willing to admit when you've done something wrong. Own it and move past it in order to keep your relationships moving forward.

July 18ᵗʰ – Identify the ebbs and flows.
All relationships will go through ebbs and flows. It's impossible for people to be 100% happy 100% of the time. In life there will always be stress, financial burdens, family drama, sickness, and even death. Beware of the people in your life that only come around when times are good; a real friend will be there for you when times are tough as well.

It's certainly much more fun to be around for the good times. It's fun to share laughter and fellowship with the people in your life; to celebrate and enjoy good times. But when things are going bad, it's important to show up and be present.

When my dad passed away, it was a really difficult time for me and my family. I tried to put on a happy face at work and not burden others with my troubles, but I know I wasn't exactly fun to be around at that time.

I still remember my friends and coworkers that were there for me when my dad passed. I remember feeling loved and cared for and grateful for their support. Looking back, I'm not sure how I would have gotten through that time, or any of the hard times, without the people who loved me and were in my corner.

Don't be the kind of person that just shows up for the good times. Be the kind of person who is there when you are needed and you can be sure that those people will be there for you when you are in need.

July 19ᵗʰ – Ask a lot of questions.
If I've learned one thing in over twenty-five years of working with others, it's that people like to talk about themselves! There is no better way to connect with someone than to ask them questions that focus on them, and that show an interest in the things they are interested in.

In our selfie-addicted society where many people are self-absorbed, sending a tweet every time they use the restroom, it's refreshing to be with someone who can shift the focus on others and takes the time to get to know people on a deeper level.

When you meet someone new, take an interest in them and ask lots of questions. Give yourself a chance to get to know the person and learn about them.

Remember, every friend was once a stranger!

July 20ᵗʰ – Show affection.
Human beings crave closeness and physical touch; and affection does not have to be reserved for romantic relationships. A hug, a kiss, even holding someone's hand, can do wonders for a person when they are feeling stressed or down.

Research has shown that there are five main types of affection. They are:

1. Acts of service
2. Gifts
3. Physical touch
4. Quality time
5. Words of affirmation

In romantic relationships, it's important to know what types of affection your partner enjoys. If your partner wants hugs and kisses and you're showering them with expensive gifts, you may be missing the mark. Subsequently, if you need words of affirmation, but your spouse thinks taking out the trash will show his love, there may be a disconnect that leaves both parties feeling frustrated.

The best way to determine how people like to give and receive affection is to ask them. By doing so, you can determine the best ways to show affection to those that are close to you.

July 21st – Practice forgiveness.
On July 4th we talked about holding a grudge. While today's topic is in a similar vein, today is all about forgiveness, of yourself, and others.

In my dealings with others, I am big on intent. Sometimes people hurt my feelings or do things that bother me, but they don't mean to; it may not have ever been their intent to hurt me. When I can be mature enough to recognize that sometimes people do things that result in bad feelings, I can get past their transgressions and forgive them for what they've done.

YOUR BEST YEAR YET!

Please understand that there are nasty people out there in the world who will do bad things on purpose, because deep down, they're not good people. Those are not the people that I'm talking about here.

I'm talking about the right people who sometimes do things wrong. Forgiving someone does not mean that you condone what they've done or that you agree with it; it just means that you value the person enough to let go of what has happened and move on with your relationship in a healthy way.

There is great power in forgiveness. I've seen powerful examples of this over the years, from the woman that forgives the man who killed her son, to the woman who forgives the man who raped her, to the man who forgives the drunk driver that killed his family.

Forgiveness is freedom; freedom from suffering and hatred, freedom from burden and guilt, and freedom from obsessing about something that you cannot change.

The most important form of forgiveness is forgiving yourself! Be sure to exercise the same kindness and patience with yourself that you do with others in your life. You deserve forgiveness as much as the next person; maybe even more so.

July 22nd – Know when to compromise.
The art of compromising means that neither party in a relationship gets exactly what they want, but they can make enough concessions to get to a place where they can learn to live with the outcome.

When compromising, please note that there are a few things you should NEVER compromise; they include:

- Your beliefs and values
- Your health and well-being
- Your honesty
- Your humanity
- Your integrity
- Your personal safety
- The quality of your work
- Your self-respect

However, when you can make some concessions in your relationships and compromise on things, you may find that you can get past hard feelings and tough times with people and strengthen your relationships through your willingness to be flexible and give a little.

The bottom line is to know when to stand your ground and know when to let go a little.

July 23rd – Recognize that relationships change.
Few long-term relationships stay exactly the same over the years; that's mainly because <u>we</u> don't stay the same!

To be sure, I am not the same person now in my early forties that I was when I was in my late teens or early twenties, or even my early thirties. I've changed a lot and so have my relationships with other people.

In my early twenties I met lots of great people at an outdoor club I used to frequent. I'd hang out for hours on end with this particular group of friends, dancing and drinking and listening to my favorite reggae band. As my life changed and my priorities changed, my relationship with the people that I hung out with changed.

I don't see those people much anymore. It doesn't mean that they aren't still great people, it's just that I don't hang out at the club anymore, none of us do, and so our relationship has changed.

There are lot of reasons why relationships may change:

- We experience a major life change – we get married, get a new job, or start a family
- We move away
- Our priorities or interests change
- We latch on to an entirely new set of friends

When you have an amazing group of friends that you love and respect and that love and respect you, it's worth putting in the time and effort to keep those relationships alive. If you can weather the changes and keep your relationships intact, DO IT! Loyal people and good friends are hard to come by!

July 24th – Live in a spirit of gratitude.

There is plenty of research to show that people who are grateful are healthier and happier and find that they end up having even more to be grateful for. If you need a reason to start practicing gratitude, here are a few you can start with.

- Grateful people are happier people
- Grateful people tend to be healthier than their ungrateful counterparts

- People who live in a spirit of gratitude develop better coping skills that can help them more successfully weather the hard times
- Grateful people enjoy their work more
- Grateful people are more attractive to others
- Practicing gratitude can make you feel better
- Being grateful for what you can have can keep jealousy at bay
- Grateful people have stronger, healthier relationships with others

I know I haven't given you a lot of exercise to do this month (it is summer after all), but I have an exercise I'd like you to do today. Pull out your journal and make a list of no less than fifty things that you're grateful for.

I know fifty sounds a like lot, but trust me, this exercise is meant to stretch you. Even if you're having a bad day or going through a particularly rough time, remember, there is ALWAYS something to be grateful for. Even if the only thing you can think to be grateful for is air or sun or a new episode of your favorite reality TV show; there is ALWAYS something to be grateful for.

You can take this exercise a step further by writing down three things that you're grateful for every night before you go to bed. Doing this is a nice recap to the day and a nice way to plant some "feel good seeds" in your brain before you go to sleep.

Starting today, live with an attitude of gratitude for all the things you have!

July 25th – Take care of yourself first.

"You cannot serve from an empty vessel."
~Eleanor Brownn

Taking care of yourself is not selfish, it's a necessity! Being at your best means that you can give your best to others. When you're tired, hungry, sick, cranky, or stressed, you cannot nurture good relationships. It is imperative that you take care of yourself so you can be fully present and engaged with others.

Sometimes the best way to be there for someone is not to be there. I have turned down many a social engagement because I knew that I was not at my best. How good of a guest would I be if I go to my best friend's BBQ with a migraine and sit in the corner like a Debbie Downer? What good would it do my mom to tell her I will take her shopping, only to show up sick and cranky and be short with her?

When you feel the urge to retreat and disconnect from others, honor that urge. Don't force yourself to be the social butterfly when every fiber of your being is screaming for you to take a break.

I am the best friend, coworker, and family member I can be when I feel physically and mentally well. Be sure that you are taking care of yourself in order to fully and enthusiastically give to others.

July 26th – R-E-S-P-E-C-T
Relationships must be built on mutual respect. That is a complete sentence; no buts, howevers, or maybes. Life is too short to spend with people who are disrespectful to you. In turn, you can't expect to enjoy healthy relationships if you are not respectful yourself.

There are lots of ways to show respect to others. We've talked about some of them throughout the month; being present, disconnecting from technology, and listening to people. Here are a few more:

- Respecting effort – Recognizing when people are giving their best effort to something
- Keeping your promises – It's as simple as doing what you say you will do, when you say you will do it
- Respecting others opinions – Not everyone will think the same way that you do
- Be polite – Practice the basics, such as saying please and thank you, holding the door open for others, or giving up your seat on the bus to an elderly person
- Don't judge – Being respectful means not judging people based on factors such as who they are, what they do, or their physical attributes
- Have respect for people's possessions – Take care when in other's homes and with other's possessions. If you borrow something, for example, take great care to return it in the condition you received it in
- Be respectful of people's time – Being consistently late shows a lack of respect for others valuable time

Think about how you can show respect to those around you today and every day.

July 27th – Learn to be alone.
Today is all about nurturing your relationship with yourself. Hopefully, you went ahead and scheduled a date with yourself earlier this month. If you didn't, shame on you; go back and do your homework!

YOUR BEST YEAR YET!

No matter how big your family is, how much you love your children or your significant other, or how terrific your friends are, there is only one person that you are with 24 hours a day/7 days a week, and that's YOU!

Learning to be content in your own presence is vitally important, after all, you are always with yourself.

Being alone was something I was never able to be comfortable with when I was younger. Being alone made me feel anxious and lonely. I often found myself making plans with people I didn't really want to see, doing things I didn't really want to do, just so I wouldn't have to be alone.

Now that I'm older (and extremely busy) I relish those moments when it's just me and the cat chilling and relaxing at home. I've even learned how to go out alone and be okay, although I still don't like to eat out by myself.

If you didn't have a date with yourself yet this month, your homework today is to schedule that date.

If you <u>did</u> have your date with yourself, today I want you to journal about the experience. Where did you go? What did you do? How did you feel about your time alone? Take some time to reflect on your experience, and if you're up to it; schedule another date!

July 28th – Choose your battles.

Arguments, disagreements, and not seeing eye-to-eye are part of life, and will sometimes creep into your relationships, no matter how solid they may be. It's important to choose your battles to protect your peace of mind.

Choosing your battles doesn't mean that you have to be a human doormat. I was a doormat for many, many years. People didn't just walk all over me; they actually stopped to wipe their feet!

Don't be a human doormat, and, please know, that you are not required to attend every argument you are invited to.

July 29th – Know when to move on.

As much as you may love your friends and the people in your life, it's important to know when it's time to move on. Every person does not deserve a place in your life. Although they may have done many things for you in the past, or have been there for you when you need-ed them, it does not mean that they get a lifetime seat at your table.

I know we started talking about these concepts in March, but we're going to get more in-depth this month. Consider this your "master class."

It may be time to move on from a relationship if:

- The thought of seeing them stresses you out
- You feel like you are doing all the giving, and they're doing all the taking
- You're doing all the work to keep the relationship going
- They've done something to break your trust and you don't feel like you can ever forgive them
- A person consistently lets you down by not keeping their word or their promises
- You are living in the past, holding on to what the relation-ship used to be like
- The other person puts you down a lot, criticizes you, or gen-erally does not support or encourage your endeavors
- Your friend is engaging in illegal activities; drugs, theft, etc.

Only you will know when it's time to move on and let go of a relationship that no longer serves you well. If you're still unsure, look back through April and read the days that talk about energy vampires and NEDs.

July 30th – A reason, a season, or a lifetime
For as long as I can remember, one of the thoughts that has stuck in my head when it comes to relationships is that people enter your life either for a reason, a season, or a lifetime.

I've learned, over the years, that not everyone stays in your life forever, and that not everyone is meant to. While it is sometimes painful when someone disappears from our life, other times it happens in a way that can make you think about the saying of the day.

When people come into your life for a **reason**, they are there for a specific purpose. It may be a blatantly obvious purpose, such as, your teachers come into your life to teach you in school; you meet a realtor because you're buying a house; you see a doctor to treat an illness.

Other times, the reason is not as "in your face." Sometimes the reason people come into your life is because there is a lesson to be learned; either by you, or by the other person.

I've noticed this most often with friends that drift off after a period of time. Nothing went wrong. There were no knock-down, drag-out fights that precipitated the end of the relationship, we just sort of drifted apart. Thinking back on those friends that have come in and out, I realize that with each one there was something I learned, something I came to appreciate, and something that I figured out, just because they were part of my life for a period of time.

223

Sometimes, people come into your life for a **season**, and while you can certainly take that literally, a schoolmate, a summer fling, etc.; I find that the season is more about a particular stage in your life. I've had many "seasonal" relationships where a person is there during a particular time or "season" of my life. These people seemed to always be going through the same stage and that created a bonding time. Of course, once one or both of us moved out of that stage, the relationship didn't seem to make sense anymore, and so, like the above, we drifted apart.

But, please don't discount the power of the reason and season relationships in your life. Those folks that seem to come into your life at exactly the right time are no less valuable than the people that stay with you forever.

It probably doesn't take a lot of explanation to tell you that the people that are with you forever are your **lifetime** people. I've been blessed to have a few of them in my life too; mostly family.

I've realized over the years how incredible it is to have people in your life for a lifetime. If you think about all the changes you've gone through over the course of your life, if you think of all the ways your life has evolved or grown or changed, you'll probably see that the YOU that you are today, is nothing like the YOU that you were yesterday, or in college, or in high school, or when you were a kid.

When you meet people along the way that stay with you for all the ups and downs and challenges and changes, that is incredibly special and valuable. These are relationships worth fighting for!

As we wind down to the end of the month, I'd like you to grab your journal and make a list of people that were in your life for a reason, for a season, or for a lifetime. For the folks that make the reason and season list, just think back about those relationships and try to think of what positive things you got out of those relationships. No action item here; just a chance to sit back and be nostalgic about old times and think about what each person brought into your life.

For the people on your lifetime list, there is a big action item. Grab some blank notecards (or make a date to go buy some) and write a thank you note to each of your lifetime people. Tell them how grateful you are to have them in your life and let them know how much they mean to you. If it's a lifetime person you haven't seen in a while, make a date to see them for coffee, or dinner, or lunch. If one of your lifetime people lives far away, see if you can set up a Skype date to catch up.

July 31st – Take responsibility for your own happiness.

This month, I've saved the best for last! I cannot stress to you enough the importance of today's entry. If you are looking for someone to make you happy, someone to help you feel fulfilled, and someone to love you no matter what, look in the mirror – that person is already with you.

It took me a long time to realize that you have to take responsibility for your own happiness. No one can truly <u>make</u> you happy; real happiness has to come from within. *Jerry Maguire* (while a great movie) had it all wrong with this whole "You complete me" business.

That's implying that unless you have someone else in your life, you aren't a complete person. I think it would have been more accurate to say, "You enhance me," or, "You add to my joy."

If your peace, joy, happiness, love, compassion, or energy is based on someone else, then there's a chance you might lose it. But, if your peace, joy, happiness, love, compassion, and energy is based on your own relationship with yourself, you will always have it with you, and it will always be part of your life.

Besides, depending on another person to supply you with happiness is a huge burden to place on another human being; and it's an impossible task.

If you have made up your mind to be unhappy, there is really nothing I can do to change your mind. I may be able to temporarily cheer you up or distract you from something. I may even be able to make you smile or laugh. But, deep down, if you are choosing to be unhappy, there is nothing I can do to make you change your mind.

So, if you have a terrific family, loving spouse, amazing children, supportive parents, fabulous co-workers, tremendous friends, I applaud you and want to remind you how lucky you are. However, don't lose sight of the fact that you are still responsible for your own happiness.

Don't have all those things? Guess what; you are still responsible for your own happiness! And, if you don't have all those supportive, loving people in your life, now is the time to start working that happiness muscle for yourself. Start by figuring out what makes you happy. What do you like? What do you get excited and energized about? Then, if you want to be happy, DO MORE OF THAT!

My July to-do list:

- I came up with my daily "kindness mantra"
- I've started to speak up for myself
- I claimed my independence from grudges
- I've become more giraffe-like in my communication with others
- I'm being more authentic these days
- I'm practicing disagreeing without demonizing
- I am practicing compassion every day
- I am learning to find the good in others
- I have practiced one act of generosity every day
- I've unplugged from my electronic devices in an effort to reconnect with those around me
- I've been practicing good listening skills
- I wrote a letter to someone I really want to reconnect with
- I've made an effort to show affection to those I love
- I am practicing forgiveness
- I am living in a spirit of gratitude
- I am consciously practicing good self-care
- I scheduled, and went on a date with myself
- I wrote notes to each of my "lifetime" people
- I am taking responsibility for my own happiness

AUGUST – MEDITATE AND RELAX

Most people find it easier to relax and slow down when the summer months hit. It's the time of year when most people go on vacation, or just start to move at a slower pace in the midst of the summer heat.

Relaxing, meditating, and keeping stress at bay needs to be a conscious effort for many of the busy people I coach and counsel, so this month, I'm going to show you some great ways to incorporate meditation into your every day.

We'll also explore relaxation tips and techniques, aromatherapy, water therapy, and stress relief on the go.

So sit back, relax, and start chanting "ohm," as we dig into the wonderful world of meditation.

August 1st – What is meditation?

Meditation is not about the act of doing something, it's about the act of relaxing, letting go, and letting your mind enjoy some quiet time. Meditation is about getting back in touch with yourself, without all the distractions that come up in the course of normal life.

There is some debate about the exact origins of meditation, but some of the earliest written records date back to around 1500 BC and have roots in Hindu traditions.

Most people think of Buddhist Monks with shaved heads sitting in a yoga pose when they think about meditation; but meditation is now practiced worldwide and for many people has become an important part of their daily self-care routine.

August 2nd – How can meditation help you?

The health benefits of meditation have been widely studied and the research has been all positive. Meditation has been shown to relieve anxiety, help with headaches, lower blood pressure, and give people a sense of peace and well-being.

While some people report having a hard time turning off their brains and relaxing, meditation is a relatively easy practice to start working on. You can do it almost anywhere, and it's completely and totally free!

Can meditation help you? Check out the list below of all the health benefits that have been associated with the practice of mediation.

- Helps people kick addictions like smoking and alcohol dependency
- Reduces anxiety
- Helps people appreciate others
- Gives people more appreciation for themselves
- Increases blood flow
- Helps lower blood pressure
- Can result in better breathing
- Helps improve focus and concentration
- Helps with headache and migraine pain
- Enhances the immune system
- Helps reduce inflammation
- Helps people get a better handle on their internal thoughts
- Helps improve your memory
- Relaxes the nervous system
- Establishes a sense of peace of mind
- Reduces symptoms associated with PMS
- Leads to increased relaxation
- Increases serotonin in your brain
- Helps promote better sleep
- Gives people a deeper understanding of others
- Gives people a deeper understanding of themselves

With all the health benefits to be gained, and nothing to be lost (except for a little time to try it out) meditation is something to be considered for sure. Most people I know don't know where to start; that's okay, I'm going to walk you through and help you get started. But first, let's gauge your stress level.

August 3rd – How stressed are you?

Grab a pen and take the quiz below. Be honest; no one needs to see your answers but you.

1. I frequently feel like there's not enough hours in the day to get things done.
    ☐ YES   ☐ NO

2. I find it hard to relax and unwind at the end of the day.
    ☐ YES   ☐ NO

3. I get impatient when I have to wait for something.
    ☐ YES   ☐ NO

4. I feel like I am stretched too thin.
    ☐ YES   ☐ NO

5. I find it difficult to fall asleep or stay asleep.
    ☐ YES   ☐ NO

6. I frequently engage in unhealthy habits like smoking or drinking too much.
    ☐ YES   ☐ NO

7. I worry often about things like finances, health, or the future.
    ☐ YES   ☐ NO

8. I feel like I do not have control of my own life.
    ☐ YES   ☐ NO

9. I find myself constantly trying to race through the day.
    ☐ YES   ☐ NO

10. I experience a variety of physical symptoms, such as frequent headaches and/or trouble with my stomach/digestion.
   ☐ YES   ☐ NO

If you answered yes to three or more of these statements, you are likely experiencing some form of stress in your life. If this is the case, the time to take action is NOW! The longer you wait, the worse you may begin to feel.

Many people I work with use the "head in the sand" technique of stress relief, which is, they simply ignore what's going on in the hopes that it will go away.

This is NOT a stress relief technique; this is a denial technique!

> *"Denial is not just a river in Egypt."*
> *~Karen Ann Kennedy*

Ignoring a problem rarely makes it disappear, and while you are ignoring it, the symptoms and ill effects of stress will continue to wear you down. Meditation may help, so get ready to dive into the next ten days; where I'm going to walk you through, step by step, how to get started on a plan of meditation. Each day, we will focus on one new aspect of the meditation process, and then, you can put it all together and start incorporating a meditation practice into your life.

There are tons of ways to get into meditation, the ten steps I'm sharing with you are the ones that I have personally used and what worked best for me. Good luck!

August 4th – Set your intention.
When I was a student of the Institute for Integrative Nutrition in New York, one of the first things we did as part of the curriculum

was to set our intention for why we were attending, and what we hoped to gain.

Since then, I've used this as a way to approach almost everything I do in life. I find that setting an intention (a lot like finding your "why") helps me decide if:

    a. this is something I really want to do, and,
    b. how important it is to me to do it.

So today, I want you to set your intention. Ask yourself the following questions:

    a. Why do I want to start meditating?
    b. What am I hoping to get out of the meditation process?
    c. Is this a good time for me to start the process?
    d. Do I feel excited about getting started?

If you don't feel like this is a good time for you to get started, don't force it. I tried to force my way into this many times, and each time it ended up badly. If this is not the right time for you, bookmark this section and come back to it when you feel like you're ready.

If you are genuinely excited about getting started and have a strong intention, read on.

August 5th – Establish time.
I don't meditate every day. Lots of people tell me that in order for meditation to be successful, you must do it every day. I don't find that to be true, at least not for me. I find that trying to squeeze a full meditation session into every day causes me anxiety (which is counterintuitive) so I commit to meditating four days a week, squeezing in a fifth day when my schedule allows.

I always do my meditating in the morning, as I find that this is the most positive way to start my day. If you aren't much of a morning person, you can meditate in the afternoon or evening, just find a time that works for you.

Today I want you to grab your planner and figure out how many days (and which days) a week you will meditate, and for how long. My entire meditation routine lasts thirty minutes. Here's a breakdown of how I utilize that time:

Prepping my space	4 minutes
Sitting and posture	2 minutes
Being still	5 minutes
Focusing on my breath	6 minutes
Saying my Mantra	6 minutes
Checking in with myself	2 minutes
Preparing to finish	3 minutes
Ending my session	2 minutes
Total time	**30 minutes**

Now you may find yourself needing more or less time on a particular step, and you should feel free to adjust your session as needed. You may also want to start out with meditating just ten or fifteen minutes each day until you get the hang of it. I just wanted to share with you the schedule that works for me.

August 6th – Establish space.
It's best to find a quiet place in your home where you can sit quietly, without distraction or interruption. If you share your home with others, consider choosing a room that has a door, and consider having a "do not disturb" sign that you can put out to let others know that you are meditating. Encourage your housemates to respect the sign and to give you some time alone.

My meditation space is in my home office. When it's time to meditate, I take my first four minutes and get my space ready. I make sure there's no clutter lying around (it's hard to relax in a cluttered room), I move my chair over, and lay down my big comfy cushion. Sometimes I light a candle (if there's not a lot of sun) and sometimes I'll put on soothing meditation music.

Once my space is ready, then I feel ready! If you have enough room to have a dedicated space that does not need additional prep, that's great! Just find a space that is quiet and comfortable and a space that you feel like you can relax and unwind in.

August 7th – Sitting and posture
One of the most important things that meditation has done for me is to improve my posture. As a writer, I tend to sit for long stretches of time, and I've noticed that my posture is not always as good as it should be.

Whenever I meditate, I sit on the floor, on my cushion, and focus on sitting straight up. I imagine that there is an invisible thread hanging down from the ceiling that is connected to the center of my head. I imagine that the thread is gently pulling my head up so that my chin comes up off my chest, my shoulders pull back, my chest pulls forward, and my spine is totally erect.

I've noticed that sitting up straight on my cushion with my legs crossed and my hands resting gently on my knees is the most comfortable position for meditating, and it also helps improve my breathing by opening up my lungs and my diaphragm. Once I have established my posture, I close my eyes and allow myself to relax. Try it!

I've had people ask me if they can meditate while sitting in a chair. Why not? Heck, I've known people who can meditate while sitting on the bus! But, I always ask people to try sitting on the floor first in an attempt to help them get that good posture that I just told you about.

The goal is to be comfortable, but not so comfortable that you begin to slouch. Try today on a cushion or pillow on the floor for ten minutes, working to find the position that feels most comfortable to you. See if you can find that invisible string on the ceiling and spend a few minutes getting your posture correct.

August 8th – Be still.

This is probably the hardest step of all for me, which is why it takes me a full five minutes to get this part down. Being still means not only not physically moving, but trying to keep your brain from moving. The mantra that comes in at step seven will help with the latter.

As a person living with adult ADHD, sitting still for more than a few minutes is really hard for me. I've noticed that through my practice of meditation, it has gotten better, but some days I still find I have to work really hard to remain still.

The following exercise has helped me tremendously in learning how to still my body. First I imagine that there is a giant weight on my rear end. If you've ever seen me in person, you know that's not that much of a stretch! I imagine that the weight is pulling me down towards the floor (grounding me). Just be careful not to let the weight mess up your good posture. Then I concentrate on my legs and I let them sink into the floor. I concentrate on my arms and allow them to feel like they are sinking as well. I allow my shoulders to relax and come away from my ears. I concentrate on every last inch of my body, letting all of my extremities get heavy and sink down into the floor.

Then I focus on letting my mind be still. I try to let go of the "to do" list in my head, the thoughts of work or school, the thoughts of what I'll do when my session is over. I try to focus instead on a single thought (my mantra) or on the music (if I'm using it in my practice).

Today, try the exercise on letting your body be still. That will be helpful as we continue to move through the other steps.

August 9th – Focus on your breathing.

One of the core principles to meditating is focusing on your breathing and getting your breathing into a good, steady rhythm. When I first started meditating, I had to actually count the breaths. This was helpful in making my breathing pattern a habit, and it also helped with stilling my mind; I was focusing on the counting, not my thoughts.

Try inhaling deeply through your nose for a full five seconds, then exhale through your nose for a full five seconds. Keep repeating this five seconds in, five seconds out pattern for three to five minutes and see if you can get to a place where the breath becomes automatic, and where you no longer have to keep count.

Because breathing is such an important part of the meditation practice, you'll notice that I spend an entire six minutes on getting my breathing pattern down.

August 10th – Establish your mantra.

Your mantra can be a noise or a phrase that you continue to repeat either out loud or in your head. The purpose of the mantra is to help you focus on one thing and keep you in the present, helping you clear your mind of the internal "chatter" and thoughts that are cycling through.

Some people I know say, "ohm" out loud while they meditate. I find I tend to get bored of saying the same thing over and over, although I now start my six minutes of mantra work with saying "ohm" a bunch of times. Then I move on to a phrase that I usually don't say out loud, but continue to say over and over in my head. I alternate between saying; "I am fully present," "I am entirely grateful," and, "Today is my day."

If you are a particularly religious person, you may want to repeat a passage that is near and dear to you, or you may want to look up some spiritual sayings that speak to you. The phrases that I use are the ones that speak to me, and I've found them to be very useful in my personal meditation practice.

Today, do a little research to find your mantra and then try saying it a few times. It's okay if it feels weird to you at first, you'll get the hang of it after you do it a while.

August 11th – Check in with yourself.
By now, a full nineteen minutes have passed (minus the prep time), so it's a good time for me to take two minutes and check-in with myself. My check-in normally consists of seeing how I'm physically doing (is my posture still good, how do my back and legs feel, is my breathing still on track, etc.) and then how I feel emotionally (do I feel relaxed, sad, anxious, am I feeling generally positive, etc.)

This is the time to make any adjustments you need to make and to think about the quality of your session.

August 12th – Prepare to finish.
I have found this step to be very helpful for me as it starts to help me focus on all the positive things that came out of the session. In preparing to finish, I stop repeating my mantra and start to bring

my thoughts back to the present. I start to become aware of each part of my body. I start to listen to the noises that are surrounding me; birds chirping, the cat meowing, the sound of the leaves, or cars going by, and I start to think about the day ahead. Not the "to do" list…but what I strive to be like as I go through the day. I strive to go through the day feeling energized and positive, and I strive to be compassionate and loving towards others.

As I begin to focus on the day ahead, I find myself feeling more positive and more open about what's to come.

August 13th – End the session.
Now that the session is ending, I slowly open my eyes and take a few minutes to look around and become reacquainted with the space; I'll stretch a little and when I prepare to stand up, I stand up slowly. Once I'm standing, I'll reach up and stretch some more and usually close the session with one uplifting thought or spoken intention for the day, such as, "I'm going to put something good out there in the world today," or, "Today, everything is stacked in my favor," or sometimes I'll just say, "God is good."

Then I put my space back to its original configuration and move on with my day.

I hope the last couple of days helped you to establish a meditation routine. If my way of meditating does not resonate with you, don't be afraid to venture out and find something else that fits your style. There is no one way to meditate and the "right" way to do it is the way that works best for you!

August 14th – Putting it all together
Now that you have all the individual steps, today is the day to put it all together. Pick a time that works for you and see if you can

meditate for at least fifteen minutes. If you can't make it a full fifteen minutes, try for ten, and see if you can work your way up. If you can't make it through all the steps, try a pared down version focusing at least on your posture, breathing, and mantra. You can always add in additional steps, if you'd like, as you increase your time.

After your first full session, pull out your journal and write about your experience. Use this to tweak and refine your subsequent sessions to get the most out of your time.

August 15th – Walking meditation

When I was first beginning to meditate, I found it nearly impossible to sit still. I didn't want to totally abandon the practice, but I needed a way to ease into it, and I found that walking meditation was very helpful.

Because I am so easily distracted, I needed to walk in a space that didn't distract me with lots to look at, so I headed out to my own backyard.

There were two ways that I walked in order to meditate; one was in a circle, the other was to walk up and down a path that was made up of six square stones. One of the nice things about doing this in my backyard, was that there weren't any people staring at me, wondering why I was walking in circles.

By not having to pay attention to where I was going, look out for traffic, or worry about bumping into another person that might distract me, I was able to concentrate on my breathing and my mantra, while still moving my body.

Since I've now been able to meditate while seated, I don't practice walking meditation as often, but every now and then, I'll still head out and try to walk along a small path where there aren't any people around. I've found this walking meditation to be especially helpful if I'm feeling particularly anxious or worried about something. The walking helps me clear my mind and center myself so I feel more equipped to handle the issue.

If you're so inclined, put on your walking shoes and find a place to walk for ten to fifteen minutes. Practice going in a circle, or up and down a short path. Remember to focus on your breathing, and practice saying your mantra.

August 16th – Is it anxiety?

If you've ever had an anxiety or panic attack, you'll likely be able to relate well to my story.

I had my first panic attack on a city bus. I grew up in Philadelphia where public transportation was my lifeline! I didn't start driving until I was twenty-two, and I relied on public transit to get me everywhere I needed to go. I had successfully ridden on "the El," the subway, the bus, and the suburban transit trains for years without incident, but one day, it just all fell to pieces.

I was riding to work with my husband and there were shuttle buses running for part of our normal train ride. I got on the bus and off we went. It wasn't overly crowded, and traffic wasn't particularly bad, but I felt anxious. About ten minutes into the ride, I started to sweat; I couldn't control my breathing, I felt like the walls were closing in, and I started to shake uncontrollably. I freaked out so bad that I felt like I was going to throw up and I made my husband get off the bus with me; in a not-so-nice section of town, I might add.

I had never had a panic attack before, but I surely had one that day. This scene would repeat itself nearly ten years later, when, while my car was in the shop, I had a panic attack again on the bus. This time, the bus was stuck in traffic on the expressway, and I had no choice but to hold it together until we got to a stop. By the time I got off the bus, I was drenched with sweat and shivering and I immediately vomited.

I bring this up because many of us feel anxious or uneasy from time to time, and most people I know worry, at least occasionally, about something that's happening in their life. If you find that you are anxious all the time, or to the point where it is interfering with your life, you may find it necessary to talk to someone about your experiences.

Thankfully, for me, I can avoid the trigger that sets me off, i.e. the bus; but if anxiety is interfering with your ability to fully engage with your life, please know that you don't have to suffer. There are lots of great resources out there to help you learn to cope with your anxiety. Start with a look through some of these sites:

ADAA – Anxiety and Depression Association of America
www.adaa.org

Anxieties.com
www.anxieties.com

NIMH – National Institute of Mental Health
www.nimh.nih.gov

August 17th – Relaxation 101

Webster's dictionary defines relaxation as:

- *A way to rest and enjoy yourself*
- *Time that you spend resting and enjoying yourself*
- *Something that you do to stop feeling nervous, worried, etc.*

Karen Ann Kennedy defines relaxation as

*"An absolute non-negotiable thing that you
must practice for yourself every day!"*

Research has shown that people who learn to relax experience a myriad of benefits including:

- Increased blood flow to the muscles
- Reduced blood pressure
- More energy
- Fewer headaches and less pain
- A healthier immune system
- Decreased muscle tension
- Better sleep

Hmmm; this list looks a lot like the one that outlines the benefits of meditation! That's because meditation is a form of relaxation, but it's not the only form. I'm about to give you some really great relaxation tips and techniques, but before I do, let's talk about why relaxation is so important.

Relaxation plays an important role in stress relief. Let's go way back to the caveman days and talk about fight or flight. Our bodies are engineered to either run in the face of danger, or, stay and fight for survival. This was an important skill back when saber tooth tigers were roaming the Earth.

But now, those tigers are no longer in existence and walking around in a state of constant survival mode is terribly unhealthy.

When we are always on alert, our bodies are continuously exposed to the detrimental effects of stress. There are behavioral symptoms such as, lack of appetite, sleep issues, and nervous habits like biting your nails; cognitive symptoms such as, memory problems, an inability to concentrate and constant worrying; emotional symptoms like feeling moody, overwhelmed, isolated, and depressed; and physical symptoms such as aches and pains, digestive issues, and a compromised immune system.

It's important to remember that relaxation and stress relief are not luxuries, they are necessities, and as I mentioned yesterday, if you are feeling really anxious, stressed, or overwhelmed, don't be afraid to reach out for help!

August 18th – Relaxation tips and techniques

What is relaxing to one person may not be relaxing to another. I know people who love to take a long drive out in the country; being behind the wheel for hours would stress me out. I like to go for a long distance run to clear my head; I have friends that would just as soon poke their eyes out with a hot poker.

The trick is to find the things that work well for you. How will you know they work? Do you feel better, calmer, and more relaxed while and after doing them? There you go!

There are lots of things you can try. Today, I want you to grab your journal and write out a list of 25 things you can do to help you relax. I'll even give you some ideas to get you started. Here are 50 things…yes 50 things…you can do to help you relax.

1. Take a walk
2. Sip some decaf, herbal tea
3. Eat a piece of good-quality dark chocolate
4. Nosh on something crunchy
5. Do a crossword puzzle

6. Take the dog for a walk
7. Pet a cat
8. Lie down for ten minutes
9. Count backwards from ten; or from one hundred if you're really stressed out
10. Close your eyes and visualize being at your favorite place
11. Put on some soft music
12. Massage your temples
13. Give yourself a hand massage
14. Sit in a chair and run your bare feet over a tennis ball
15. Take a warm bath
16. Take a hot shower
17. Take a cool shower
18. Jump into a swimming pool
19. Spend ten minutes sitting in the sun
20. Turn the lights up in your home
21. Watch a funny cartoon, TV show, or movie; and laugh… A LOT
22. Get up and stretch
23. Journal about how you're feeling
24. Dance around your house
25. Dig in the garden
26. Buy yourself some flowers
27. Try aromatherapy
28. Bake some cookies
29. Call a friend
30. Get a hug from a friend
31. Write a thank you note to someone
32. Eat an orange
33. Give yourself a pedicure
34. Take a nap
35. Exercise
36. Play with your pet

37. Hug a pillow
38. Play in the sand
39. Walk barefoot in the grass
40. Write down all the things you are grateful for
41. Drink a glass of cold water
42. Squeeze a stress-relief ball
43. Kick something (not someone)
44. Do something nice for someone else
45. Read an uplifting passage from a book
46. Brush your teeth
47. Put on something brightly colored
48. Don't forget to breathe
49. Chew gum
50. Look at pictures that make you smile

There you go. Now get started on your own list!

August 19th – Can yoga help?

Over the years, I have dipped a toe into the world of yoga, and as much as I'd love to say I practice it regularly, I've never quite been able to work it into my life. I haven't totally given up, I just haven't done it...YET!

Many of my friends and clients LOVE yoga, and I can totally see why. The health benefits are amazing and I've yet to meet a yogi that is stressed out and angry!

My yoga-loving friends all tell me that their fitness levels and flexibility have improved; some are using yoga to help manage chronic illnesses and conditions, and all of them have reported that they have reduced their stress levels.

There are all types of yoga to choose from; it's just a matter of finding the discipline that works best for you.

- There's **Bikram Yoga** which you do in 105 degree heat
- **Hatha Yoga** which is a more relaxing and gentle form of yoga
- **Yoga for runners** with specific movements that help improve your most-used running muscles
- **Vinyasa Yoga** that's all about flow and movement
- You could practice **Kundalini Yoga** to work your core or **Ashtanga Yoga** if you really want a physically demanding workout
- There's **Restorative Yoga** to help with relaxation and **Prenatal Yoga** for, well, you know, moms-to-be

The idea is to find the type that most interests you, find a reputable studio in your area where you can practice, and then practice!

August 20th – Can running help?
While I can't speak firsthand about yoga, I can definitely tell you all about running.

Running, for me, is as much about my mental health as it is about my physical health; maybe even more so.

Running releases endorphins that can make you feel less stressed and running helps you focus on your breathing.

The best thing running does for me is give me time to work out my issues. Some of the best business ideas I've had or creative ideas I've come up with have come during a long run. Nothing cures a bad day and a bad attitude more than lacing up my sneakers and hitting the open road.

Running may or may not have the same effect on you. Even if running does help you relax, don't expect that it will work that way in the beginning.

When I first started running, it was all I could do to control my breathing and think about anything besides the fact that I might die! Now that I've been at it for a while, I find that I can run and think and it relaxes me.

One word of caution, if you're running outside, you must always be aware of your surroundings. Don't get so caught up in your thoughts that you stop paying attention to traffic and people, etc.

If you're interested in running, start by looking for running clubs in your area and see if you can get involved with them. Running may not solve all your problems, but it's worth giving it a try!

August 21st – Quick stress busters

Quick! Your kid just dropped a full gallon of milk on the kitchen floor, the dog threw up his food all over the hallway, you can't find your left shoe, your husband is out on the road with a flat tire, and your in-laws are due to arrive on your doorstep in ten minutes.

Ever have a day like this? How can you possibly sit and meditate, go for a run, or haul yourself out to a yoga class in the midst of all this chaos? You can't! But, there are some quick things you can do to calm yourself down when you're in the thick of it.

1. Focus only on the most immediate issue at the moment. To me, in the scenario above, the most immediate issue is

getting the milk off the floor. If you start trying to focus on everything, you won't be able to focus on anything, and you'll find yourself walking around in circles stressed out about the entire picture. Ever hear the saying, "first things first?" That's what we're talking about here. Take care of the milk first, then move onto the dog puke, then find your shoe, etc. You can only do one thing at a time.

2. Do not forget to breathe. Ever notice when you are scared that you have a tendency to hold your breath? This is a natural response, but not a healthy one. In the moment of stress, make a conscious effort to breathe. You may even want to say the word to yourself over and over again so that you can focus on your breath and not the thing that is causing you stress. Once you start to breathe normally, you will start to relax and that can help you see things more clearly.

3. Do not make a small issue into a big issue. Speculation and overthinking can cause you to become more stressed out than you need to be. Okay, so your husband is out on the road with a flat tire. Suddenly, you start to think that he's in the middle of the road, that a tractor trailer is going to come by and rear end him, that it's going to rain and he's going to get wet and sick, that some unscrupulous tow truck driver is going to try to scam him out of money; WHOA, slow down. You don't know if any of these things are happening. So if you don't know whether or not they are happening in real life; why let them happen in your head?

4. Count to ten. This has helped me out of a jam a number of times. When I am feeling stressed and want to lash out, instead, I count to ten and focus on my breathing. While

my brain is focusing on the counting, it is letting go of the thoughts and feelings that are causing my stress.

5. Take a walk. Just the act of physically moving your body can help lower your stress levels. If you are in the middle of something stressful that you can't walk away from, even the act of pacing back and forth can help you expel some of that nervous energy.

August 22nd – Music therapy

Music has always played a huge role in my life, in both good times, and in bad. I have cried over more than my share of songs following a break-up; I listened to music to calm me down and distract me on the 36-hour flight I took to Saudi Arabia during Operation Desert Storm; and I've listened to my iPod to drown out the noise and cut down on my anxiety over a root canal.

I've also celebrated with music! Music has helped me cross the finish line at two full marathons and over a dozen half marathons; has kept me and my sister singing and laughing on a nine-hour drive to Ohio for my nephew's college graduation; and has served as the back drop at countless house parties, barbeques, baby showers, bridal showers, etc.

There's even a national organization dedicated to increasing awareness about music therapy; the American Music Therapy Association, www.musictherapy.org.

You don't need a ton of research to know how music affects you. Today, spend some time with your favorite tunes. Notice how much you enjoy the music; make yourself a playlist of music to pump you up, to calm you down, and to help you relax.

August 23rd – Aromatherapy

Have you ever noticed that just a whiff of a certain scent can instantly transport you to another time or place? While scent can evoke things in your memory, it can also improve your mood, help with concentration, and even affect your appetite!

I use aromatherapy essential oils all around my home. You must be careful; some of the oils are very potent and are not meant to be digested. Some are often so strong that they can irritate bare skin. Your best bet is to check the labels on your essential oils carefully before use. You can also do some research on aromatherapy and essential oils at www.naha.org, the website for the National Association for Holistic Aromatherapy.

Here are some ways to incorporate essential oils into your home:

- Mix a few drops of your favorite oil with some water in a spray bottle and use it as an air freshener.
- Add a few drops to a diffuser ring (which you can find at your local craft store) and sit it inside your lamp near the light bulb. The heat from the lamp will heat up the oil and leave your home smelling amazing. Can't find a diffuser ring? You can put a few drops of oil right on the light bulb.
- Add a few drops of lavender oil to your bath at night to help you get a restful sleep.
- Add a few drops of a citrus oil, like lemon, orange, or lime to your bath to energize you.
- Mix a few drops of tea tree oil into some warm water and baking soda and soak tired feet at the end of a long day; tea tree oil helps with foot odor.
- Cotton balls and essential oils are a terrific pair. If you have a problem with mice, put peppermint oil on some cotton balls and place them in areas where you've seen mice; hide

a cotton ball soaked in your favorite essential oil inside a dried flower arrangement to refresh it.

- If you're feeling tired, just open up a bottle of rosemary essential oil and take a whiff. Rosemary has been shown to promote alertness. Consider sending your college-bound kids off to school with a small bottle of rosemary for those late night study sessions.

Today, head down to your local health food store, Trader Joe's, or Whole Foods, and check out the essential oils available to you. Most of these stores have tester bottles where you can smell the oils before you buy them. Find some scents that you enjoy and try some of the tips above to add some scent to your home.

August 24th – Stress relief on the go

If you're someone that travels frequently for work, or even for fun, you probably know that traveling can be stressful. It's easy to relax when you have your favorite products and accessories at home, but when you travel, you may not have all of your favorites available.

Time is also a factor when traveling, especially for business. All-day conferences, late-night dinners, and nightcaps with colleagues may leave you feeling burned out and cranky. Tack onto this the joys of lost luggage, delayed flights, and unpredictable weather conditions, and it's enough to send even the most seasoned traveler into a spin.

Don't worry, if you're planning to take a late summer vacation, travel for work, or are planning to travel over the upcoming holiday season, I've got you covered.

Below are some of my favorite tips to bust stress on the go:

- If you're traveling and have to catch a plane, set your alarm for a half hour earlier than you think you need. That extra time will give you a chance to deal with any last-minute emergencies that come up. If everything goes smoothly, and you have extra time, use it to sit quietly for a few minutes and take deep breaths to relax yourself.

- Keep a list of everything you need to pack and cross each item off as it goes into the bag. My friends have made fun of me for years about this, but it stops me from having that panic of wondering if I actually put my emergency undies in the bag!

- If you're a nervous traveler (e.g. afraid of flying) take your journal with you and spend some time in the airport writing down all the things you're excited for upon reaching your destination (seeing friends or family, lying on the beach, or exploring a new museum) then, when stressful times hit during the journey, you can look at what you wrote and remind yourself that the hassle is worth it.

- If space in your carry-on bag allows, pack a light blanket from home, or something else from home that makes you feel secure and comfortable. Pack an eye mask for the plane if you plan to sleep. Don't want to carry liquid on the plane? Put a few drops of lavender oil on your eye mask at home and put it in a Ziploc bag to protect the scent. Then take your eye mask out on the plane and inhale deeply to help relax yourself.

- If you're on a long flight, be sure to get up and stretch every hour. Walk up and down the aisle of the plane or use the restroom so you can stretch your legs. Taking a long car ride? If you're the driver, be sure to stop at rest stops along the way and get out to stretch; if you're the passenger, do some light stretching while you are in the car, a few neck stretches, shrugging your shoulders, pointing and releasing your toes, and twisting in your seat will help.

- Limit caffeine and other stimulants before you travel. I find that I feel like I'm on high alert when I'm traveling, and that just adds to my stress levels. If this happens to you as well, be sure to limit your caffeine consumption to help you keep stress at bay, and be sure to hydrate properly. A few days before your trip, boost your water intake and be sure to catch a few more winks of sleep in preparation for your travels.

August 25th – Breathing exercises

We talked about the importance of breathing earlier this month when we talked about meditation, but you don't have to be in the practice of meditating to practice proper breathing. Paying attention to your breath can help relax you and calm you down when stress hits, and ensures that your body is getting the oxygen it needs to work at its optimum levels.

Have you ever noticed that when you get frightened or when you're extremely angry that you tend to hold your breath, or that your breathing becomes rapid so you are no longer taking deep breaths in and out? This is perfectly normal. Today, I want to give you three breathing exercises that you can do anywhere at any time to relax you and help you feel more in control.

1. Abdominal Breathing - Put one hand on your chest and the other on your stomach, take a deep breath in through the nose and make sure that your belly extends (not your chest). Then let the air out through your mouth and pull your stomach in. I've found that doing this in the doctor's office before a test or bloodwork has helped me to relax.

2. The Bellows Breath – Inhale and exhale rapidly through your nose, keeping your mouth closed. I do this ten times in a row and then on the last exhale, I breathe out all the way; then I inhale deeply for a count of five, exhale deeply for a count of five, and then start over. This is a noisy exercise, so I suggest doing it some place where you won't be embarrassed. I do this one in my car before I go to a stressful meeting; sometimes I do it at home before I go out for a run to help me clear my head.

3. Cooling Breath – Part your lips slightly and curl your tongue so it rests on the roof of your mouth. Breath in slowly through your mouth so you can feel the air hitting the underside of your tongue. I usually hold my breath there for a second or two before breathing out through my nose. I do this when I'm feeling physically hot, or when I'm angry. I practice this exercise often after a workout when I want to cool down.

Try all three and pick the exercise that you like the most. Use this as your "go to" exercise when your stress level rises and you need a way to relax and regroup.

August 25th – What is mindfulness?

If you do a Google search for mindfulness you'll see lots of definitions, including the Webster's definition that defines mindfulness as, "the practice of maintaining a nonjudgmental state of heightened or complete awareness of one's thoughts, actions, or experiences on a moment-to-moment basis."

My own definition of mindfulness is very simple:

> *"Mindfulness is paying attention, on purpose, to everyone and everything that is happening in the present moment."*
> *~Karen Ann Kennedy*

For me this means giving 100% of my attention to whatever is happening RIGHT NOW. If I'm out having coffee with friends, it's focusing 100% on what my friends are saying, how I'm feeling, how the coffee tastes, how the air feels on my face. It's not thinking about what I have to do when I leave there, it's not checking my email on my phone, it's not letting my attention drift back to something that happened yesterday, or ahead to something that is going to happen tomorrow.

My quest to practice mindfulness was born from the fact that I have ADHD. If I don't "pay attention on purpose," my mind will naturally wander to the point that I am not paying attention at all to what's happening right in front of me. This does not mean that I don't want to give my friends the respect of paying attention, it's just that my mind will naturally go off somewhere else and I have to be vigilant about pulling it back.

A lovely "side effect" to my practice of mindfulness has been an increased appreciation for things that would normally have gotten by me in the past. If I'm sitting at the park, instead of incessantly checking my email, I take the time to think about the leaves on the trees. I listen to the sound they make when the air rustles them; I look at the different colors; I watch the squirrels run up and down the tree. This brings me fully into the moment and I find myself enjoying the time and relaxing, instead of thinking about things that have either happened already, or are yet to happen.

Multitasking has been the death of mindfulness in my opinion. We rarely do one thing at a time, and that robs us of enjoying the experience of doing even the simplest of things, like eating a meal or watching our children play in the park.

I have a very simple exercise to help you practice mindfulness today. I call it "Mindful Coffee," but you can use tea, or wine, or even water, if you're not a coffee fan.

Here's how it goes:

Brew yourself a cup of coffee, paying close attention to every single step along the way. I open the bag and sniff the coffee, enjoying the aroma. I put the coffee into the machine and I watch as it drips. I continue to smell it, I listen to the noise of the drip, I let myself anticipate how it will taste. When the coffee has brewed, I pour in my coconut sugar and coconut milk and watch how the color of the coffee changes from dark black to creamy caramel.

Before I sip the coffee, I take time to prepare my spot. Usually, I'll sit in my office on my comfy chair and if it's a nice day, I'll take a moment to enjoy the breeze coming through the open window. I take a deep breath and savor the aroma once more before I take my first sip.

I let the coffee swirl around in my mouth for a minute and then I swallow it. I don't think about anything else except the way the coffee tastes, the warmth of it, the breeze blowing. In that moment, it is all about the coffee and my experience of drinking the coffee.

Sometimes "Mindful Coffee" can last for ten minutes, sometimes it can go on for twenty minutes, but at least once during the day, I have practiced the art of being fully present in the moment. I try to extend that exercise to other moments in the day as well, to keep me 100% alert and in tune with what's happening.

Try "Mindful Coffee" today if you can, and see how it feels for you. Don't forget to grab your journal afterwards and write down your experience.

August 27th – Let it go.
Not just a popular song from a Disney movie; learning to "let it go" can be a powerful tool to help you relax and live a more peaceful life, too.

I can be as stubborn as a dog with a bone when I want my way. Don't we all want to get our way? I've learned that some things are not worth fighting over and letting them go creates a sense of peace in my life.

As I'm getting older, I realize that nothing is perfect and I don't have to stress over every little detail. My obsessive need for perfectionism has caused me to get stressed out over the smallest most inconsequential things in life, and has robbed me of peace and joy.

Letting things go doesn't mean letting people walk all over you or take advantage of you. It means picking your battles. I like to do things in a particular way, but when my friends do it a different way, it doesn't mean either one of us is right or wrong, it's just different. The old me would obsess about it and want to "fix" it, the new me, the "let it go" me understands that at the end of the day, it really doesn't matter.

Today, think of some things that you can let go of. Maybe your husband folds the laundry differently than you; maybe your wife takes Oak Avenue to get to work and you prefer Beech Street; stop and ask yourself if it really matters! If it doesn't; let it go!

August 28th – The benefits of massage

There has been extensive research done over the years about the benefits of massage. Few can argue that massage just feels good, and it also can:

- Alleviate specific pain in the body such as low back pain and migraine headaches
- Increase your immunity by stimulating lymph flow
- Ease your dependence on pain medications
- Help to exercise and strengthen your muscles
- Help athletes recover from strenuous workouts
- Help ease the symptoms of anxiety and depression
- Release those feel-good endorphins

Clients that I've talked to who believe in regular massages report that they sleep better, feel less anxious, have more energy during the day, enjoy improved concentration, and feel more limber and physically healthier.

I don't know about you, but I don't have the funds to get regular massages, so I've discovered self-massage as a way to relax and unwind. Certainly, if you have a partner or friend that you can trade massages with, go for it! That's a lovely way to spend an evening, but if you live alone, like I do, don't abandon the idea of a massage just yet. Try out a few of my self-massage techniques.

Hand Massage
1. Hold your left hand up, palm facing out, and use your right hand to pull your fingers back towards your wrist. Feel that stretch? Do the same thing with your other hand until you feel the stretch.
2. Rotate your wrists in a circular motion first clockwise, then counterclockwise until they feel loosened up.
3. Spread your fingers wide for five seconds then curl your fingers down toward your palm. Repeat a few times until your fingers feel loose.

Foot Massage
1. Soak your feet in some warm water and tea tree oil and then dry thoroughly. Sit on the floor in a butterfly stretch, with your feet touching each other and your knees down to each side. Run your thumbs up the soles of your feet from your heel to your toes.
2. Run your thumbs on the top of your foot from your ankle to your toes.
3. Grab each toe with your thumb and forefinger and wiggle it around. Repeat on the other foot.
4. For an extra enjoyable experience, use a thick lotion or massage cream on your feet, paying special attention to dry, cracked heels.

Additional Foot Massage:
1. As a runner, I find this massage very soothing after a long run where my feet take a beating. I do the same massage as listed above, then, I finish off with a frozen water bottle.

2. Take your frozen water bottle and lay it on the floor underneath your left foot. Gently roll your foot up and down the water bottle, giving extra attention to the arch in your foot. Repeat this step with your right foot.

3. When I want an extra cooling boost, I put peppermint lotion or gel on my feet and then roll the water bottle under both arches. It instantly cools me off and soothes my feet.

Hip Massage

1. Lie on the floor on your back with your knees bent. Gently let both knees fall to the floor on one side. Using your hands, reach down and gently massage the hip that is facing up. This is one where a good massage oil will help you get a deep massage.

2. Use your thumbs to rub around your hip bone in a circular motion until you've massaged the entire hip area.

3. When finished, let your knees fall to the opposite side and repeat on the other hip.

Back Massage

1. Take a ball, any size from a tennis ball to a basketball, and press it up against the wall with your back.

2. Move your body around in a circular motion to move the ball around.

3. I find the tennis ball to be most effective when there is a particular area of my back or shoulders that needs attention; I use the basketball for an overall massage.

Neck and Scalp Massage

1. Sitting comfortably on the couch or a chair, gently bend from the waist and allow your head to rest between your legs.

2. If you have long hair, you can flip your hair over to expose your neck.

3. Using your thumbs, gently massage the back of your neck in upward strokes towards your head.

4. Using all of your fingers and both thumbs, gently massage your head, working your fingers in a circular motion from the back up your head up to your forehead. Alternate between pressing your fingers deep into your head, and gently rubbing your head.

There you have it! A massage that you can give yourself at home. Try some of these moves and see which ones are the most enjoyable for you.

August 29th – The relaxing bath

Nothing seems to relax me as much as a nice hot bath at the end of a stressful day. Whenever I have extra time, my bath becomes more like an event than a way to get clean. There are a million ways to treat yourself to a relaxing bath; here's what I do.

1. Make sure the bathroom is clean. It's impossible to relax when the room is a mess.

2. Start the bath water (as hot as you like it) and add one cup of baking soda, one cup of Epsom salts, and a few drops of your favorite essential oil (I use lavender).

3. Turn off the lights and light some candles.

4. Put on some soft music.

5. Sink into the tub.

I usually do some breathing exercises while I'm in the tub for added relaxation. I try visualization if I'm having a really hard time unwinding; picturing myself on a beach or out on a lake. I soak until the water turns cold and then I get out, lather myself up with lotion, dry off, and slip into my jammies.

One last tip, after getting out of the tub, I usually treat myself to a glass of cold water with lemon. I know many people that enjoy their bath with a glass of wine or tea, but I find that a hot soak makes me feel thirsty and dehydrated afterwards. If that's your thing, go for it!

The next time you find a few minutes to yourself, try treating your-self with a relaxing bath to destress and help you relax.

August 30th – Relaxing beauty

As a rule of thumb, I try to keep my beauty routine down to the bare minimum. Most mornings I can get out the door in twenty minutes flat, and that includes time to do my hair and my makeup. It's not that I don't like to look nice, it's just that over the years I have pared down my beauty routine a lot.

There are lots of ways that you can use your beauty routine as a way to relax. I employ some of these tips when I have extra time, am feeling like I need a little extra TLC, or when I'm getting ready for a special occasion or event that requires me to do a little more primping than usual.

- Sit comfortably on a chair and flip your head over between your knees. Brush your hair from the nape of your neck down to the tips of your hair in one long continuous stroke. Brush as many times as it feels good to do so, then flip your head back up and brush your hair from your forehead down to the ends of your hair with the same long strokes.

- Fill your bathroom sink with hot water and add a few lemon slices, some fresh rosemary or mint, or an essential oil that energizes you. Lean into the sink and put a towel over your head to keep the steam in. Keep your face close to the water (without touching it) and breathe in the scents. The steam will help open your pores and make your skin feel soft and smooth. After about five minutes, let the water go down the drain and rinse your face with cold water.

- When applying lotion to your face, start with your neck and apply the lotion in long strokes working from the base of your neck up to your jawline. Apply lotion to chin, cheeks, and forehead in a circular motion, treating yourself to a mini facial massage.

- When applying lotion to your body, spend a few extra minutes massaging areas that might need extra attention, such as your calves, thighs, shoulders, upper arms, and even your derriere.

I don't recommend trying to do this on a Monday morning when you're rushing out the door to get to work, but if you're planning a date night with your spouse, or are going to an event like a reunion or a wedding, the extra primping helps make the event seem even more special, and the extra pampering will have you looking and feeling great!

August 31st – Make relaxation a daily habit.
Don't wait until you are already stressed out to practice some of the relaxation tips we went over this month. Sneaking a few minutes into your every day to help you relax and unwind can help prepare you to better deal with life's annoying and stressful moments as they come up.

Think of at least one or two things you can do each day and strive to do them at a certain time so they become part of your daily routine. Perhaps you can meditate in the morning, take a walk at lunch, and have a relaxing bath each evening. Maybe your schedule is really hectic so you do some breathing exercises in the morning, repeat them again at lunch, and then practice mindfulness as you prepare dinner for your family.

Whichever methods work best for you, the key is to try to incorporate them into your daily routine so you can make self-care, rest, and relaxation a habit.

My August to-do list:

- ° I took the "How Stressed Are You?" quiz
- ° I set my intention for wanting to practice meditation
- ° I established a time to meditate
- ° I established a space to meditate
- ° I went through the ten-day meditation sequence
- ° I practiced walking meditation
- ° I wrote out my list of ten things that help me relax
- ° I explored the various types of yoga
- ° I spent time listening to my favorite music
- ° I tried a few essential oils
- ° I practiced the breathing exercises and found one or two that I really enjoy
- ° I did the "Mindful Coffee" exercise
- ° I thought of some of the things I could let go of in my life
- ° I practiced self massage
- ° I had a relaxing bath experience
- ° I tried at least one of the relaxing beauty methods

SEPTEMBER – KEEP LEARNING

As a kid, I went to school because that's what everybody did. There were parts of school that I enjoyed, and lots of parts that I didn't. As an adult, I learned to appreciate the value of education, both formal and informal.

I consider myself a life-long learner and a life-long student (although my wallet doesn't always support that thinking!) I enjoy learning new things and opening my mind to new challenges and new possibilities.

Now, I look for every learning opportunity I can find. Let's start to explore the concept of learning together this month.

> *"The mind, once stretched by a new idea, never returns to its original dimensions."*
> ~Ralph Waldo Emerson

September 1st – The lifelong learner mindset

I'll be the first to admit that I was not a good student in school. As an adult with ADHD, I realize that growing up I was a child with ADHD, but it wasn't socially recognized back then. When you got out of line in school in my day, your mom just cracked you on the butt and you did your best to stop "acting up."

Even in my college years, I don't think I fully appreciated the value of education and learning. I enjoyed what I was studying and I was at a school I really wanted to be part of, but I still didn't appreciate the value of what I was learning.

Now, I know how important education is, but more than what can be learned in a classroom, I've discovered the joy of informal learning.

One of the most effective ways to adopt the lifelong learning mindset is to look at every challenge and every setback as a learning opportunity, and to welcome each new experience as a chance to learn about something new in life. So this month, open your mind to the world around you and think about all the wonderful things there are in life to learn about.

September 2nd – What do you want to learn?

Grab your journal and find a few quiet minutes to sit down and write a list of some things you've always wanted to learn. There's no set number of things for this list; you can have twenty things, ten things, six things, or just one thing that you want to learn more about. I always wanted to learn martial arts, and when I got the chance to take classes, I was really grateful for the opportunity.

I have a few things still on my list. I want to learn salsa dancing and swing dancing; I want to learn to speak French; and I want to learn to play the piano, even if it's just being able to get through "*Chopsticks.*"

Write down in your journal the things that you want to learn.

September 3rd – Is it for pleasure or purpose?

Looking at the list of things you want to learn, you'll need to decide whether you are learning for pleasure, or, are you needing to learn for a purpose; such as to advance your career, get a promotion at work, or for the express purpose of being able to teach it to someone else?

All of the things on my list are for pleasure, but there have been many times in the past when I've had to learn things for my work. Both are equally important in my life, but different in many ways. Often when learning something for work, there's a deadline for completion and some type of test or benchmark at the end.

In the end, it doesn't really matter why you are learning, but knowing why may help you make some decisions about timing, financial commitment, time commitment, and the like.

September 4th – Do your homework.

Today, I want you to spend some time researching what you want to learn. Find out what's involved, what kind of classes are in your area, how much time you need to dedicate to learning, and what the financial implications are. Today is not meant to be about hardcore action plans or action, it's about daydreaming online and allowing your mind to explore the different options available to you.

You may find that what you are interested in becomes even more attractive the more you explore, you may be completely turned off by the activity or class, or, you may end up finding something else that you have even more interest in. Before you begin your search, be prepared for any possibility, and keep an open mind.

September 5th – Gather your resources.

Now is the time to get serious about figuring out what you will need in order to learn whatever it is you want to learn. If you want to learn to paint, you may need to find a class, and you'll certainly need to buy some art supplies.

If you want to learn salsa dancing, like I do, you'll have to find a friend who can teach you, or a class that you can take.

I always say that people make the best decisions when they have the most information, and now is the time to get the information you need. You may find that you can't make the time commitment needed to really learn this particular skill right now, or, you may find that you want to just try it out a few times to see if it's what you really want to do.

I always thought I wanted to take Zumba. It just looks like so much fun, and the people are smiling and laughing. I love music and dancing, so it seemed like it would be perfect for me. I tried a class once and realized that it was NOT for me. Not because it wasn't fun, or because the instructor was bad, but because I am so unco-ordinated and I don't know my left from my right!

When everyone was moving to the left, I was going to the right. If they were moving forward, I was going backward. By the time I got a move down, the group was already onto the next thing and I left feeling frustrated. I'm glad I didn't plunk down a lot of money to go all out with Zumba classes.

Start gathering your resources today and figure out what you truly need to start learning your craft.

September 6th – Gather your tribe.

Do you have friends or family members who want to learn the same things you do? Some activities just lend themselves to being group activities. When I first started running, I would run with my friend Dana in the mornings. Having a buddy helped me stick with it and stay focused, and it was a way for us to spend time together.

There was a time when I took karate with several friends and I found that to be fun as well. Having friends to take on challenges with is sometimes a fun way to learn new things. I know friends that have taken painting classes together, I have a friend who is learning another language with his wife, and plenty of couples I know take dance classes together.

Deciding to share your learning experience with others is a really personal thing. You may want to use your activity as a way to disconnect from others and take some time for yourself. Only you can decide if a group learning experience is right for you. If you think it is, reach out to some of your family and friends and gather your tribe.

September 7th – The power of reading

I am an avid reader. I have committed myself to reading for at least an hour every day. I read mostly personal development-type books, business books, and books on leadership, and occasionally will read a good fiction book, just for fun.

Even if you aren't reading for the express purpose of learning, reading anything for any reason will help you enhance your learning and self-development. Reading is a great way to travel the world without ever buying a plane ticket; learn about a new culture from the comfort of your own home; or experience what it's like to climb a mountain, run a marathon, or run with the bulls by reading about the experience of those who have already done it.

See if you can carve out even just a half hour every day to sit down and read. It doesn't matter what you read, it just matters that you carve out the time to read. Start small and see if you can work your way up. If all you can squeeze in is the time it takes you to read this book every day, that's fine, but see if you can add in a half hour of reading, and work your way up to an hour.

Today, ask a few friends for some book recommendations, or take a trip to your local bookstore and spend some time browsing the shelves. Buy a few titles that interest you, and try to spend some time every day reading for a little bit.

September 8th – Don't let money stop you.
Sometimes the thing that stops us from learning what we want to learn is the money that it takes to learn it. To be sure, some things you want to pick up will have costs associated with them. There are supplies, or tools, or classes, or equipment that you may need in order to do it right.

Now is the time to think outside the box. Perhaps there is an opportunity to trade for services. Maybe you can't afford to pay for swing dancing lessons, but you offer to clean the dance studio twice a week in exchange for free classes. Maybe you want to learn to make a soufflé and you have a friend who would be willing to teach you.

There was a time when taking karate classes became too expensive for me, but I didn't want to quit. I talked to the owner of the karate studio and was able to barter to keep attending class. If there's something you want to learn but you don't have the funds to take it on, look around and see what other options are available to you. Don't let money stop you from learning what you want to learn. A little creativity could get you exactly what you want and need.

September 9th – Learning is a gift.

Education and learning is a true gift in life. The ability to be able to learn new things and then apply those in the quest to live the best life you can live is a true blessing. We are lucky to live in a place that offers so many opportunities to learn and grow; and it's important to remember that education and learning are not readily available to many others in other parts of the world.

If you take a moment to think about all the things you already know in life, it truly is amazing. It's even more amazing to think about all the things you still DON'T know. There's a whole world out there full of things that you have yet to experience.

There are things that I still want to learn and know more about, but plenty of things that I'd be okay never finding out more about (i.e. swimming with sharks, or hunting).

Whenever you have the opportunity to embark on a journey of education and learning, approach it with a spirit of gratitude and go into the situation with an open mind. Be a sponge and soak up all you can.

September 10th – Learning is self-improvement.

When I started the journey of writing this book, there were very definite reasons for structuring it the way I did. By giving you a passage to read every day, it was my hope that it would keep self-improvement at the top of your mind.

Even if you only spend a few minutes every day with the book, that is a few minutes each day that you are dedicating to your own self-improvement, and that hopefully will inspire you to do a little more for yourself each day.

Keeping self-improvement om the forefront, to me, means spending a little bit of time each day doing something that helps you become a better version of yourself. Enhancing your skills and life experience through learning is a great way to help you grow as a person. We only have a few more months until the end of your best year yet, so continue working your way through the book until you reach the very end. And go you!

September 11ᵗʰ – Finding the fun in learning

Let's be honest here, everything that you aspire to or need to learn in life is not going to be fun. A few years back I needed to study to earn my certification in human resources management for my job. While I love my job, going to school one night a week for four hours at a time after working all day was not the most fun thing I've ever done. And spending four hours talking about employment law, collective bargaining agreements, and compensation and benefits was not exactly buzzworthy.

Nevertheless, I tried to make the best of the experience by making my time in class as much fun as I could. I bought the most fun notebooks and pens I could find, spent some time getting to know my classmates; on random weeks I'd bring cookies for everyone, and I'd always participate in class discussions so I could get the full experience.

Just because the subject matter isn't fundamentally fun, it doesn't mean you can't make the learning process fun.

As a corporate trainer, I've had to give classes on some pretty serious subjects like incivility and workplace harassment and discrimination laws. While I respect the seriousness of the subject matter, I also know that infusing some fun helps the participants retain the information.

Whenever you have the opportunity, try to find the fun in learning.

September 12th – How we learn

Because I work mostly with adults, I've spent a good amount of time studying how adults learn. I've learned that there are three distinct types of adult learners:

Visual learners prefer to see what they are learning. They are people that respond well to visual aids such as PowerPoint presentations, charts, graphics, and pictures that represent the main points being made. Visual learners also need written instructions if they are expected to master a skill and be able to apply the skill long after the learning process has ended.

Auditory learners like to learn by hearing information. This can be done through audio tapes or lectures. Auditory learners can benefit greatly by having someone talk them through the steps of a project while they actually perform the task. Having the instructions told to them helps them remember the information when they repeat the task on their own later.

Kinesthetic learners need to actually move around, touch things, and perform the tasks. They generally don't do well with lectures and discussion, they need to be able to have a hands-on experience.

The first step to really embracing learning is to figure out which type of learner you are. Some people will have elements of all different types, but there is usually one prevailing type that comes through. I am a kinesthetic learner that enjoys a good lecture from time-to-time.

Once you know what type of learner you are, you'll be able to go ahead and tackle your specific activity or class in the way that best suits you.

September 13th – Awe and wonder

Opening your eyes to the world around you and appreciating the wonder of the little things in life is another wonderful way to embrace learning. Think about the miracles that happen every day. The sun always rises and sets; the ocean ebbs and flows; the moon and the stars come out at night; and the world continues to turn.

Ever wonder why these things happen? It's fun sometimes to dig a little into the things that we take for granted. I never gave much thought to the fact that my heart beats all day every day, and that I never have to think about how my lungs work; they just do.

When I was in the middle of my nutrition studies, I studied a lot about the human body on my own and found it fascinating to learn more about how it works.

Today, grab your journal and make note of at least three things that happen every day in your life and then make it a point to dig down deep and learn more about them. It's a great way to pique your interest in learning and to find out more about what makes the things in your life tick.

September 14ᵗʰ – The child's mind

Have you ever watched a little kid try a new food for the first time? Or go to their first movie? Or go to the beach for the first time? I had a lot of opportunity to experience things all over again through my nephew when he was a baby. It was fun to watch the look on his face when he tried a new food, or how excited he was when his toes touched the sand or when we took our first train ride.

Kids get excited about every new experience because they haven't yet been jaded by the things that could go wrong. They just know that they are curious about what's going on and they want to experience the things that they see others engaging in.

At some point in life, we start to think about the things that could go wrong. If I try ice skating, I may fall and break my wrist and then I won't be able to work. If I eat something I haven't eaten before, it might make me sick. If I try learning how to cook, I might burn myself.

I'm not suggesting that you throw caution to the wind and just run out there and engage in dangerous or risky activities, but I do want you to think about limiting beliefs that hold you back from trying the things you really want to do.

When you want to embark on something new, take some time to think about the risks versus the rewards and then decide on whether it's something you want to take on. Don't be afraid to try some new things., and approach them with the mind of a child, with the utmost curiosity and wonder.

September 15ᵗʰ – No education is a waste.

Many, many years ago, I went to school to be a Pastry Chef. Being a kinesthetic learner, the thought of sitting in a classroom for four years of college sounded like torture to me. I wanted to learn a trade and be able to move around, work with my hands, and be creative.

Being a Pastry Chef is a far cry from being a Certified Health Coach, and people often remark, "Isn't it a shame that you wasted all that education in cooking school?"

I actually don't feel like any education is a waste. I may not be doing what I went to school to do, but I learned a lot during my time in cooking school and I don't feel at all like it was time wasted.

Throughout life, you'll learn lots of different things at different times. The truth of the matter is most of the people I know are not currently working in the field that they went to school for; and that's okay!

I've had lots of different jobs over the years and with each different role, I've had to learn new things and more things. I'm glad that I have had the opportunity to expand my knowledge base though my collective experiences. I've been a cook, a waitress, an HR Director, a soldier, and a magician's assistant!

Whenever you have a chance to pick up a new skill set, take it! You may never apply it literally to your life, but you will surely learn something new that may help you as you move through your life.

September 16th – Learning is growing.
We're halfway through September. I hope by now, you've figured out what new things you might want to learn and have done some research to figure out what you'll need to start learning this new skill.

Learning is a form of growing, and with each new thing you learn, there is an opportunity to grow. Once you've learned something, you can't "unlearn" it. You may forget some things along the way, but you really can't unlearn.

Sometimes this learning and growing can be painful. As I've continued to go through the years and learn more about myself, I've had to make some difficult decisions about what is really best for me and what works well in my life. The hardest thing I ever did was to be honest with myself about my life and then start to make changes.

Today, I want you to spend time writing down what's working in your life, and what's not working. If there's a chance someone else might see this, do not put it in your journal. You want to be able to write honestly, so put it on a piece of paper that you can destroy after the exercise if you must.

Learning about yourself is the ultimate exercise in personal growth. Take time today to answer some of the following questions:

1. What is working well in my life?
2. What is not working in my life?
3. What do I like to do?
4. What don't I like?
5. What am I willing to put up with?
6. What am I absolutely unwilling to put up with?
7. What are some areas where I am experiencing positive growth?
8. What are the areas where I feel stunted?
9. What changes do I know I need to make that I've been unwilling to make?
10. What in my life is currently causing me the most pain?

September 17th – Sneak a little learning into your every day.
Whenever I find myself with a few minutes of downtime, I like to play word games, or problem-solving games to exercise my brain. Whenever there's a chance to learn something new, I jump at it.

Sneaking in a little everyday learning doesn't have to be very complicated or take up a lot of time. Get yourself a word-of-the-day calendar, or visit a website like www.freerice.com that not only allows you to expand your vocabulary, but donates rice to countries in need each time you play.

The goal is to make learning a little bit every day a daily habit.

September 18th – Expand your world.
When I was a kid, going to the beach each summer for family vacation was the highlight of my year. In my little six-year-old world, there were really only a few places that existed; my house, school, the grocery store, my best friend's house, and the beach. It never occurred to me that there was a whole world out there.

When we started to learn about different cities and different countries in school, I started to wonder what these places were like. When I graduated high school, I enlisted in the Army and went off to basic training in South Carolina. Talk about expanding my little world!

Over the years, I've been fortunate to travel to places like Paris and London and Jamaica; and I certainly hope I'm not done yet!

Traveling always takes two things that there never seems to be enough of; money and time. Although I haven't been able to physically get to many of the places I dream about, whenever I need a mini vacation, I log onto my computer and I take a virtual vacation.

283

Just recently, my friend Gina and I took an online "e-vacation" to Bali!

It's fun to learn about other cities, countries, and cultures, and I try my best to go on these e-vacations at least once or twice a week. Not only do I get to learn lots of new things, but it's relaxing to look at some of the beautiful countries and get away from every day stresses for a few minutes.

Think about some exotic locations that you'd like to visit or learn more about and then go ahead and take your own "e-vacation." If you really want to get into it, make a pina colada before you "travel" to Hawaii; dine on some fish and chips for a jaunt over to London; or put some reggae music on as you look at the beautiful sites of Jamaica.

September 19ᵗʰ – Reality check

While I'm a fan of learning and trying new things, I'm also a realist! There are some things that (if I'm being honest) I know are not smart for me and because of that, I have a healthy respect for which things I want to try.

Since I'm deathly afraid of heights, I'm not interested in trying skydiving. Some have told me I should try it, as a way to face down my fear, and while that may work for some people, I can tell you that it's not happening for me.

I've found that people can get very passionate about hobbies and activities that they love, but that doesn't mean it's the right thing for everyone. I love marathon running, but have lots of friends that have no desire to run that long and that far. As much as I love running, I'm not interested in mud runs, color runs, or obstacle runs;

although many of my well-meaning friends tease me about doing them all the time.

When you want to learn something new, take some time to be honest with yourself about what it all entails. If your friends indulge in a hobby that you can't afford to partake in, or you don't feel like you can physically tackle, you should be honest with them about it. Instead of focusing on things that you can't do, focus your energy on things that you can do and that you like to do!

September 20th – Utilize the KISS principle.

Are you familiar with the acronym KISS? Keep It Simple, Silly! One of the most fascinating things I've seen in working with my clients is their amazing ability to make things 100% more complicated than they need to be.

Life is hard! Why not try to make things as easy for yourself as possible? You can apply the KISS principle to most anything in your life, and that includes how you learn.

If you're about to embark on something new; learning a new language, computer program, or learning how to do something physical, like skiing or snowboarding, here are three simple ways to put the KISS principle into practice:

1. Ask someone that has learned this before you. Often, when you talk to someone who has already learned the skill that you want to learn, they can tell you lots of stories about what they did wrong in the beginning. The beauty of this is that it can help keep you from repeating the same mistakes. Learning from someone else is like taking a master class in learning, because you can cut out a lot of time and errors in the beginning.

2. Check out more than one avenue. Let's say you want to learn a new language; you don't want to just buy the first computer program or sign up for the first class that you stumble upon in your town. You want to check out all the ways of learning that are available to you so you can choose the best one for you. Don't limit yourself to just one way of doing things! You can take that class at the local community college while you work your way through language-learning software on the side.

3. Break up a large learning objective into manageable chunks. Patience will surely be your friend when you are learning something new. When I first began learning Tae Kwon Do, I was frequently frustrated when I wasn't able to pick up on a certain move that I needed. One of my instructors, Sensei Mark, would always say, "Stop saying you 'can't' do it. It's not that you can't; it's just that you haven't gotten it…YET!" That really stuck with me! Some of the things you need to learn may come really easy for you, and at other times, progress may seem like it will never come. Don't allow the frustrating moments to keep you from following through. Break up the learning process into manageable chunks that you can easily manage, and don't be afraid to just get started!

> *"Faith is taking the first step even when you*
> *don't see the whole staircase."*
> *~Martin Luther King, Jr.*

September 21st – If not now; when?

We often put off things we want to do because we are too busy or don't have enough money. I challenge you today to go back to the beginning of the month and think about something you said you really wanted to do and then ask yourself this question:

If not now; when?
~*Karen Ann Kennedy*

As I get older, and life gets busier and busier, I think about all the things I have wanted to do and I feel a little sad for not starting some of them sooner. Now to be sure, it's never too late to start something new; I started karate in my thirties and ran my first marathon as my 40th birthday present to myself. But I do wish that I had started these things much sooner in life.

"In the end, it's not the years in your life that count. It's the life in your years."
~*Abraham Lincoln*

If you haven't yet done any of the action steps to get you started on learning what you want to learn, grab your journal and let's answer these questions:

- What is keeping you from moving forward?
- Is there a way to get creative in learning what you want to learn? Can you trade services with someone to get your training for free? Can you swap babysitting services with a neighbor to buy you more time to devote to your learning?
- Is this really the right time for you to pursue this endeavor? If not, commit to looking at your calendar and figuring out the right time.

And then, ask yourself this really big question. On a scale from one to ten:

> *How bad will I feel a year from now if I don't do anything today to start learning what I've always wanted to learn?*

If learning something new is really important to you, do what you can to find a way to make it happen! You'll likely enjoy what you're doing, and you'll be proud of yourself as you begin to learn and master the skill.

September 22nd – The falsehood of failure

When I work with my clients and talk to them about their dreams and goals, the two most quoted reasons for not moving ahead are lack of time and lack of money. But I find when I dig a little deeper, that one of the biggest things that holds people back is a fear of failure.

I used to be petrified of failure, and that held me back from doing anything new and different. I'd ask myself questions like:

"What if I look foolish doing it?"
"What if I'm awful at it?"
"What if people laugh at me?"

This kind of negative, self-sabotaging thinking kept me from trying things that I probably would have really enjoyed.

What got me out of this negative thinking was the realization that our whole lives are spent doing new and different things. Think about all the new and different things you've done in your life:

- Learned to walk
- Learned to talk

- Learned to drive
- Started a new job, or two, or twenty
- Learned to read
- Learned to work a computer
- Made new friends

That list could fill up the rest of this book! We don't always fail, sometimes we get redirected, or we learn what doesn't work for us, or we change direction, or our interests change.

Approach every new learning opportunity with the idea that, if nothing else, you will get an opportunity to see something completely new and then decide if it's something that's right for you! Don't let the fear of what <u>might</u> happen, stop you from experiencing all the good that <u>could</u> happen.

September 23rd – What's holding you back?
Now that we've talked about failure and "if not now, when?", it's time to really examine what's holding you back if you're feeling stuck.

Grab your journal and turn to a blank page. We're going "old school" here! Draw a line down the center of the page and on one side we're going to capture the pros and the other side we're going to capture the cons.

What's good about embarking on a new learning opportunity, and what's not-so-good about it?

Go back to your entry on March 22nd and read through "exploring your 'why'." This is a good time to rediscover your "why muscles." If your desire to learn is for pleasure, your "why" will be really important. If you have to learn new things for school or for work, the "why" is already built in for you; you need to do it because it is a requirement.

But if you are embarking on this activity for pleasure, a strong "why" may help you break through whatever is holding you back.

On the next blank page of your journal, start writing down all the thoughts and feelings you have about the activity. Don't worry about punctuation or spelling, just write free flow all the things that are going through your mind. Once you've done that, grab a highlighter and read back what you wrote. Highlight the key words or phrases that stand out to you. This exercise will help you get to the root of what's holding you back and keeping you stuck.

By the way...the purpose of this whole month on learning is to help you live your life to the fullest by doing all the things you really want to do. It's about helping you think about the activities, hobbies, or educational opportunities you want to explore and then helping you take that first step to doing what you really want to do!

Go get 'em!

September 24th – Learning is empowerment.

> *"The mind, once stretched by a new idea, never returns to its original dimensions."*
> *~ Ralph Waldo Emerson*

Learning is truly one of the most empowering experiences a person can have. There is pride in mastering a new skill and a knowledge base that enhances your view of the world., and learning can boost your confidence.

After each new skill that I've learned in life, I've tackled the next new thing with even more confidence. Learning makes me feel powerful and in charge of my life. I recognize learning as something that is good for me, like eating right and exercising. The boost in confidence from learning new things has truly empowered me throughout my life.

Give yourself the power of learning and experiencing new and different things. Your mind will be expanded in ways that you can never imagine.

September 25th – Learning is pride.

At the time of this publication, I've been studying martial arts for six years. As I progressed, there was testing to get to my next rank or belt level. I remember my very first belt test and how nervous I was, but more than that, I remember the pride I felt when my instructor slipped that new belt around my waist.

Over the years, I got to experience that feeling many, many times, culminating in the day that my instructor slipped my black belt around my waist. In that moment, I felt a wash of pride that I've felt only a few select times before. It wasn't about the belt, it was about the hours of practice, learning and refining my skills. It was about the journey of gathering the knowledge and seeing how far I had come.

Anyone who has ever had an experience like mine will understand that feeling. Just writing about it gives me goose bumps! Take a few minutes to think back to those learning opportunities you've had in the past that have given you the goose bumps.

Getting your high school or college diploma, completing a certification course, performing a task that you've studied how to do for months and months. These things are all learning opportunities that can lead to moments of great pride.

September 26th – Know what you don't know.

There are three things that I have learned in life:

1. There are things that I know.
2. There are things that I don't know.
3. There are things that I don't know I don't know!

One of the most liberating things about realizing this in life is that it helps me keep an open mind about learning. I recently saw a quote that says:

> *"If you're the smartest person in the room,*
> *you are in the wrong room!"*
>
> *~Unknown*

So often we look at things we don't know as a weakness. I often wonder why. We live in a world where there are billions and billions of things to know. So many languages, cultures, sciences, types of art, species of animals, and the list goes on and on.

Stop for a minute and think about how ridiculous it is to expect yourself, or anyone else, to know everything about everything!

Acknowledging that you don't know what you don't know is healthy; the danger comes when we pretend that we know everything!

Admitting that you don't know something, asking lots of questions about an unknown topic, and asking someone else for help is not a sign of weakness. It's the sign of someone with an open mind that wants to learn all they can.

Don't be afraid to acknowledge that you don't know it all and allow yourself the freedom to learn more!

September 27th – Learn by teaching.
In my research on how adults learn, which I use extensively through my training and consulting, I've learned that there are four proven stages of competence.

1. Unconscious incompetence – When a person does not understand or know how to do something and they don't recognize that not knowing is holding them back. They don't understand how the skill they need to learn will help them in their daily lives. This, for me, as a trainer, is the toughest stage to break through. I have to help them understand the need for the learning.

2. Conscious incompetence – This is when a person does not understand or know how to do something, but they recognize the need to learn it. This happens often for me in corporate settings where someone may not necessarily want to learn a skill, but they recognize that they need to learn it in order to move up and continue to grow.

3. Conscious competence – This is when a person understands and knows how to do something, but they have to think about each step in the process of performing the task. This involves heavy concentration when working through the process, often requiring the person to read back on notes they may have taken or asking others to help them as they work through the process.

4. Unconscious competence – When a person knows how to perform a task so well that it becomes second nature to

them, they are experiencing unconscious competence. This is also the level at which a person can start to teach others what they know.

Going back to my martial arts experience, I learned so much as a student, but have learned so much more as a teacher. Things that I thought I had "aced" through my learning stumped me when it came time to break down the steps and help someone else learn them. It was a humbling experience to go through.

Teaching others what I know helped me to gain a deeper understanding of the task and helped me reach a whole new level of learning. This is a classic win-win situation in which I help someone else learn something they want or need to learn while increasing my understanding.

When you get to the point that you feel comfortable and confident in your abilities, spread the wealth by helping others learn as well. You'll feel terrific when you can use your knowledge to help others.

September 28th – There is always room to improve.
While perfection should never be your goal (unless maybe you are a brain surgeon), recognize that there is always room to improve on what you've learned.

One of the most dangerous places to be is the place where you feel you've got nothing left to learn. There is always more to learn and always room to improve on what you already know. Getting my black belt was not the end of my martial arts journey; it was just the beginning. While I am proud of all that I *do* know, I am acutely aware of all that I still *do not* know, and I actually get excited about all that is still left to learn.

I also get excited about being able to refine and polish what I've already learned. This is true in so many aspects of my life; from karate to cooking to writing. I am always excited when I find a way to make something even better than it was before.

When you've learned something new, enjoy the experience. Don't obsess about perfection, but be open to the concept of expanding your knowledge and improving on what you already know!

September 29th – You don't need to be the authority.
While I enjoy the role of teacher, mentor, trainer, and coach, I never see myself as the "authority" on things. I have found that taking the stance of authority, expert, or guru, keeps me from being open to learning.

I can't tell you how many training sessions I've led where I have learned something new from the participants. While I am definitely there to teach people (a responsibility I take very seriously) I am still open to the idea that someone in the room may be able to teach me something I don't know, help me see something in a different way, or give me a different perspective on something.

I am honored to be called upon to teach or coach someone and always give 100% to helping that person or group learn as much as they can so they can be at their best, but I approach each of these opportunities with an open mind and a hope that I'll also learn something new in the process.

If you find yourself in a position to teach, mentor, or coach someone, go into it with that same lifelong learner mindset that we talked about at the beginning of the month. You may be surprised at how this can enrich the experience for both you and the people you are educating.

September 30th – Make the world your classroom.

Can you believe we are at the end of September? Check in today with yourself about your learning mindset, the activities you still want to try, and if you've started to learn a new skill, give yourself a great big pat on the back for taking a step forward, and take some time to appreciate how much you've already learned,

I am not a "book smart" person. I was never a good student and found sitting in a classroom borderline painful, but I've learned so much through the course of my everyday living because I have consciously made the world my classroom!

There is learning to be done nearly every place you go, with every person you meet, and in every experience you go through. I've learned about relationships by having them and paying attention to them. I've learned about teaching and training by researching and then getting out there and doing it. And while I've learned much of my information about health and wellness through formal schooling, I've learned just as much from living life and seeing what works for me.

Today, as we close the month of September, I challenge you to find the learning opportunities in your everyday life. I challenge you to embrace new experiences and to open your eyes to the amazing world we live in. With the advent of the internet, learning is even easier today than ever before. As you move through your daily interactions and question things you see, hear, and experience, research them. Learn more about what's happening in the world around you.

See yourself as a lifelong learner!

My September to-do list:

- ○ I made a list of things that I'd like to learn more about
- ○ I have determined which things on my list are for purpose and which things are for pleasure
- ○ I did some research on my interests
- ○ I gathered my resources
- ○ I gathered my tribe
- ○ I got book recommendations
- ○ I have discovered my learning style
- ○ I completed the "awe and wonder" exercise and am making a conscious effort to learn more about the things I encounter in my daily life
- ○ I answered the questions about learning and growing
- ○ I found a way to sneak in a little bit of learning every day
- ○ I took an "e-vacation"
- ○ I've practiced applying the KISS principle
- ○ I answered the questions of "if not now; when"
- ○ I've explored what's holding me back from learning
- ○ I'm committed to making the world my classroom

OCTOBER – GET COOKING

Welcome Fall! I LOVE, LOVE, LOVE the Fall; the leaves changing, the fresh air, the bright colors, and of course, Halloween – my favorite holiday! I also love the fall because it's when I feel most like getting into the kitchen.

Who wants to cook during the dog days of summer? I eat lots of salads and fruit in the warm summer months, but as soon as the first leaves start to fall from the trees, it's time to hunker down with hearty soups and stews, casseroles, fresh baked bread, and delicious baked desserts; all healthy of course!

So let's give the kitchen a good scrubbing, pull your pots and pans out of the cabinets, restock the cupboards and let's get cooking!

October 1ˢᵗ – Grab some cookbooks.

I know, I know, you can find tons of recipes online, but for me, there's just nothing quite like cracking open an actual cookbook, looking at the pictures, and flipping through the pages for inspiration (we'll talk about that in the coming days).

There are so many cookbooks out there, that you may not know where to start. The best place to start is in your own kitchen with the cookbooks you currently have. Take an inventory of your current cookbooks and decide if you need some new ones. Maybe you're just tired of the ones you have, or maybe there is a category of recipes that you're missing. You may have a lot of dessert cookbooks, but not a lot of cookbooks for soups or stews. Or maybe, like me, you had a lot of cookbooks but the way you cook and eat has changed and you need new ones to support your new lifestyle.

Below is a list of some of my favorite cookbooks to get you started:

"The Eat Clean Diet Cookbook" by Tosca Reno
"Forks Over Knives – The Cookbook" by Del Sroufe
"Salads" by Elsa Petersen-Schepelern
"Vegan With a Vengeance" by Isa Chandra Moskowitz

October 2ⁿᵈ – Feast on your cookbooks.

Call me crazy, but one of the things I love most, is to sit down with a good cup of coffee or tea and thumb through a cookbook. I love to look at the pictures, read the ingredient list, and get inspiration for my next cooking session. There is something lovely and wonderful about cookbooks.

This is a great exercise for both the hardcore cook and the not-so-sure-of-themselves cook. If you are a seasoned cook or budding chef, you'll love to envision yourself making the dishes in your own kitchen. If you're a new cook or a cook that's not so confident in your skills, looking through the cookbooks will help you familiarize yourself with cooking terminology, ingredients, and techniques.

So, grab those cookbooks and curl up on a comfy chair with your beverage of choice. Be sure to have plenty of post it notes or slips of paper to bookmark the recipes that intrigue you. Savor the pages and enjoy the experience of discovering new meal ideas.

October 3rd – Research some recipes online.

Yes, you really can forego the traditional cookbook and get lots of recipes online. This is especially helpful when you don't have the money to buy several cookbooks, or you don't have space to store the books. You can get fresh recipes online and with sites like Pinterest, you can create an online cookbook that you can reference whenever you need. Check out some of these really great sites for recipes:

www.allrecipes.com
www.chow.com/recipes
www.food.com/recipes
www.foodnetwork.com/recipes
www.myrecipes.com

There are also sites where you can enter in the ingredients you have on hand and you'll get recipe ideas based on what's available to you. How cool is that? Check out:

www.myfridgefood.com
www.recipekey.com

www.recipematcher.com
www.supercook.com

October 4th – Start your recipe binder.

Keeping your recipes in digital format is certainly an option, but for me, I love to have a printed recipe on the kitchen counter that I can follow along with as I cook. I've started a really great recipe binder that I organized by category and can pull out and follow along with each time I cook. Over the years, the binder has become more than just a collection of recipes, it's become almost a keepsake. There's my mother's mac and cheese recipe, my girlfriend's recipe for granola bars, the recipe I used to make my first Thanksgiving dinner, and recipes that I've collected from my friends over the years. Each time I look through the binder, it's more than just a way to get dinner ideas, it's a trip down memory lane!

It doesn't have to cost a lot to start your binder. Grab a good sized three-ring binder and a set of dividers from your local office supply store. Then, as you gather recipes from friends, family, or from the internet, just slip them in under the correct tab. If you have a little extra to spend, invest in some clear sheet protectors that you can easily wipe clean if they get messy in the kitchen.

Half the fun is gathering the recipes, so don't be shy about asking your friends and families to contribute to your binder with some of their favorites!

October 5th – How to read a recipe.

Believe it or not, there is a proper way to read a recipe. I found this extremely helpful when I was just starting out as a cook and find that even now, I still use these tips to make sure I fully understand the recipe, and that I have all the ingredients that I need on hand.

There's nothing more frustrating than to start cooking a dish and get halfway through the process before you realize that you are missing a key ingredient!

Follow these steps to read your recipe:

- Always read through the recipe in its entirety at least once, so you know that you can perform the cooking techniques, have all the ingredients, and know all the steps in the preparation process.
- Figure out whether or not you need to preheat the oven. Over the years, I have been "burned" (pardon the pun) by getting the entire meal prepared and then realizing that I didn't turn the oven on.
- As you read the recipe, visualize each step to be sure you know what to do, and also to ensure that you have the proper tools in your kitchen.
- Don't just discount a recipe because it has an ingredient you don't like. I've modified many recipes by making a simple swap such as vegetable broth for chicken broth or olive oil for butter. If that's the case with a recipe, be sure to make note of the swap before you start the cooking process.

Reading the recipe a couple of times before you get started will help you feel confident and will make the cooking process much more enjoyable.

October 6th – Clean the kitchen.

Just as we talked about not being able to relax and unwind in a messy bathroom or bedroom, you can't fully enjoy cooking in a kitchen that is messy and dirty. Before you start the cooking, you've got to get to the cleaning.

Now is the time to empty your fridge and give it a good scrub. The best time to clean your fridge is when it's nearly empty, before you go out to restock. Use a cooler or a sink filled with ice to contain perishable items while you clean. Take everything out of the fridge and use a hot soapy sponge or rag to wipe down all the shelves, removing and washing shelves or bins that are removable. As you take items in jars and containers out, things like salad dressing, pickles, and sauces, check their expiration dates. Anything that is past its prime should be tossed.

After cleaning the inside of the fridge, put items back, organizing them in the way that best makes sense for you with labels facing out, grouping "like" items together.

After the inside of the fridge is clean, give the outside a good wipe down as well and wipe down the rest of your appliances (follow your manufacturers suggested cleaning method).

Clear off kitchen counters and wipe everything down. Go through your pantry items and organize them, ditching those that have gone beyond their expiration dates. Create space to work in your kitchen by keeping on your counter only those items that you use regularly.

Once the kitchen is clean, treat yourself to something that will enhance the cooking experience or will brighten your kitchen. Invest in some new oven mitts or kitchen towels or buy a plant to cheer up the space.

Starting out with a clean kitchen is the first step to making your cooking experience more pleasant and more productive.

October 7th – Make cooking joyful.
Cleaning the kitchen and buying a few items to make the space cheerful will certainly help to enhance the experience of cooking,

but there are other things you can do to make cooking a joyful experience.

The biggest reason given by my clients for why they don't cook is that they don't have time; the second biggest reason is that they just don't enjoy cooking. But there are things you can do to help you turn the task of getting dinner onto the table into a delight-fully creative experience.

You can often find me on a Sunday afternoon in the kitchen with the radio turned up, enjoying my favorite music, looking at color-ful artwork on the walls, standing on my comfort-padded floor mat, drying my colorful dishes with colorful towels, and cooking delicious, healthy food surrounded by fresh flowers and a bevy of cool plants in funky pots.

By the way, my kitchen is not a huge Italian cucina, it's a 6x6 kitch-en in my apartment in the city! You don't need a huge space or top-of-the-line appliances to make your cooking experience a joy-ful one. You just need a clean space, stocked with the essentials, infused with a little bit of fun. You also need to find the time to cook (which we'll talk about later) and willingness to be a little adventurous.

So get in there and spruce up your space and have fun with the experience!

October 8th – Gather your tools.
Okay, confession time, I'd love to have a kitchen full of cookware from Williams Sonoma, but my wallet has other ideas. Believe it or not, my kitchen collection is a mishmash of tools from K-Mart, Wal-Mart, Kohl's, Ikea, and the dollar store!

With just a few key basics, you'll be getting in touch with your inner Julia Child in no time. Here's the checklist of items you'll need:

- Baking sheet
- Bread knife
- Can opener
- Chef's knife
- Colander
- Cooling rack
- Corkscrew
- Glass casserole dish for the oven
- Grater
- Jar opener
- Kitchen shears
- Kitchen timer
- Kitchen towels
- Ladle
- Loaf pan
- Measuring cups
- Measuring spoons
- Meat thermometer
- Metal spatula
- Mixing bowls
- Muffin tins
- Nonstick frying pan
- Nonstick saucepan
- Oven mitts
- Paring knife
- Pie pan
- Plastic cutting board
- Pot holders
- Potato masher

- Roasting pan
- Rolling pin
- Round and square cake pans
- Rubber spatula
- Serving dishes
- Serving spoons
- Slotted spoon
- Spatula
- Storage containers
- Tongs
- Trivets
- Vegetable peeler
- Whisk
- Wooden cutting board

With just these basics, you should be able to whip up fabulous culinary creations from the comfort of your own kitchen. Take a few minutes and go through your kitchen cabinets now, making a list of any items that you don't currently have, but need to buy. Once your kitchen is cleaned and fully stocked, you'll be ready to go!

October 9th – Mise en place

Many years ago, in another lifetime, I was a pastry chef student at the esteemed Restaurant School at Walnut Hill College in Philadelphia. It was a really fun experience, and although I am not baking for a living, I learned a lot during my time in school. One of the things that I learned, that I still practice today is mise en place.

Mise en place is a French term that literally translates to "putting in place." When we practiced mise en place at school, it meant getting all of your items in place prior to cooking. Before I begin to cook any dish, I determine what ingredients and equipment I need and I lay it all out prior to diving into the actual cooking.

If you went through the exercise of reading the recipe once or twice before you start, then you'll already know what you need, and it will be much easier to get through the cooking if you aren't searching for things in the middle of whisking, stirring, and heating things up.

The easiest way to practice mise en place is to take out all the items you need and pre-prepare them. If your recipe calls for diced onion, dice the onion and put it in a small bowl so it's ready to go when you're ready for it. Pull out and measure all your spices, chop any fresh herbs, take out your oils, and have everything sitting out within easy reach.

For refrigerated items, cut, chop, or otherwise prep them in advance, but keep them in the fridge, in easy reach, until you're ready for them.

Having all your items gathered will make the cooking much easier and can help ensure that your attention is on the cooking once you start with the actual cooking process.

October 10th – Whip up some trial dishes.

Now comes the fun part; you get to turn your kitchen into a laboratory where you can experiment and try new dishes. Today, go through your recipes and pick two or three that interest you and that you'd like to try. If you're feeling really adventurous, invite some friends over to try some of your new dishes. If you're not sure how adventurous you're really feeling, start with a dish that is familiar to you and cook it in a new way.

Something like pasta can be cooked in hundreds of ways, so if you know you already like pasta, use that as your base and try cooking it in a way that you never thought of before. Trying some new foods, new recipes, and new cooking techniques will help you expand your culinary repertoire and discover new tastes and new dishes for you and your family.

October 11ᵗʰ – Host a recipe party.
A really fun way to get some new recipes, test out your new dishes on others, and spend some quality time with friends, is to host a recipe party. Here's how it works:

1. Invite some friends over for a potluck party where each guest brings a dish.

2. Along with the dish, each person needs to bring one copy of the recipe for each of the people attending.

3. You make a dish or two and make enough copies of the recipe for each of the people that are coming.

4. You can invest in a few inexpensive and fun folders from the office supply store or dollar store and as your guests come in, collect the recipes and put them in the folders to give your guests a nice keepsake of the evening.

5. Invest in a few blank table tents and markers and have your guests write down the name of their dish and put the card next to each dish so people know what they're eating.

6. Make your party a BYOT (Bring Your Own Tupperware) party, having guests bring empty containers to take leftovers home with them.

Get that planner out and start planning for your recipe party now.

October 12th – Find your "go to" dishes.

If you're anything like me, you don't have a lot of time to cook. As much as I love to be in the kitchen and value my time creating dishes, I often don't have a lot of time, so I have a rotation of dishes that are my "go tos" when I just need something that I know will taste good, be good enough to serve to company, and will come out perfect every time.

As you go through your recipes and start to collect the ones you really enjoy, start to find five to seven dishes that you can put into regular rotation. It's helpful to have those dishes that you and your family love for those nights when you don't have time to spend experimenting in the kitchen. In a few days, I'm going to give you the Family Recipe Score Card, to get feedback from your family on what they like. This will help you pick the "go to" dishes that you know your family will eat.

Some clients I work with have four or five "go to" dishes for each season, which you can certainly do, but don't make it too complicated! The idea here is to lighten the load in the kitchen, so feel free to do what works best for you.

October 13th – Schedule cooking time.

On most Sunday afternoons (when I'm not writing a book) you'll find me in the kitchen whipping up enough grub to get me through the week! I don't have much time to cook on weekdays, and while the occasional dinner of a frozen veggie burger and salad is okay, that gets old rather quickly. I love to spend Sunday cooking up good food that will keep me well fed during the week. It's comforting to know that on Wednesday night, I'll be eating a delicious and healthy home cooked meal, instead of running through the fast food drive-thru.

311

For me, Sunday cooking is like an event! I throw open the windows, turn up the radio, gather my supplies and take the time to savor the smells and tastes that I am able to create. The cat usually lays at the edge of the kitchen floor sniffing right along with me. I actually think he enjoys my singing as well!

I especially enjoy my Sunday cooking events in the Fall, whipping up big batches of hearty soups and stews, crusty breads, and roasted winter vegetables.

Sunday not your day? That's alright! Pick a day that works for you and get in the kitchen! Enjoy the experience, and then, savor the food you get to enjoy all week long.

October 14th – Get your kids in the kitchen.

Getting your kids in the kitchen has many, many benefits. While it certainly can add to your prep and cooking time, you can enjoy the experience of cooking with your kids while making it a time for learning and fun.

The most important tip I can give here, and I cannot stress this enough, is to be sure that you have the time to spend with your kids. If you feel rushed, have a pounding headache, or are stressed to prepare food for guests, you don't want to have the kids under foot.

The experience of cooking with your kids should be a pleasant one. You want your children to associate being in the kitchen with you as a pleasurable bonding experience. If you're feeling rushed and pressured, your kids may very well sense the tension.

Studies have shown that when children have some involvement in choosing and preparing food, they are more likely to eat what is made, and to eat more healthy foods.

Have your kids help you with age-appropriate tasks (we'll cover those tomorrow). Let them help you set the table, wash vegetables, mash potatoes and crack a few eggs.

Use your time in the kitchen as a way to teach your children. You can teach your kids about math; how many half cups are in a cup? Teach them about reading; have them read the recipe for you and explain what the steps mean. Of course, there's plenty of science in the kitchen, like what makes a cake rise?

Use your time in the kitchen as family time and get your kids excited about cooking. Teaching your kids about healthy food and helping them learn to cook is an important lesson that will help them a great deal when they get older and get out on their own.

If you don't have kids, grab a niece, nephew, or grandchild and share your cooking experience with them.

October 15th – Age-appropriate kitchen activities for kids
As we talked about yesterday, having your kids in the kitchen can be a wonderful learning and bonding experience, but you certainly don't want your five-year old chopping vegetables with a giant chef's knife! You want to make sure that you choose activities that your children can easily handle. Below are some guidelines to help:

Activities for 2 – 3 year olds:
- Knead bread dough
- Rinse off fruits and vegetables
- Shake ingredients in jars and bottles, such as salad dressings
- Stir ingredients in a bowl
- Take items to the trash
- Tear lettuce for salad
- Wipe down the table and countertops

Activities for 4 – 6 year olds:
- Mash soft items like bananas with a fork
- Measure ingredients
- Peel oranges
- Set the table
- Use kitchen shears to cut items like herbs

Once your child becomes proficient in an area, you can start to make that their job. It will give them a sense of responsibility and will help you cut down on prep time.

October 16th – My best cooking tips
Over the years, I've learned how to cut my time in the kitchen by picking up a series of little tips and tricks to make cooking even easier. Some of these are tips that I picked up in cooking school, some on the internet, and some just by trial and error. I hope they'll help you the way they've helped me over the years. Enjoy!

- After working with particularly pungent foods like onions or garlic, hold a stainless steel spoon and run your hands, and the spoon, under cold water; it will take the smell off your hands immediately, and don't worry, the spoon won't stink afterwards
- After you slice a cake in half, brush some simple syrup (sugar melted in boiling water) on the cut side before you frost to keep the cake moist.
- Brew a pot of coffee and pour it into an ice cube tray. Then, when you make iced coffee at home, you can drop the coffee ice cubes in your brew to cool your coffee without watering it down.
- If you don't have a knife block and keep your knives in a kitchen drawer, use a cork at the tip of the knife to protect you from getting cut when you reach in the drawer.

- If you want to use whipped cream, but don't have time to make it fresh, you can "doctor up" store bought whipped cream by putting a splash of good quality vanilla in it. The vanilla cuts the "container taste."
- Invest in a foldable plastic cutting board to make getting small pieces like diced onions and celery into a bowl or pan easier
- Lay a wooden spoon over a pot of boiling water to keep the water from spilling over the sides of the pot.
- Remember that cooking is an art, but baking is a science; do not skip the important step of carefully measuring your ingredients when preparing baked goods.
- Spray measuring spoons with a little shot of cooking spray before measuring out sticky stuff like honey or molasses.
- When you have fresh herbs and spices that you want to use before they spoil, put them in an ice cube tray and pour olive oil over them. Once frozen, you can grab an "ice cube" when you need it, heat it up in a pan, and use it as a base for sauces or to cook vegetables.

October 17th – Clean as you go.

I know this sounds like a really cliché thing to say, but I have to tell you that cleaning while I cook has made both the cooking and the cleaning much easier and much more enjoyable. There's nothing worse than getting to the end of cooking a fabulous meal and then looking at your horribly messy kitchen and knowing you have to clean it up.

As you're cooking, take time to wipe down counters, put items in the dishwasher, or rinse or wash items when you can. Once you get things started either in the oven or on the stove, take a few minutes to put items like spices and oils back in their original "homes" when you're done with them.

Taking those steps to keep the kitchen clean while cooking will save you lots of time and a headache at the end.

October 18th – Explore the farmer's market.

I love the Fall. I love the smell of the crisp air, the colors of the leaves, and I love the colors and textures of Fall foods like pumpkins and squashes. Getting to the farmer's market on a Saturday morning is so enjoyable and relaxing. I love to walk up and down the aisles and peek into each merchant's stand to see what they have to offer.

I get so much inspiration from looking at the items and often get excited about what I'm going to do with them once I get them home. Plus, shopping outdoors in the crisp fall air and talking to the local merchants is much more pleasurable than running my items down a conveyor belt under the fluorescent lights at the grocery store.

There's one other thing I love about shopping at the farmer's market; and that is supporting the local farmers. I can almost guarantee that if you stop shopping at your local grocery store, they won't notice you've gone. But, if you spend your money buying the products of a local farmer or merchant, that money will go a long way towards supporting their families and their trade.

Grab a newspaper, look for fliers in your neighborhood, or ask some friends and neighbors if they know of any farmer's markets in your area. Then, grab some reusable bags, maybe a friend or two, and cup of hot coffee or apple cider and head on out to experience the joy of shopping fresh and local.

October 19ᵗʰ – Discover new cuisines.

The world is a big place with lots of culinary offerings for the adventurous. With just a few new ingredients and recipes and an open mind and sense of adventure, you can take a trip around the world in the comfort of your own kitchen.

Don't be afraid to experiment with new cuisines and flavors from other cultures. While you can certainly have Chinese delivered, or hit up your favorite Italian bistro, trying your hand at making some of these dishes on your own can be fun. Plus, when cooking at home, you can make the items even healthier by controlling the amount of salt, sugar, and fats in your dishes.

Try some of these around-the-world favorites:

- **Chinese**
- **Greek**
- **Indian**
- **Italian**
- **Japanese**
- **Mexican**
- **Thai**
- **Vietnamese**

Grab those cookbooks, visit some of the recipe websites from a few days ago, and take your taste buds on a trip to another country.

October 20ᵗʰ – The family recipe scorecard

As promised, here it is; the family recipe scorecard. As you start to experiment with new and exciting foods, and as you search for your "go to" recipes, it's helpful to get input from your family to

317

find out what they really like. A fun way to do this is to offer your family a recipe scorecard that they can fill out and leave their comments and compliments to the chef.

If you have access to a copy machine, make a few copies of the score card and make the cards available to your family whenever you cook something new.

YOUR BEST YEAR YET!

Family Recipe Score Card

Name of Dish: _____

Date Prepared: _____

Name of Chef: _____

Circle the words below that best describe the dish:

Salty	Sweet	Sour	Juicy	Dry
Slimy	Gooey	Nasty	Icky	Yummy
Spicy	Hot	Greasy	Tasty	Cheesy
Hard	Soft	Bitter	Buttery	Mushy
Chewy	Creamy	Crunchy	Heavy	Light
Eatable	Enjoyable	Fishy	Hearty	Burnt
Frozen	Cold	Grainy	Mellow	Mild
Delicious	Messy	Mushy	Hard	Soft

The thing I liked best about this dish is:

_____
_____

The thing I liked least about this dish is:

_____

_____

Should we have this dish again? ☐ **Oh yeah!** ☐ **No way!**

October 21st – Spice guide

Cooking with herbs and spices can give a lively kick to your dishes. Not only are they flavorful, but many herbs and spices have medicinal and/or healing properties. You can certainly buy fresh herbs and spices, when available, but I often use dried spices as well. The key is to store your spices in a cool, dry place, and pay attention to the shelf life.

Below is a list of some of my favorite cooking spices. Make a commitment to buy at least two or three things that you haven't tried before and research ways to work them into your dishes. You'll be flavoring it up like Chef Emeril Lagasse in no time!

- Basil
- Bay leaves
- Cardamom
- Cayenne pepper
- Chili powder
- Cilantro
- Cinnamon
- Cumin
- Curry powder
- Ginger
- Mint
- Mustard powder
- Nutmeg
- Oregano
- Paprika
- Parsley
- Pepper
- Pumpkin pie spice
- Red pepper flakes
- Rosemary

- Saffron
- Sage
- Tarragon
- Turmeric

October 22nd – Healthy substitutions

As a Certified Health Coach, I regularly coach my clients on healthy eating and healthy cooking. With just a few simple swaps, you can cook really delicious meals that are still healthy and nutritious. There are many swaps you can make every day; below are some of my favorites.

Swap:

- Almond flour for whole wheat flour (if you need something gluten-free)
- Brown rice for white rice
- Cacao nibs for chocolate chips
- Coconut milk for dairy milk
- Dark, leafy greens for iceberg lettuce
- Frozen, pureed bananas for ice cream
- Graham crackers for cookies in pie crust
- Greek yogurt for sour cream
- Kale chips for potato chips
- Lettuce leaves for wraps in sandwiches
- Mashed banana for butter or oil
- Mashed cauliflower for mashed potatoes
- Nutritional yeast for cheese
- Nuts for croutons in salad
- Quinoa for oatmeal
- Steamed, grated cauliflower for rice
- Unsweetened applesauce for sugar
- Whole wheat flour for regular flour
- Whole wheat pasta for regular pasta

October 23rd – Cook once, eat two or three times.

Since we've spent the last ten months together, I think it's time to come clean and tell you that I am inherently lazy! I do love to cook and experiment in the kitchen, but most days it's all I can do to find clean clothes to wear to work and keep gas in the car.

This is why I've learned how to cook something once and then eat from it two to three times after that. Here's a few ideas that may help you with this kitchen hack. Try a few out and see how they fit.

- On Monday, I cook a big batch of brown rice to have for dinner. On Tuesday, I take a little of that same brown rice, heat it up with some coconut milk, cinnamon, and raisins, and enjoy it for breakfast. On Wednesday, I take some of the brown rice and wrap it in a tortilla with some sliced avocado and black beans for lunch.

- On Thursday, I cook chicken (okay, when I used to eat chicken) and have it for dinner with a side of potatoes and a veggie. On Friday, I slice some of the leftover chicken and top my salad with it. On Saturday, I saute some carrots, onions and celery, mix the vegetables with some chicken broth and shred the chicken for a healthy and quick chicken soup.

- On Sunday, I cook a big pot of beans and serve them on a bed of lettuce with some shredded cheese and sliced avocado for a Mexican taco salad. On Monday, I take the beans and mash them, serving them with a fried egg on top for a hearty breakfast. Finally, on Tuesday, I mix those same beans with brown rice and a dash of hot sauce for a zesty rice and beans dish served alongside a veggie burger.

Of course there's lots of ways to employ this time-saving tactic in your own kitchen. Think of a few that you can use to save time as you prepare your weekly meals.

October 24th – Kitchen timesavers

Now that the proverbial cat is out of the bag on my lazy gene, I thought I'd share with you a few more of my favorite timesaving tips. I hope you can use these to get you in and out of the kitchen in no time.

- *Buy pre-minced garlic* – It honestly tastes just as good in cooking, and it saves a lot of time and trouble.
- *Clean your grill with aluminum foil* – Ball up a piece of foil and use it to scrub your grill. It will clean your grill completely and quickly.
- *Ditch your trash can* – When you're cooking a lot of food, keep a large bowl on the counter to throw your scraps into. Dump the bowl at the very end and voila; just one trip to the trash can.
- *Keep markers* – Having markers in your kitchen allows for quick and easy labeling of items going in the fridge or freezer.
- *Pre-pack your lunch* – If you're going to eat the same dish for lunch for several days, pre-portion the containers so you can grab them and be on your way.
- *Quickly peel a kiwi* – Cut the ends off your kiwi and instead of peeling off the skin, run a spoon around the inside and pull the flesh out away from the skin.
- *Use an egg slicer* – It will quickly and easily slice your strawberries.
- *Use a straw* – To hull a strawberry, pull a straw up through the bottom of it and the core and stem are quickly removed.

October 25th – Forget about Bobby Flay.

While it sucks to spend lots of money and a whole day in the kitchen on a dish that doesn't turn out quite right, experimenting and trying new things can help you discover a slew of new dishes that may just become your favorites.

Cooking, as we've established, is supposed to be fun, so please, ditch the notion that you have to be a Michelin Star chef to whip up a healthy, flavorful, and all-around fabulous meal!

It's fun to look at cookbooks and magazines with colorful and beautiful pictures of food, but you need to know that there are actually people who work as food stylists. Their entire job is to make food look appetizing and beautiful for magazines, cookbooks, and websites. Here's a little something I learned from cooking school; some of that "food" isn't really food!

Food stylists often use inedible substitutes like glue mixed with water to make milk, a succulent chicken that's been perfectly stuffed with paper to keep it looking plump, or that decadent vanilla ice cream that's actually store-bought cake icing mixed with powdered sugar.

The whole point of wanting you to get in the kitchen this month is to have fun and discover new foods, it's not to turn you into a celebrity chef. Enjoy the process and give up the need for perfection in the kitchen. Let loose and realize that in every kitchen, a little cheese must fall.

October 26th – Quick breakfasts

Most days, I pack breakfast to eat at my desk when working outside of my home. I don't have much time to get out the door in the morning, so I'm always looking for something quick that I can grab and get on the road with. Here are some of my favorite quick breakfast ideas:

- Sliced banana and peanut butter topped with granola
- Oatmeal with cinnamon and raisins
- A fried egg topped with salsa
- A fried egg sandwich on whole wheat toast with sliced avocado

Or, whip up one of these quick smoothies:

- Frozen banana with cinnamon, cacao powder, and coconut milk
- Frozen mixed berries with coconut milk
- Fresh or frozen strawberries with coconut milk and a splash of vanilla
- Frozen peaches with a tablespoon of peanut butter, coconut milk, and a dash of cardamom and cinnamon
- Frozen blueberries and peaches mixed with coconut milk (turns a *wonderful* shade of battleship grey, but tastes really awesome)

October 27ᵗʰ – Quick lunches

Lunch is another meal that I often pack and eat on the go. There are lots of healthy and quick lunch options that you can put together relatively easily as you run out the door. Try a few of these:

- Top salad greens with peas, bacon, and some fresh grated parmesan cheese.
- Ditch the bread and make chicken lettuce wraps. Wrap sliced, grilled chicken and avocado in a large lettuce leaf.

- Make a quick-cook couscous and mix with feta cheese, black olives, diced red pepper, and diced cucumber for a light Greek couscous salad.
- Fill a whole wheat pita with turkey, avocado, and cucumber for a light and tasty sandwich.
- Mix canned, rinsed chickpeas with olive oil, fresh parsley, diced cucumber, diced tomato, and diced avocado. If you wish, you can add some tuna, chicken, or tofu for an extra serving of protein.
- Make a tuna pasta salad by mixing cooked corkscrew pasta with tuna and black olives. Mix with a light dressing of olive oil, red wine vinegar, and a pinch of red pepper flakes.
- Fill a tortilla with brown rice and beans. Sprinkle with shredded cheese and warm in the microwave until the cheese melts. Top with your favorite jarred salsa and enjoy.

October 28th – Quick dinners

I am the girl that used to eat cereal for dinner – often. All that milk and sugar lying in my stomach at bedtime was wreaking havoc with my digestive system and truth be told, it wasn't very healthy! If there happens to be a week when I haven't had my usual Sunday cook-a-thon, I find that I need a few quick go-to dinners to satisfy me at the end of a long day.

Here are a few:

- Make a stir fry with a frozen stir fry blend from the grocery store, mixed with some pre-cooked frozen chicken.
- Zap a veggie burger, top with hummus and serve on a warm slice of pita bread with lettuce, tomato, and sliced onion.
- Mix cooked brown rice with jarred salsa for a quick side of Mexican rice. Serve with some veggie sausage and a fresh veggie.

- Whip up a pizza by topping English muffins with pasta sauce, cheese, and toppings such as mushrooms and pepperoni. Serve with a side salad.
- Grab a pre-cooked rotisserie chicken from the grocery store. Shred and cook in some vegetable broth and a jar of salsa verde for a quick Mexican-style chicken soup.
- Cook some angel hair pasta and top with tuna, capers, black olives, and jarred pasta sauce.
- Have breakfast for dinner! Mix avocado with a little cilantro, lime juice, and salt to make a quick guacamole, top with a fried egg and serve with a side of the Mexican rice above.
- Whip up a tuna melt by topping an English muffin with prepared tuna fish and a slice of Swiss cheese. Melt the cheese under a broiler, and serve with a side salad.

October 29th – Quick desserts

Even though I am a healthy eater, I still love dessert! I don't eat it all the time, but every now and then, I just want a little something sweet. As a reformed pastry chef, I could whip up an elegant cake, decadent brownies or cookies, or a delightful English trifle, but I don't want to make a large portion (I'll eat it all), and these days I tend to gravitate toward lighter, healthier options.

Here are a few dessert ideas that you can quickly whip up the next time your sweet tooth comes a-calling!

- Slice fresh strawberries and top with fresh whipped cream and a few chocolate chips.
- Make a dairy-free ice cream by pulsing a frozen banana in the food processor with honey, a squeeze of lime juice, and a dash of cinnamon, until it becomes the consistency of ice cream.

- Mash up a few graham crackers and mix with a little bit of honey, line the bottom of a small dish with the graham cracker mix and top with fresh blueberries and whipped cream.
- Make the world's easiest and healthiest cookies! Mash a banana with a cup of oatmeal, a bit of honey, and some cinnamon. Bake at 350 degrees for 15 minutes.
- Make an easy English trifle as a dessert for company. Using a glass bowl, layer store-bought angel food cake with apricot preserves, whipped cream, and fresh raspberries.
- Need a chocolate fix? Warm a mugful of milk and mix with a tablespoon of cacao powder, a dash of cinnamon, and honey to taste. Top with whipped cream and chocolate shavings.

October 30th – Quick snacks

Who doesn't love a good snack? While I definitely don't want to eat all day, I do snack regularly to stave off hunger and keep me from overeating at meal time. I do my best to keep snacks under 100 calories. But forget those expensive, chemical-laden 100-calorie packs at the store! Try some of these snack ideas instead:

- Half an apple dipped into a tablespoon of peanut butter
- Six strawberries dipped in good-quality dark chocolate
- One cup of frozen grapes
- Ten baby carrots with two tablespoons of hummus
- A smoothie made with half of a banana, a quarter cup of vanilla yogurt and ice
- Ants on a log – fill a stalk of celery with a tablespoon of peanut butter, place raisins on top
- Baked apple – core one medium-sized apple and fill with a teaspoon of brown sugar and cinnamon; bake at 350 degrees until tender

- Cucumber salad made with one medium-sized cucumber mixed with two tablespoons of chopped red onion and 2 tablespoons of apple cider vinegar

October 31st – Halloween treats

HAPPY HALLOWEEN! I have to tell you that Halloween is absolutely my favorite holiday! I don't know if it's just because I love this time of year so much, or I love the idea of dressing up and becoming someone or something else for the day, but I just get giddy on Halloween.

If you're considering hosting a Halloween party, or need to make some treats to take to your children's school, I've got you covered. Below are some easy, and fun treats that you can make with the kids. Nothing spooky, nothing scary, nothing that goes bump in the night; just some awesome treats to make and share.

- *Bloody good punch bowl* – Mix a two-liter bottle of orange soda with two liters of fruit punch and a half gallon of vanilla ice cream.
- *Deviled egg eyes* – Prepare deviled eggs using whatever recipe is your favorite. Instead of topping with paprika, cut large manzanilla olives in half and lay on top like eyeballs.
- *Graveyard cups* – Top chocolate or vanilla pudding in small cups with crushed up Oreo cookies as dirt and candy gummy worms
- *Marshmallow ghosts* – Dip marshmallows in melted white chocolate and use mini chocolate chips for the eyes. Lay marshmallows on wax paper and let cool in the fridge.
- *Mummy dogs* – Wrap hotdogs (or veggie dogs, if you're me) in pre-packaged crescent rolls. Once baked, use dots of mustard to create the eyes on your mummies.

- ***Tombstone cupcakes*** – Top frosted cupcakes with crushed Oreo cookies for dirt. Insert a Milano cookie into each cupcake to serve as the tombstone.
- ***Wizard wands*** – Dip pretzel sticks in melted white, milk, or dark chocolate and cover in Halloween-themed sprinkles. Package in individual cellophane bags (you can get these at your local craft store) and tie with festive black and orange ribbon.

My October to-do list:

- ° I bought new cookbooks
- ° I spent time looking through my cookbooks and book-marked some new recipes to try
- ° I researched recipes online
- ° I started my recipe binder
- ° I asked friends and family to share their favorite recipes
- ° I gave my kitchen a good cleaning
- ° I gathered my cooking tools
- ° I tried two to three new dishes
- ° I hosted (or have scheduled) a recipe party
- ° I discovered a few "go-to" dishes
- ° I scheduled some cooking time
- ° I cooked with my kids
- ° I practiced cleaning as I cooked
- ° I visited a local farmer's market
- ° I tried some new cuisines
- ° I utilized the family recipe scorecard
- ° I tried some new herbs and spices
- ° I tried out some of the healthy substitutions
- ° I prepared one of the quick breakfasts
- ° I prepared one of the quick lunches
- ° I prepared one of the quick dinners
- ° I prepared one of the quick desserts
- ° I prepared one of the quick snacks
- ° I whipped up a Halloween treat

NOVEMBER – PRACTICE GRATITUDE

Thanksgiving is this month; a day when many of us get together with family, friends, and loved ones and give thanks for the many blessings we have in our lives. But, do we have to wait until Thanksgiving to be thankful and grateful for all that we have?

I will admit that over the years I've spent a lot of time focusing on what I didn't have, bemoaning my place in life, and complaining about every little thing that didn't go my way. As soon as I started to change to an attitude of gratitude, lots of things in my life changed for the better.

This month, I want you to start to be grateful for everything in your life. It's not as hard as you may think. Each day for the month of November, I'll give you some tips, tricks, and techniques that will help you incorporate a little bit of gratitude into every single day.

November 1st – What is gratitude?

Webster's dictionary defines gratitude as "a feeling of appreciation or thanks."

Call it gratitude, gratefulness, being thankful, or showing appreciation, this kind of thinking can change your entire life. I know that may sound very "pie in the sky," but it's absolutely true.

Gratitude is a way of feeling and a way of thinking; it's about things you can do for others, and it's a powerful and moving philosophy on life.

Start November with an open mind and an open heart; one that lets gratitude come in.

November 2nd – Benefits of gratitude

There have been many studies done on the benefits of expressing gratitude. Some of the most prominent conclusions are:

- Higher levels of physical, mental, and emotional wellbeing
- A more optimistic outlook on life
- Less jealousy
- A higher level of spirituality; feeling more connected to life
- More desire to help others through giving

With all of these amazing benefits, the only question to ask is – why not start this practice? You can begin reaping the benefits of gratitude right away. So, let's get started.

November 3rd – What are you grateful for?

Grab your journal and get to a quiet spot where you can sit for a few uninterrupted minutes to write. Set a timer for ten minutes and start writing a list of all the things you are grateful for. The first few may come easy for you; your family, your home, your health, but after a few minutes, you may find it harder to come up with items. Keep going! Don't quit until your ten minutes are up. Even if all you can think of is your gratitude for air, water, and food, write them down.

If you recall, we started the conversation about gratitude back in July, so if you did some of the exercises we talked about then, you may feel like this is a bit of a repeat. Resist the urge to skip over today's exercise. I promise that we only scratched the surface of gratitude this summer; consider this month the gratitude master class.

November 4th – Focus on the little things.

While much of the advice you hear in life mirrors the sentiment to "not sweat the small stuff" and "let go of the little things," today, I want you to pay close attention to the little things.

Part of cultivating gratitude is living in the moment and being thankful for everything that is coming your way. Imagine what it would feel like to:

- Wake up in the morning and be grateful for your bed and a good night's sleep
- Be grateful for running water in your home while you brush your teeth
- Appreciate every sip of your cup of coffee; giving silent thanks to the growers that made the coffee possible

- Take a deep breath when you walk out the door of your home, giving thanks for your lungs and the air that goes into them
- Be grateful for your car, or for the bus driver that gets you to work
- Be grateful for a job to go; a job that pays your bills and puts food on the table
- Show appreciation to your coworkers and colleagues; the people you spend your days toiling alongside at the job
- Take your lunch outside and feel thankful for every tree, every bird, and every blade of grass
- Be thankful for the food on your plate, savoring each bite
- Show appreciation for your family, ensuring that they know how much you love and care for them
- Go to bed with a heart that is full of love and gratitude for every single thing that filled your day

Wow! How can anyone not feel good after a day like that? Today, focus on the little things. Take the time to pay close attention to all the little things that make up the fabric of your day.

November 5th – Just for today, don't complain!
At some point today, whether you read this book in the morning, in the afternoon, or before bed, I want you to stand in front of a mirror, look yourself straight in the eye and say:

> *"For the next 24 hours, I WILL NOT complain, not about any person, any thing, or any situation!"*

And, I want you to stick with it! The time you normally spend complaining will be much better spent being thankful. When you find yourself feeling a complaint creeping up on you, stop yourself from thinking about it by replacing the complaint with an expression of gratitude.

- Instead of complaining about the long line at the coffee shop, be grateful you have money to spend on coffee
- Instead of complaining about the mess the kids made in the living room, be grateful for the love and joy your children bring to your life
- Instead of complaining about traffic, be grateful for having a place to go
- Instead of complaining about the weather, be grateful to be alive to experience it

Take your journal with you today and record each and every complaint "trigger" you experience. Notice the things that happen during the day that cause you to want to complain; but don't do it! Instead, replace that negative thought with an expression of gratitude.

Don't be afraid to look in the mirror more than once today and repeat the mantra above!

November 6th – Always say thank you.

November 6th – Always say thank you.
In all my years working with people, both in volunteer management, and in human resources, no one has ever come to me to complain that they were thanked too often. People enjoy hearing those two little words, "thank you." It takes so little to do it, but is so often overlooked as we rush through life, hurrying from one thing to another.

It's sad to say, but true, the people we should thank the most are the ones we thank the least. When is the last time you thanked your spouse for picking up the kids or taking out the trash? When is the last time you thanked your parents for providing for you as a child? When was the last time you thanked your teenager for cleaning his or her room?

"But they are *supposed* to do these things," you say. Who said? It's important to show your appreciation for the people in your life and for the things they do for you. When is the last time your spouse thanked you for picking up the kids or taking out the trash? When was the last time your kids thanked you for feeding them, or your teenager thanked you for clean socks and underwear?

How would you feel if they thanked you? Wouldn't you feel good? What if they're not thanking you because you are *supposed* to do these things? You may look at this situation differently when the shoe is on the other foot!

Never be afraid to thank someone too often. I promise you, it doesn't get old.

November 7th – Keep a gratitude journal.
If you started your gratitude journal in January, good for you! If you kept up with it, then I'll be really impressed! It's quite possible that you've adopted this practice as part of your daily routine, if you have not, I want to encourage you to revive the practice, and I'll make it even easier for you.

Keep a journal next to your bed. It could be the journal you've been using throughout this year, or you may want to buy a special journal that you use exclusively for this exercise. Every night before you go to bed, write down three things that you are grateful for.

If you've had a particularly rough day, it might be hard to come up with three things, but I promise you, as I've said before, there is *always* something to be grateful for. Even if the only three things you can come up with are:

1. I woke up
2. I ate today
3. I get to go to sleep

Write them down! Thinking about what you're grateful for before you go to sleep is a lovely way to close the day and drift off to sleep with loving thoughts on your mind. The other thing that I've noticed when I practice this exercise is that I pay closer attention during the day to the things I am truly grateful for.

Starting today, before you go to bed, jot down those three things you're grateful for. It shouldn't take more than a few minutes to do, and it will be time well spent on your gratitude journey.

November 8th – Keep positive thoughts with you at all times.
There are hundreds and hundreds of quotes on gratitude that you can read and re-read whenever you need to be reminded to practice being grateful.

You can find some books with inspirational quotes, or do a Google search for quotes on gratitude; but, find a few that you really like and that really resonate with you and keep them in a place where you can refer to them often. Write them on 3x5 cards and read through a few before bed, tape them on mirrors in your house, write a few of your favorites on small slips of paper you can keep in your wallet, or keep a few on your smartphone and read them when you have a few minutes.

Here are a few of my favorite quotes to get you started:

"When we give cheerfully and accept gratefully, everyone is blessed." ~ *Maya Angelou*

"An attitude of gratitude brings great things." ~ *Yogi Bhajan*

"Enjoy the little things, for one day you may look back and realize they were the big things." ~ *Robert Brault*

"If the only prayer you said was thank you, that would be enough" ~ *Meister Eckhart*

"The deepest craving of human nature is the need to be appreciated." ~ *William James*

"We must find time to stop and thank the people who make a difference in our lives." ~ *President John F. Kennedy*

"True wisdom is being able to say 'it is what it is' with a smile of celebratory wonder on your face." ~ *Eric Micha'el Leventhal*

"Piglet noticed that even though he had a very small heart, it could hold a rather large amount of gratitude" ~ *A.A. Milne, from Winnie-the-Pooh*

"The more grateful we are, the more we practice this in our everyday lives, the more connected we become to the universe around us." ~ *Stephen Richards*

"Trade your expectations for gratitude and the world changes instantly." ~ *Tony Robbins*

"Feeling gratitude and not expressing it is like wrapping a present and not giving it." ~ *William Arthur Ward*

"Gratitude can transform common days into thanksgivings, turn routine jobs into joy, and change ordinary opportunities into blessings." ~ *William Arthur Ward*

November 9th – Share your gratitude journey with others.

When you eat at a really fabulous restaurant, do you tell all your friends to patronize it? When you find the most perfect little flower shop on the corner, do you tell all your friends to go there? When you find the best boutique, pet groomer, car repair shop, etc, don't you tell everyone you know about the good thing you found?

Why not tell others about your journey to gratitude? Invite the people around you to participate in the process with you. Open up their eyes to the wonderful benefits of living with an attitude of gratitude. Let others see the way gratitude has enriched and enhanced your life.

Sharing your journey can also be a way to let others know that you are no longer answering invitations to "pity parties," are no longer living at the corner of "bitchy and petty," and are no longer tolerating the gossiping that tears others down.

Will some of your friends think you've gone off the reservation? Maybe. Should you care? No. Be firm in your belief that gratitude and compassion for others is the only way to live. Let go of the negative and live in the positive.

November 10ᵗʰ – Give away a smile.

What if I told you that you could give away a free gift every day, and that there is no limit to how many of these gifts you can give or who you can give them to? You know I'm talking about smiling here; flashing those pearly whites!

I smile as often as I can to as many people as I can in the course of a day. Some people will smile back, others will move to the opposite side of the train, but I don't mind if they think I'm crazy. Even if the recipient of my smile doesn't understand or reciprocate, giving that smile makes me feel good.

> *"Let us always meet each other with a smile,*
> *for the smile is the beginning of love."*
> *~Mother Teresa*

Today, make it a point to smile at people. You never know what a smile might do for someone, how it might lift them up, or comfort them. Go on now; don't be stingy with that grin!

November 11ᵗʰ – Learn to appreciate even the bad times.

Let's have a reality check here; life is not all rainbows, kittens, and unicorns. I don't fart rainbows, my breath doesn't smell like cotton candy, I don't live in a bubble that keeps me dry when it rains, and I certainly don't relish the times when I get beat down, insulted, rejected, or feel abused.

Life is hard. There you go, I've done my job; you can close the book and call it a day now! I realize this is not a news flash. I've gone through things in life that have been hard to live with and hard to get over; illness, rape, physical abuse, and loss. I can tell you with 100% certainty that it's hard to appreciate anything in life when you're in the thick of a personal crisis.

But even in the bad times, I worked really hard to try to find something to be appreciative for.

> *"When you lose, don't lose the lesson."*
> *~Unknown*

I can tell you that this is a difficult thing to do, and it takes a lot of practice. I pray that you won't have a lot of difficult times in your life to practice with, but should you run up against something that seems insurmountable, don't forget to breathe and try these few quick exercises:

1. Try to find at least one good thing about what has happened. Even if you just appreciate the fact that it's over. Looking for the silver lining, if nothing else, can be a distraction to keep you from focusing on what has gone wrong.

2. Give yourself the appropriate amount of time to be angry, sad, or hurt. Practicing gratitude doesn't mean that you stuff those other feelings. Those feelings are important and are an essential ingredient to healing. Allow yourself to feel what you feel, but try to keep an underlying current of gratitude in mind.

3. Be sure to deconstruct what has happened to either avoid getting into the same situation over and over again, or, to help you handle a same or similar situation in the future.

Life is hard. Sometimes love hurts. People get sick. People pass away. Do not let it steal your attitude of gratitude.

November 12ᵗʰ – Mentally change places.
A few months ago, for no reason at all, I started to get really down on myself. I was so focused on what I didn't have, what was going wrong, and all the things I wasn't doing. I texted my friend Mark and whined for a while. He reminded me in his not-so-gentle way, that there are people out there who are happy with a lot less than what I have. His message helped, but it didn't stop me from wallowing.

After a long and draining week at work, I met my marketing consultant on a Friday night for coffee. It was a snowy and cold night and as much as I wanted to go home and crawl into my pajamas and my bed, I didn't want to cancel.

At the end of the meeting I walked my friend to the train. The streets were icy and slippery and I shuffled my way gingerly towards my car to go home. As I shuffled, slipped, and slid along, I bitched under my breath about the cold and snow. I found myself generally whining about everything that I felt was going wrong in that moment.

As I whined, grumbled and groaned, I saw a homeless man lying on a steam grate, covered in dirty blankets and a thick piece of plastic. It was maybe all of six degrees by this time of night and the wind was howling. In that moment, I cursed myself and thought, "Who the hell are you to whine about anything in your life?" I was ashamed of myself for being so selfish and ungrateful, and for being so unappreciative of everything that I had.

I mentally changed places with the man on the grate. I thought about what it might feel like to sleep outside on the street, look for food, and protect myself from the elements.

When you put yourself in someone else's shoes it can give you a reality check that reminds you of all the things you have to be grateful for in life.

When you find yourself taking things for granted, stop and put yourself in someone else's shoes. Remind yourself of the good you have and the people and things you have to be grateful for.

November 13th – Thank a higher power.
Whether you believe in God, Allah, HaShem, or some other type of higher power, it's good to take time to get in touch with your spiritual side and give thanks for all there is in the world. If you stop and look around, there are so many things to be thankful for; sun, rain, animals, trees, birds, and even squirrels.

If you believe in a higher power, take some time to give a quiet thanks to them for the wonders of nature we get to experience every day.

November 14th – Examine your heart.
Often, in times of both extreme joy and extreme sorrow, you feel it deep down in your heart. I don't know how to explain it; I don't know if you <u>can</u> explain it, but if you've felt it, you probably know what I'm talking about.

In times of extreme joy, it's a wonderful exercise to examine your heart and how you feel. That feeling of fullness in your heart, where it seems you could literally explode with love and gratitude is a wonderful feeling; and who wouldn't want to have it? When you are in those moments of extreme joy, savor it!

Take some quiet time in the midst of the good and feel that feeling. If you feel inclined, grab your journal and write about it. It doesn't have to be anything structured, in fact, free flow writing literally "pouring your heart out" will feel good, and, give you a nice memory to read back on long after the moment has passed.

In times of extreme sorrow, it's easy to want to shut off our feelings. It's a natural thing to want to push your feelings aside, sleep more, distract yourself with unhealthy habits like eating too much or drinking too much; but it can be very cathartic to let yourself feel the feelings that are in your heart. Acknowledge them, and then honor them.

If you are going to allow yourself to examine that feeling of sadness deep down inside, give yourself permission to do so and then set parameters around it. The first parameter is to give yourself a timeframe. If you decide that your Saturday afternoon will be spent examining the sadness and then moving on, you avoid the risk of falling into a depressive state that can last for days.

You also want to set a parameter around the <u>way</u> in which you will examine your heart. Instead of engaging in an unhealthy behavior, use the time in a way that is self-nurturing and loving towards yourself. Commit to a day of watching comedies, taking a hot bath, ordering something from your favorite takeout place. Allow yourself to feel the feelings that are in your heart. Resist the urge to stuff and stifle them.

November 15ᵗʰ – Give back.
Giving back, to me, is putting your feelings of gratitude into a tangible act. Whenever I've had an opportunity to give to others, I've walked away from the experience feeling very grateful. I feel grateful that I have enough to be able to share, and grateful for the experience of sharing with others.

If there are charities that you currently support, kudos to you! If you're able to continue to give to them, please do. Even if you can only spare a little, that little bit will surely go a long way to helping the charity reach its goals.

Having spent most of my career working in the non-profit world, I have seen, first-hand, the good that donations from generous people like you can do. It's a blessing to receive a gift and know that we can serve so many with the generosity of others.

If you don't have a charity that you currently support, but would like to find one, I encourage you to spend some time today doing a little research on charities with missions that resonate with you. If you're an animal lover, there are plenty of animal charities. I give as often as I can to the animal shelter where I adopted my beloved cat, Felix.

If you are interested in the health and welfare of children, or furthering education, there are many charities that do work in that arena that may appeal to you. If you lost a family member or loved one to a particular disease, you may want to give to a charity that conducts research to find a cure.

When choosing a charity, use these helpful hints to be sure you are giving to a reputable group that will use your donations in the most ethical way.

- Check out your charity online to be sure that it is an established charity and not a scam.
- Be sure that the charity is the one you think it is. There are many unscrupulous "sound-alike" groups out there that are hoping to confuse you in order to get your money. Again, research the group and be sure it's the correct one.

- Find out if your gift is tax-deductible, if this is something that is important to you.
- Take time to understand the organization's mission to be sure that it is in alignment with your personal values. For example, if animal rights are important to you, and you're interested in giving to an animal shelter, you may want to ensure that the shelter is a no-kill shelter.
- Ask the charity about their income and expenses. Many charities will put out an annual report that gives detail on where and how their donations are spent. Don't be afraid to ask for this information.

Giving back is the ultimate win-win situation where the charity of your choice gets much-needed funds to continue their important work and you get to experience the joy of giving.

November 16th – Bring back the thank you note.

Among my friends and coworkers, I'm known as the queen of the thank you note. When someone has given me a gift, helped me with something important, or just does something to brighten my day, I make it a point to jot down a quick note to thank them for their kindness.

It doesn't take a lot of time or money (you can usually find thank you cards at your local dollar store), but it seems to mean a lot to the recipients. Sure, you can send an email, or even a text message, but to me, it's just not as personal and special as putting pen to paper and expressing your gratitude in writing.

I imagine my coworkers going to their mailboxes, expecting to find the usual; memos, junk mail, budget reports, and timesheets, and instead finding a little envelope with their name emblazoned on the front. I imagine it's a little something that will brighten their day, the way they brightened mine.

Make it a point today to make a trip to the store and pick out some thank you notes that you can keep handy in your desk at home or at work. If money is an issue, you can do what I do, and grab some value packs from the dollar store. If you have a little money to spend, and time to shop, browse around a stationary or card store and check out the cool designs available.

The next time you feel the need to express gratitude, put it in writing! I know it's an old- school practice, but I love the thought of the thank you note, and I am quietly hoping it makes a comeback!

November 17th – Remind yourself of all the good in the world.
If you watch the news on even a semi-regular basis, you may find yourself feeling discouraged about the world around you. I, for one, have made it a point to stop watching the news (except for the weather). It seems that the media is filled with stories of war and sickness, murders and robberies, and being constantly bombarded with this type of information can really get you down.

Instead seek out those "feel good" stories that tend to get buried under the sensationalized stories the media highlights. If you look around you'll see lots of stories of people working with others, neighbors helping neighbors, kids giving back to their community, and kittens being rescued from trees.

When you're feeling especially down, or ungrateful, look for these stories as a nice reminder of all the good that is out there in the world. It really is there if you take the time to look for it!

November 18ᵗʰ – Think of others.

It can be very easy for us to get wrapped up in our own lives. When we spend a lot of time wrapped up in our own thoughts and feelings, we can easily forget that we share the world with so many others. Gratitude can be a very contagious thing if you practice it with others in mind. Whenever something good happens to you, chances are, the people in your life that love and care about you will be happy for you and will be grateful on your behalf. When you have an opportunity to engage in an activity that will bring you joy, look for ways to include others in the experience. Your gratitude and joy can be multiplied by sharing it with others.

November 19ᵗʰ – Keep visual reminders of gratitude nearby.

Earlier in the month, I gave you some quotes on gratitude that you could keep nearby and reference often. Today, I want you to focus on visual cues of gratitude.

If you're grateful for the vacation you took with your kids to the beach, keep some seashells and pictures from that trip in a place where you can see them often and enjoy the memories they invoke. If you're grateful for your spouse and all the things he or she does for you, keep wedding pictures and loves notes in a place where you can see them to remind you of all the things you love about them.

You can also make yourself a gratitude book with pictures and mementos that remind you of all the good things in your life. If you have children, helping them create their own gratitude books is a nice way to help them feel good about what they have. In a world that bombards kids with commercials showing all the latest toys, and birthday parties that rival some weddings, it's nice to remind your children about the really important things in life, like family, pets, home, and love.

351

Having these visual reminders nearby helps keep things in perspective and helps you remember all the things you have to be grateful and thankful for.

November 20th – Volunteer.

Remember in January when we talked about the power of volunteering? If you weren't able to take the leap to volunteering earlier in the year, I hope you'll consider spending some time exploring volunteer opportunities now.

The holiday season is the perfect time to donate your time to organizations and causes that are meaningful to you. And, just like giving money and resources can make you feel appreciative and happy, giving of your time can be just as rewarding, if not more so.

Many organizations are in need of extra help over the holiday season. Soup kitchens start preparing for the Thanksgiving holiday, there are coat drives and toy drives for children, and homeless shelters can start to fill up with people looking for refuge from the cold.

Volunteering and helping those who are less fortunate than you can serve as a gratitude wake-up call for those who tend to focus on what they don't have, instead of what they do have. You'll likely stop coveting that pair of designer shoes when you spend the day serving food at a soup kitchen where the people coming for a meal don't have any shoes at all.

Spend some time looking for a charity in your area that can use an extra set of hands, or, in case you need it again, check out www.volunteermatch.com to find volunteer opportunities near your location.

"Volunteers do not necessarily have the time; they just have the heart."
~Elizabeth Andrew

November 21st – Celebrate everything!

When I say everything, I mean EVERYTHING! Got out of bed this morning? Be grateful for it. Made the bus on time? High five a coworker when you get to work. The perfect cup of coffee? THAT deserves a happy dance!

Sound crazy? Sure, but, it's fun to celebrate all the good things that happen to you in the course of a day, no matter how trivial or minute they may seem.

Today, as you go through your daily routine, look for all the nice little things that happen. If you feel really ambitious, keep a little notebook or piece of paper in your pocket and write each thing down. Then celebrate, celebrate, celebrate, and be grateful for each and every one of them!

November 22nd – Appreciate a service worker.

When I was younger, all through high school and college, I worked at the local Pizza Hut waiting tables. I met a lot of people in the many years I spent slinging pizza, some folks were mean and ornery, but most of them were pleasant and appreciative folks that would thank me for taking care of them during their visit.

Think about the many people that provide service to you during your average day, week, month, and year. Your letter carrier, the barista at your local coffee shop, the dog groomer, the cashier at the grocery store, your mechanic, your hairstylist, the trash collector.

Many of these folks are working hard for you and you may never even know who they are. You may never even see them working behind the scenes to provide service to you. So when you have an opportunity, thank someone for the work that they do. Leave a thank you note in the mailbox for your letter carrier, tell your mechanic how much you appreciate him keeping you safe on the road, thank the person who bags your groceries on your weekly shopping trip.

I can tell you as a former service worker how much it meant to me when someone would thank me for taking care of them. Sure, leaving a tip for a waiter or waitress is standard, and I was certainly always grateful for that; but there was just something extra special about someone approaching me for the express purpose of thanking me for my work.

Who can you thank in your life? Make a list, and then get to thanking!

November 23rd – Compliment others.

Thanking people is certainly a way to show gratitude, but there's also another, albeit more subtle way to show that you care, and that is through complimenting others.

Think about how you feel when someone compliments you on how your hair looks, or on your new shoes, or how well you did with your presentation to the "big wigs." It feels pretty good; right?

Every day you have lots of moments where you can help other people feel that way as well. It costs nothing and takes so little time to pay a compliment to someone. One caveat here, don't give fake compliments. People know when you're being disingenuous. Compliment people when you mean it; the object is to mean it more often!

Starting today, and for the rest of this week, make it a point to compliment at least three people each day. When you do, notice how good it makes you, and them feel!

November 24ᵗʰ – Grateful or hateful

I have found that it is impossible to hold onto more than one emotion at a time, so when I start to feel angry, annoyed, or deprived, I stop and ask myself whether I want to be hateful or grateful.

I want to make it perfectly clear here that I am no Mother Teresa. I get angry, irritable, spiteful, jealous, and petty just like most other people I know, but I really do my best to catch myself in these moments and ask myself if I am currently being grateful or hateful.

When I find that I'm feeling hateful, I do my best to turn that feeling around to something grateful. This isn't much different than what we talked about in March with CANCEL CANCEL, but let's be honest, the alliteration here is kind of fun!

Try it out and see if it helps you switch gears when the hateful thoughts start to creep in.

November 25ᵗʰ – Imagine life without.

At the time of my writing this book, I am lucky to have a very good, very stable job. I love many of my coworkers and I've moved up over the years at my company to a position that I never thought I would one day hold. As much as I love my job, my coworkers, and my boss, there have been plenty of times in my nearly ten years at this company that I've loathed the thought of going to work.

I went through a period when I completely hated my job and contemplated, very seriously, finding something else. One day, as I pulled my car in the parking lot at work, I started to feel that familiar icky feeling that I didn't want to go inside. I turned off the ignition and sat in the car for a few minutes, eyes closed, and started to imagine my life without my job.

355

I imagined not being able to see my friends every day, not being able to pay my rent, not having any money for food. I could get evicted from my apartment. What if they repossessed my car? What about health insurance? As aggravated as I was with my current situation at work, I was incredibly grateful for my job.

When your spouse is driving you crazy, imagine your life without them! When you have one nerve left and your kids are dancing on it, imagine your life without them! This one simple but powerful exercise can create a very deep feeling of gratitude. Today, pick something, anything, and imagine your life without it. Then, when you're done, do something to express gratitude for that something.

November 26th – Make today "Thank You Day."

Earlier this month, we talked about the importance of saying thank you. Today, we're going to create a new holiday called Thank You Day! And the best thing about Thank You Day, is that you get to play a game.

There are 24 hours in a day. Granted, you probably sleep for about eight of them, but that still leaves you with approximately sixteen hours to work with. In order to "win" the game, you must say thank you at least twenty-four times today. Each time you say thank you, make a check mark somewhere, in the notes on your smartphone, on a notepad, or a piece of paper you keep in your pocket.

Once you hit your twenty-four thank you's, you've won! And, guess what? All the people that you've thanked have won too! If you reach your goal of twenty-four thank you's, treat yourself to something. Take yourself for a latte after work, have a decadent snack after you put the kids to bed, buy yourself a new belt, or shirt, or tie.

The more you say thank you, the more it becomes a habit to do so. Now get going – you have twenty-four thank you's to get to!

November 27ᵗʰ – Make every day Thanksgiving.
When I really stop and think about my life, the first thing that comes to mind is how incredibly lucky I am! I really do have so much to be thankful for. In my family, we didn't pray before meals, and being that we weren't a very "mushy" family, we didn't get all sentimental before Thanksgiving dinner.

It used to bother me that our Thanksgiving meal did not resemble that of the Waltons; but I got over that in favor of diving into the mashed potatoes. Now, whenever I have an opportunity to share a meal and enjoy fellowship with someone else, I treat it as a Thanksgiving meal.

Since I live alone, I often eat my meals alone. Breakfast and lunch are normally at my desk while I work, and dinner is alone in my apartment, so eating with other people has really become like an event for me.

Each time you have the opportunity to sit down and "break bread" with others, treat it as sacred and as special as you do your annual Thanksgiving meal. It will change your entire outlook on the experience.

November 28ᵗʰ – When you're happy and you know it…
When you are happy, living in gratitude, and feel good about yourself, use your positivity to serve as a light for others. Earlier this month we talked about giving and volunteering, but your efforts to lift someone else up don't need to be a hugely calculated effort.

Listening to someone, offering comfort in times of need, or celebrating and laughing with someone can have a big impact on their life. When you're feeling good and have lots to be thankful for, don't be afraid to shine that light! Celebrate for yourself all the wonderful things in your life, and shine your light for those around you.

November 29th – Remember you are human.

As I recounted to you earlier this month my story of the homeless man lying on the steam grate to stay warm, I told you about feeling sorry for myself and bemoaning my life and my circumstances. I was pretty hard on myself about the selfish nature from which I was operating, however, I want to tell you (and remind myself) that we are all human.

There will be times when despite having a good home, good friends, good health, a stable job, a loving marriage, and well-adjusted children, you will still feel ungrateful, unhappy, or envious of others. This is human nature.

It is inevitable that sometimes you will still end up in that place; the trick is to not unpack your bags and live there!

You can always go back to the exercises where you wrote down things that you're grateful for; re-read your old journal entries, or look around and take stock of everything you have. You can also take time to feel your feelings, honor your emotions, and even examine what is causing you to feel the way you do.

If you are jealous of a coworker for what you perceive he or she has that you don't have, give yourself the space to examine this. Also, remind yourself that what you see with this person is merely a snapshot of their life. You don't know exactly what's happening in their life, just as they don't know exactly what's going on in yours

When negative feelings pop up, resist the urge to beat yourself up over them. Acknowledge them, and then move on from them. You are human!

November 30th – Why I'm thankful for <u>you</u>.

As we come to the end of the month, and are winding down to the end of this year-long journey together, I want to take a moment to say why I am thankful for <u>you</u>. Writing this book has been a labor of love and a life-long dream of mine. I always wanted to write a book, but I never really knew if I would or what it would be about.

My goal in writing this book was to write something that would truly help people live their best life. To give you real-life, real-world information that you could adapt and modify to fit your own life; I hope I've done that for you.

As we close out the month of November, the month of Thanksgiving, let me pause for just a moment to give thanks to you, my reader. Pause for a moment and close your eyes. Do you feel that? It's my virtual hug to you; it's my long-distance expression of thanks and gratitude.

My November to-do list:

- I completed the ten minute gratitude exercise
- I practiced focusing on the little things
- I spent a full 24 hours NOT complaining
- I kept up with my gratitude journal
- I wrote down my inspirational quotes
- I spent a day smiling at people
- I mentally changed places with someone
- I thanked a higher power
- I found a charity to support
- I bought thank you notes
- I made a gratitude book
- I looked into volunteer opportunities
- I spent a day celebrating EVERYTHING
- I appreciated a service worker
- I spent a day focusing on complimenting at least three people
- I imagined my life without
- I had a "Thank You Day"

DECEMBER – REFLECT AND RESET

We made it! It's almost the end of our glorious year and our glorious journey together. For many of us, December is about the holidays, whether you celebrate Christmas, Kwanzaa, Hanukkah, Festivus, or some other holiday, December is normally a time for friends, family, and celebration.

In the midst of all this merriment, I want to encourage you to take some time to reflect on this past year and reset yourself so that you can have your second best year yet!

Thank you for being with me on the journey. Just 31 more days left; let's go!

December 1st – Welcome December!

I don't know about you, but December is such a mixed bag month for me. I am not a big Christmas fan, it's okay, but you know Halloween is my day! I often find myself feeling depressed around the holidays. That's not unusual, as many people find the holidays depressing and stressful.

While part of me is kind of "meh" about December, there is another part of me that gets excited about resetting and refocusing myself for the New Year. I get excited about getting ready for a fresh 365 days to conquer my fears, slay my dragons, climb new mountains, and meet new challenges.

This month, much like my attitude about December, will be a "mixed bag" of getting through the holidays, taking care of yourself, celebrating with loved ones, and planning and preparing for the new year. Get ready.

December 2nd – Organize your month.

While we haven't done this every month, because December tends to be so hectic for many of us, I'd like you to grab your planner and organize your month. I'd like you think carefully about what's going to be happening this month, scheduling and/or paying careful attention to the following items:

- Scheduling time off from work
- Finding time to meditate and relax
- Building in alone time
- Making, confirming, or mapping out your travel plans (if you'll be traveling)

- Figuring out what things you can delegate to others
- Planning the holidays, from the travel, to the cooking, shopping, cleaning, etc.
- Finding time to shop for the things you'll need for the New Year (new planner, journal, etc.)
- Scheduling time for regular self-care
- Building in times/ways to give back
- Planning for the new year

So, grab your planner, look at all the days, and see when you can start scheduling the things that need to be done this month. While you are doing this, please schedule a day for self-care (perhaps a movie and a massage) and make sure you build in extra time to meditate and relax. When you are busy, it's easy to let these things slide, but trust me, this is when you need to do them the most!

December 3rd – Set your holiday expectations.

I love the movie *National Lampoon's Christmas Vacation!* What's not to love? The characters are funny, the underlying message is endearing, and there's a squirrel jumping out of a Christmas tree!

What I love the most is the funny interpretation of a holiday that did not go quite as planned. We all have visions of what the holiday is going to be. Well-behaved children in their adorable pajamas running down the stairs on Christmas morning in euphoric excitement about their gifts; a perfectly cooked turkey to feed your loving family; singing carols by the fire. Do you have this holiday? Yeah, me neither!

Today is the day to set your holiday expectations and to make them known to others. This is the time when you may have to break the news to your mother-in-law that you're not driving six hours to

Michigan to visit. You may have to break the kid's hearts when you tell them that they are not getting that $400 gaming system they've been eyeing up all year. And sadly, you may have to tell your friends that you can't make the annual "ugly sweater party" this year.

While I'm sure you don't want to disappoint or upset anyone, helping others manage their expectations (especially children) is important. In the end, it can actually help to ease the disappointment.

It's much better to tell your kids today that they're not getting a puppy, than it is for them to wake up on Christmas morning expecting a little Fido or Spot to be there. When you have the conversation now, you can talk about why they are not getting what they want, and have a dialogue about it that can help avoid the tears and tantrums that may come around on December 25th.

Today, grab your planner AND your journal. Look at the schedule you put into place yesterday and now, knowing what the month will look like, set those expectations. Then hold firm, make them known, and move on with the rest of the month.

December 4th – Learn to say no.

Personally, I hate to disappoint anyone, but I'm getting to that age and stage where keeping my sanity is more important than disappointing others. In my younger days, I've accepted more than one invitation to something I didn't really want to go to in an effort just to "save face," or, "not make waves."

Saying no is an act of courage, and it's an act that is worth doing! Learning to say no is also a form of honesty, in that you exercise the freedom to be honest with yourself and with others about what you want to do.

Don't be afraid to tell your mom that you can't afford the cashmere sweater she wants this year, or to tell your sister-in-law that you can't make their party, or to tell the kids that they can't have the toy that they wanted.

Saying no and setting boundaries is always important, but even more so during the busy holiday season when there seems to be even less time to do what needs to be done.

By the way, I know we talked about it earlier this year, but I just want to remind you that "no" is a complete sentence! Resist the urge to over-explain and over-apologize. A polite, "no, thank you," is all that needs to be said.

December 5th – Relax your standards…a little!
Since it is the holidays and things may be a bit more hectic, it's okay to loosen the reigns a little. It's okay to indulge in a few more desserts that usual, and a drink here or there, and while you certainly don't want to undo all your good work (we'll talk about that tomorrow), it's okay to let loose a bit.

- Let the kids stay up a little later than usual
- Let the kids watch a little more TV than usual
- Allow yourself to stay up a bit later
- Don't obsess about keeping the house so spotless
- Let go of your vision of the "perfect holiday" and meet the reality of your situation where it is
- Indulge in a few more treats than you normally would
- Feel free to skip *a few* workouts in order to get some other things done

Finally, don't be too hard on yourself. In just a few glorious weeks, you'll have a whole new year to get back on track!

December 6ᵗʰ – Don't undo all your good work.

People tend to obsess about what they eat from Halloween to Christmas, but I think what you eat from Christmas to Halloween is so much more important!

Having said that, you do not want to undo all the good work of the last eleven months by going off the reservation in December. You want to be sure that you are still being conscious of your health during the busy holiday season; especially when it comes to what you're eating.

Below are some of my best tips for surviving holiday eating. I hope they help!

- Always circle the buffet table BEFORE you put anything on your plate. If you load up on the stuff that's at the beginning of the buffet, you may not leave room for something else that you really want later down the line, and that can lead to overeating in a hurry.

- Focus your splurges on things that you can't normally get during the year. If the holidays are the only time you can enjoy Aunt Rita's homemade pumpkin pie, then don't waste your appetite (or your calories) on store bought biscuits. Ditch the biscuits and enjoy the pie.

- For every alcoholic beverage you consume, drink a glass of water! Or better yet, take a break from the holiday booze and enjoy a non-alcoholic beverage, such as cranberry juice and seltzer water with a splash of lime, or "skinny" eggnog of coconut milk mixed with a little whipped cream and topped with nutmeg.

- Use party time as catch up time with friends and family. Focus on the friendship and fellowship and less on the food. Find a place to sit or stand that is not convenient to the buffet table, eat slowly, paying attention to the conversation.

- Pack a small travel toothbrush with you and slip into the bathroom to brush your teeth after you've had dessert, or chew strong peppermint gum. This should keep you from going back for a second dessert.

- Do not allow yourself to go to a holiday party hungry! Eat an apple and drink one to two full glasses of water before you go. Otherwise, you will immediately take your ravenous self to the food and start chowing down.

December 7th – Be sure to meditate.

Hopefully, you've been able to establish and maintain some sort of meditation practice this year. If you have, please be sure to build in some time to do it during this hectic month.

If you have not yet been able to meditate on a regular basis, try to at least go back to the exercise we did on August 14th and see if you can work in a few days when you can try meditating. It might be tougher to do this time of year with all the extra-curricular activities taking place, but that's even more of a reason to try to carve out that downtime!

December 8th – Commit to paring down.

For some, the holidays are a time of excess. Too much partying, too much focus on materialism, too many people. For an introvert like yours truly, all this excess makes me anxious. After one too many holiday get-togethers, I get the urge to crawl into my pajamas, hop into bed, pull the covers over my head and stop answering the phone.

As you're planning for the next few weeks, I want to challenge you to commit to paring down. Your children do not need sixty-five gifts under the tree, you do not have to cook a dinner that would put the best chefs in America to shame, and your house does not need to look like a Norman Rockwell painting.

Grab your journal and write down at least five things you can do to pare down this season. Whether it is spending less money, eating less food, buying a few less gifts, putting up less decorations, or inviting less people to your home this season, write down your five things and COMMIT TO DOING THEM!

Do not allow yourself to get pressured into doing more than you can do. This is where saying no will be most helpful to you.

December 9th – Choose peace.

"Let there be peace on Earth, and let it begin with me."

The lyric referenced above is from a popular song written by Jill Jackson Miller and Sy Miller in 1955, and is a song that is generally quite popular around the holiday season.

Starting today, I want you to choose peace. What I mean by that, is that I want you to not allow yourself to get caught up in petty arguing, bickering, family drama, or the opening of old wounds that sometimes come up with families get together.

Whenever something starts brewing that makes you feel uncomfortable please remember this:

> *"You do not have to attend every argument you are invited to!"*
> *~Unknown*

Whenever you have a chance to make a choice, choose peace. This is a purely selfish endeavor as choosing peace will help you save your sanity and not push you into a confrontation or situation that will make you feel uncomfortable.

Choosing peace means walking away from any situation that you feel is unhealthy or unproductive. You've spent a good part of this year practicing things that bring you joy and happiness, do not let the stresses of the season ruin this!

December 10th – Covet your alone time.
If you have not yet booked a day to yourself, please do so now. It is so important that amidst the holiday hustle and bustle, you find time to be alone to relax, unwind, recharge, and rejuvenate yourself.

It does not matter what you choose to do with your alone time, it only matters that you take it. You may choose to watch a funny movie, cook yourself a nice dinner, go to the local coffee shop and read with a gourmet latte, or just take a hot bath, slip into your favorite jammies, and go to bed early.

Book your day, take your day, and enjoy the precious time you allow yourself to spend in your own company.

December 11th – Travel smart.

You may, or may not, be traveling for the holidays. If you are not traveling, you can skip today (or read it to pick up tips for a future trip).

Traveling can be quite stressful. Traveling around the holidays can be downright frightening. Here are some tips that, I hope, will help you travel smart:

- If you are traveling by train, save yourself the stress of trying to take gifts with you. Arrange to have gifts delivered to your destination ahead of time. Many companies will (for a small fee) wrap your gifts for you. If that is not an option, it's likely your host will have the trappings to wrap gifts when you get there.

- If you are traveling by car, ensure that your car is road-ready prior to embarking on your journey. If you live in an area where bad weather (ice, snow, and the like) are common this time of year, take extra care to prepare your vehicle. Have the tires checked and the oil changed, and be sure to keep an emergency kit in your trunk. Having items like bottled water, extra blankets, a pair of old boots, and some non-perishable food items will come in handy in case of an emergency.

- Prepare the little ones. Remember that children are creatures of habit and taking them out of their routine can cause them (and you) to feel stressed out. Be sure to pack plenty of snacks and activities to keep little ones busy, and try to stick to their regular routine as much as possible. Keep at least one or two rituals the same (or close to) the ones you practice at home (i.e. a story before bed, sleeping with a favorite stuffed animal, or eating a snack that is familiar). Also, spend some time with the kids letting them know what the schedule will be like and help them get excited about their destination.

- Think like Santa! He makes his list and checks it twice; you should do the same thing with your travel plans! Make sure you confirm your airline reservations in advance; call the hotel a day or two ahead and be sure that your room accommodations are set; and prepare a contingency plan for any last-minute changes. This is not the time to leave things to chance!

- Try to build in as many shortcuts as possible. It may cost a little more to take a few extra days off from work, upgrade to first class seating, or rent a car that is bigger and roomier than the compact car you normally take, but these things will pay for themselves in comfort and peace of mind. Please, only do these things if your budget will support them, and if it does, invest in them as a way to make the journey more enjoyable.

December 12th – Delegate, delegate, delegate!

With all the things you have to do this month, now is a good time to see what things you can delegate to others. There are often college students home for the holiday break. Could you pay one of them to watch the kids for a few hours so you can shop? Can you pay one of them to shovel snow for you? Can you afford to hire someone to clean your house while you wrap gifts or do your meal planning?

Can you swap services with a neighbor to buy some time; he'll shovel the drive and you'll bake cookies?

You are not Superman or Superwoman! This is the time to drop that cape off at the dry cleaners and let it spend some time there. Enlisting the help of others, when feasible, is a nice way to give yourself a break and buy something that you can't get at the department store; TIME!

Think of some things today that you can easily and safely pass off to others, and get a firm list of who those "others" might be. Then, start reaching out and scheduling things as appropriate to free yourself up to take on some tasks that must be done by you.

December 13th – Check in with yourself.
We're just about halfway through the month. Now is a good time to check in with yourself and see how you're feeling. Are you feeling stressed or anxious? Are you excited about the holidays? Are you feeling a little overwhelmed? It's important to check in and see how you're feeling so you can adjust things as needed. If you are overwhelmed and your dance card is full, you may need to decline a few invitations that are coming your way, and that's okay.

Please do not let the fact that things are busy keep you from spending the time to examine how you feel. Having this check in may keep you from having a meltdown later. Take ten minutes to write free flowing in your journal how you feel. Don't worry about grammar or misspellings, just write. If your mother-in-law is pissing your off, write it down; if you're children have been extra loving to you, write it down; if your boss has been extra generous, write that down too!

December 14th – Plan the holiday.

Over the summer, we talked about visualization in the context of your athletic pursuits. Today, I want you to visualize the holiday. I want you to play out the entire day or days that will make up your holiday celebration.

This is a great exercise, especially if you are hosting something at your home. Visualizing how the day will play out will help you to pre-determine any pitfalls that may happen. Suppose your Aunt Helen and Uncle Sy are coming to stay, but you realize that the guest room is where you've been storing the gifts; what will you do? You've created a fabulous menu for dinner, but realize that your cousin Sherman is coming, and he's a gluten-free vegan; do you have something that he will be able to eat?

What if you planned on having a huge party for the family on Christmas Eve, but then realize that your sister and her boyfriend are flying out to Mexico on December 23rd?

As you mentally walk yourself through the holiday, you can start to map out what you need, what adjustments need to be made, and what could potentially go wrong.

Thinking about Aunt Helen and Uncle Sy before their arrival gives you time to move the gifts to the attic, away from the prying eyes of the little ones. Knowing that cousin Sherman can't eat your world-famous mashed potatoes and turkey, gives you time to build in a trip to the local health food store to pick up some gluten-free and meat-free alternatives. And, perhaps you need to move that big family party up to December 18th!

Today, grab a blank pad and pen and spend some time mapping out the logistics and specifics of the holiday. The time you are spending to do this today will pay huge dividends when the big day actually arrives.

December 15ᵗʰ – Look back through your journal.
Let's switch gears today and get off the holiday merry-go-round. Today, I'd like you to take some of that alone time that you carved out earlier this month and use it read through your journal.

Pick a quiet place where you can sit undisturbed, light some candles, put on some music, grab a highlighter, and curl up with your favorite beverage. Take time to read through your journal and highlight some of the milestones that have occurred over the past year.

This is a time to make note of any items that you want to carry over and work on in the New Year, but mostly, it's a time to be proud of yourself for any growth and change you've experienced over the last twelve months.

Remember running your first 5K? Remember when you "graduated" from that art class? Remember how it felt the first time you spoke Italian to your grandmother? Go back and recall how you felt when you took that fabulous vacation with your family.

Treat this time with yourself like a special occasion, because it is. After all, what could be more special than celebrating YOU?

December 16ᵗʰ – Buy a new journal.
While you're out doing your holiday shopping, make it a point to stop and pick up a new journal for the New Year, and don't forget to grab some fun pens and highlighters while you're out there!

December 17ᵗʰ – Buy a new planner.

I sincerely hope that you didn't punk out and not buy a planner in the beginning of the year. If you did buy and use your planner, I hope it was a helpful tool for you as you went through this year.

If it was helpful, please be sure to pick up a new planner for the New Year. When you're shopping for your new planner pay special attention to how this year's planner worked for you. Perhaps you need one that is slightly bigger, has a place to store receipts, or has more room to write notes in it. There are hundreds of different types of planners to choose from, so take the time to pick one that will work for you. After all, you'll be using it for another 365 days!

December 18ᵗʰ – Take in the wonders of the season.

December is normally cold and snowy here in Philadelphia, and while that sometimes bums me out (I am a summer girl through and through), I do remind myself to take time to enjoy the wonders of the season.

I usually enjoy the beauty of the first snowfall. I take to the park and look at the snow-covered trees, the pond frozen over, and the glistening branches blowing in the wind, and I enjoy the crisp, cool air.

I also try to enjoy the things that really only come around this time of year. I like going to the local tree seller and picking out my little Charlie Brown Christmas tree. I love to watch my cat, Felix, lay under it and sniff away. I enjoy listening to holiday music, and going into town to watch the famous light show at the Macy's Department Store.

I watch holiday movies, my favorite, *A Christmas Story,* and watch the old holiday cartoons, *How the Grinch Stole Christmas,* is my own personal religion!

There are things that happen over the holiday season that don't happen any other time of the year, so be sure to savor and enjoy them before they disappear.

December 19th – Remember those that are at risk.
Not everyone is cheerful and feels good about the holidays. If you are feeling stressed out, anxious, or depressed, the kind of feelings that are not a sign of the normal hustle and bustle of the season, please reach out for help.

While the CDC has done extensive studies that prove that higher suicide rates during the holidays are in fact, a myth, the holidays are a time when some people tend to experience depression.

If you, or someone you know is going through or exhibiting any of the warning signs of suicide, such as:

- Talking about suicide
- Seeking out lethal means
- Expressing that they have no hope for the future
- Vocalizing their self-loathing
- Getting their affairs in order or starting to say goodbye to people as if they won't see them again
- Withdrawing
- Engaging in risky behavior such as increased alcohol use, reckless driving, or unprotected or risky sex
- Displaying a sudden sense of calm after being extremely depressed

Get help immediately! Talk to someone who can help you! You can reach out to organizations such as:

The National Suicide Prevention Hotline at 1-800-273-8255 or www.suicidepreventionlifeline.org

American Foundation for Suicide Prevention at 1-800-273-TALK (8255) or www.afsp.org

December 20th – Fight off holiday loneliness.

While the holidays are a time for people to spend with friends and loved ones, there are many people who are alone during the holiday season; perhaps you are one of them.

If you can, carve out some time to spend with someone who might be alone this holiday season.

- A service person that is stationed far from home
- A military spouse whose husband or wife is away
- An elderly neighbor whot is celebrating alone
- A colleague or friend that is new to the area whose family is not nearby

While dropping off a small gift to these people is a lovely gesture, the gift of your time will probably be so much more impactful. If you know someone that may be alone over the holidays, invite them to a holiday get-together, ask them out to coffee, or visit them in their home. Even just a few minutes of your time will make them feel cared for and can ease the loneliness they may be feeling.

December 21st – Have fun and reconnect.

If it's at all possible today, grab the family and do something fun! Go cut down your own tree, go skiing, play in the snow, build a snowman, make cookies together, head out to a movie, or curl up at home with popcorn, hot cocoa, and a funny flick on TV.

Today is a day to reconnect with your family in a way that is not tied to the holidays. No Christmas shopping, fighting lines at the mall and running around in circles looking for that last minute gift for Aunt Lisa. No grocery shopping, no gift wrapping, no holiday parties. Make today about you and your family. Reconnect and spend some time together. Unplug, unwind, and savor the best gifts of all, the gifts of love and time well spent.

December 22nd – Take a self-care day!

Since yesterday was all about family, I want today to be all about you! If you can't spare a whole day for yourself, at least carve out an hour or two to engage in some self-care. Get your hair cut, get a manicure or pedicure, or get a massage if you can. If your budget is tight (as it often is this time of year) set up a relaxing spa bath and practice some self-massage (we did this back in August).

The key here is to spend time taking care of your body. Consider it a gift that you give to yourself! Take time to honor yourself and thank your body for everything it does for you each day. Remember, this body has gotten you through the last 356 days; doesn't it deserve a little treat?

December 23rd – Give yourself a gift.

Today, I want you to give yourself a gift. "But wait"…I can hear you saying "I've had to buy gifts for so many people, I can't afford to get something for myself!"

I want to challenge you on that. Can you spend a few dollars on something that will make you feel special? Can you buy something that you can use as a reward to celebrate your transformation over the past year? Maybe a fancy pen to use next year when you journal? Could you buy yourself a framed inspiration quote to put in your success corner? What about a photo album to put all of next year's pictures in?

The object of the gift is not really the gift itself, but the opportunity to give yourself something that has value and meaning to you to commemorate the great strides you've made this year.

If you find yourself running out for last minute items, make sure one of those items is something for yourself!

December 24th – Establish new traditions, or rekindle old ones.
If you celebrate Christmas, like I do, then you may have something planned for tonight, Christmas Eve.

My Christmas Eve hasn't always been the same the past few years, but there are a few traditions that I always honor, even if the evening doesn't always look the same.

I always give Felix a special treat on Christmas Eve, tuna flake, or extra crunchy treats. I always curl up with decadent hot cocoa (complete with mini marshmallows) and watch *A Christmas Story.*

I pull out my hardcover copy of *How the Grinch Stole Christmas* and read it – out loud. I indulge in a spa-quality bath and always put on a pair of red pajamas!

Whether I've spent time visiting somewhere on Christmas Eve, or hosted friends at my place, it just doesn't feel like Christmas Eve until I've done my rituals.

If you have tried and true traditions that are meaningful to you and your loved ones, be sure to honor them. Or, think about some traditions you can introduce with your family this year.

These rituals and traditions have a way of bringing people closer and making the holidays seem even more special.

December 25th – Celebrate!

MERRY CHRISTMAS! There is nothing for you to do today, but celebrate! Enjoy good food and good times with family and friends, take time to savor the day, enjoy the fellowship, create warm memories, and celebrate! Tonight, if you have a few minutes, recap the day in your journal so you'll be able to look back on it in the future with fondness and nostalgia. Enjoy!

December 26th – Take the family on a "feel trip."

Notice I didn't say "field trip," I said "feel trip." Today is a day to think about others; perhaps those that are less fortunate than you. It is a day to take your family on a "feel trip," where you can spread a little joy to others.

- Take a tray of cookies to a police station or fire station and thank the men and women who work so hard to ensure your safety
- Volunteer to take a shift at a soup kitchen
- Hit day-after-Christmas sales and stock up on toys to take to a women's shelter
- Go to a local children's hospital and hand out $5 coffee gift cards to the
- Take advantage of those sales to get warm socks, gloves, hats, and scarves and donate them to a local homeless shelter

- Take a holiday plate to your elderly neighbor and spend some time with him/her over a meal
- Volunteer to read stories to kids at a shelter or kids that are spending the holidays in the hospital

After a day of receiving, it's a nice thing to spend some time giving. Make this a tradition for your family; a way to acknowledge all that you have in your life while giving to those that may not have.

December 27th – Think about your goals for next year.
Okay, you've had the big holiday, you've hosted, visited, cooked, gifted, and given back. Now, get rid of everyone and focus on yourself! Carve out some time today to sit down with your journal and your planner and think about the goals you want to create for next year.

Were there goals that you had this year that got pushed off? Can you revisit them in the New Year? Plan for them in the coming year. Were there healthy habits or new ways of living that you developed this year that you'd like to carry over to the New Year? Start to structure things so you can continue to engage in these healthy activities.

My hope is that after thinking about your goals today, you'll be excited about the coming year. Get energized, it's almost here!

December 28th – Prep your home for the New Year.
This is certainly not the time to engage in a heavy clean of your home. The tree (if you have one) is likely still up, as are the rest of the holiday decorations. You may even still have house guests.

If you have been traveling, and are still away from home, you won't be able to do much physical prep, but you can take a few minutes to make a list of things that need to be done upon your return.

Mentally walk through your home and make a list of a few things that you can do to help you prepare for the New Year.

If you're home, you can start to put these things into place. You may want to:

- Freshen up your meditation space and success corner
- Clear out the fridge of any expired foods or holiday leftovers
- Make any preparations you'll need to make for New Year's Eve
- Gather any materials you'll need for the New Year (get your planner and journal if you haven't already, get supplies for a new vision board or binder, give the house a quick once over if you have clutter that's been bothering you)

December 29th – Start scheduling.

You can certainly wait until the first of the year to do this if you wish, but if you have the time to do it now, you can start off the year in a really great position!

Grab this year's planner and your shiny new planner and start to transfer important days over. Things like birthdays, anniversaries, etc. should be recorded. If you have an exercise schedule that's working for you, feel free to put it in your new planner (even if you just fill in the month of January). Start to think ahead about family vacations, business trips, or other big events that you think may be happening this year.

I love starting the New Year with my planner already pre-filled with the things that I anticipate coming up. You may not want to schedule things too far in advance, but if you can at least get the beginning of January "on the books," it will help you transition into the New Year much more effectively.

December 30ᵗʰ – Check in, again, with how you feel.
We've had two check-ins this month so you can see how you are feeling. Today's check-in is meant to be focused around how you feel about this past year. Are you proud of yourself, disappointed about the progress you made, anxious that you didn't follow through with the book each day?

Grab your journal, one last time, and record these feelings. If the feelings you have are shifting toward the negative, try to come up with some action you can take to help address them.

DON'T SKIP THIS EXERCISE! Doing this is like literally and figuratively "closing the book" on this year. This is, after all, the last time you'll be utilizing this year's journal. Plus, putting down your feelings about this year gives you the freedom to let them go and prepare yourself for a whole new set of days to learn, experience, grow, and live your life!

Whatever you did or didn't do this year, please try to look back fondly on the time. Once you've made your last journal entry, close the book, take a deep breath, find a "home" to store your book, and get ready for all the new things to come.

December 31ˢᵗ – Read your inspiration jar.
I so hope that you started an inspiration jar in January! Hopefully you've been adding things into it this year. Since this is the last day of the year, New Year's Eve, a time when we celebrate all that has happened and look forward to all that is to come, if you can, steal away for a little bit of alone time, and grab your inspiration jar. When I do this, I make it something special. I light some candles, grab some champagne (it is, after all, New Year's Eve) put on some music, and sit in a comfortable spot.

Open up your inspiration jar and take out your slips of paper, one by one. Read each one. Look at the date. After you read it, close your eyes and try to remember what was so special about this moment or event. It must have been special to you, after all, if it wasn't, it wouldn't have made it into the jar!

Some people save their slips of paper, or at least some of the most meaningful. I save certain ones and put them in an envelope with the date on the front. It's nice to know that I have them, if I need a boost and want to review them again.

Be proud of yourself for your accomplishments. Look back fondly on all these moments that have made up the last 365 days. Use this time to not only to reflect on the past year, but to create excitement for yourself about the New Year.

My December to-do list:

- I organized my month
- I set my holiday expectations
- I practiced saying no
- I relaxed my standards – just a tad
- I practiced healthy eating habits at parties and get-togethers
- I took time to meditate
- I committed to paring down
- I chose peace
- I enjoyed some alone time
- I delegated tasks
- I visualized the holidays
- I looked back through my journal
- I bought a new journal
- I bought a new planner
- I took time to enjoy the wonders of the season
- I carved out some time to help others
- I took a self-care day
- I gave myself a gift
- I took a "feel trip"
- I thought about my goals for the New Year
- I prepped my home for the New Year
- I started scheduling for the New Year
- I read through my inspiration jar

And, there you have it; 365 days of little changes that I hope added up to big results for you. I hope you enjoyed reading the book as much as I enjoyed writing it.

Feeling inspired? I'd love to hear from you!

Visit me at www.thecaringcoachingcenter.com, or on Twitter @caringcoaching, or, send your thoughts, comments, or questions to me at karen@thecaringcoachingcenter.com.

Congratulations on completing what I hope has been *Your Best Year Yet!*

Be well,

Karen

ABOUT THE AUTHOR

Karen Ann Kennedy's commitment to wellness and service defines her life and career. With a black belt in Tae Kwon Do, the decorated US Army veteran, certified health coach, and longtime human resources director is no stranger to setting and achieving goals.

As president and CEO of The Caring Coaching Center Kennedy provides health and wellness coaching to individuals, groups, and corporations. She regularly contributes healthy living articles to *The Huffington Post*, and frequently presents at schools and businesses in the Philadelphia area.

Born, raised, and still residing in her beloved Philadelphia, Kennedy served with the US Army for eight years, including a tour of duty in Saudi Arabia during Operation Desert Storm. In addition to coaching, she loves cooking, marathon running, and writing her blog, *Carrots Don't Scream When You Boil Them*.

CPSIA information can be obtained at www.ICGtesting.com
Printed in the USA
BVOW02s2225140115

383401BV00009B/83/P